A KINGDOM STRANGE

I

R

N

G

O

O

K

Ramushouuo

Ohaunoock

I

Moratuc

Catokinge

Tandaquomuc

Metocuuem

Waratan

Mascoming

CO

AN

Mequopen

WEA

Chepanuu

MEO

Tramasquecoock

Pasquenoke

Dasamonquepeuc

Roanoac

Trinety harbor

Hatorask

Paquiwoc

MERIDIES

A Kingdom Strange

The Brief and Tragic History of the Lost Colony of Roanoke

JAMES HORN

A Member of the Perseus Books Group

Books published by Basic Books are available at special discounts
for bulk purchases in the United States by corporations,
institutions, and other organizations. For more information, please
contact the Special Markets Department at the Perseus Books
Group, 2300 Chestnut Street, Suite 200, Philadelphia, PA 19103,
or call (800) 810-4145, ext. 5000, or e-mail
special.markets@perseusbooks.com.

Designed by Brent Wilcox

Library of Congress Cataloging-in-Publication Data

Horn, James P. P.
    A kingdom strange : the brief and tragic history of the lost
colony of Roanoke / James Horn.
       p.   cm.
    Includes bibliographical references and index.
    ISBN 978-0-465-00485-0 (alk. paper)
    1. Roanoke Colony.   2. Roanoke Island (N.C.)—History.
I. Title.
    F229.H79 2010
    975.6'175--dc22

                                                2010000563

            10 9 8 7 6 5 4 3 2 1

*For Sally, Ben, and Liz
with love.*

To seek new worlds for gold, for praise, for glory.

—SIR WALTER RALEGH

Contents

JOHN WHITE'S LAST LETTER

On a cold winter's day in 1593 in the small settlement of Newtown, County Cork, an old man stood at his window staring at the dark clouds gathered along the horizon. Sleet had begun to fall, washing the landscape a dreary gray and glazing the bare trees with a thin layer of ice. But John White did not notice the frozen rain or numbing chill that had seeped into the room; he had drifted to another time and place. He pictured himself onboard a ship, the wind filling the sails and the restless Atlantic stretching away as far as the eye could see. Once more, he tasted salt spray on his lips, felt the swell of the ocean beneath his feet, and heard the dull boom of breakers beating monotonously against a distant shore.

He had gone over what happened countless times before, had thought of little else in the long years since he left his family and countrymen on Roanoke Island to return to England for help. He remembered the last hours as if they were yesterday: his efforts to convince the settlers that as their leader it was his duty to remain, and the hope in their eyes when he finally agreed to go. No one else, they said, would be able to persuade Sir Walter Ralegh, the venture's sponsor, to send a relief expedition immediately. Reluctantly, with heartfelt farewells and a firm promise to be back within six months, he boarded his ship and sailed away.

How had things gone so badly wrong? They had set out in April 1587 for Virginia (as the colony was called for the virgin queen, Elizabeth I) with high hopes—118 men, women, and children, many known to him personally, including his daughter, Eleanor, and her husband, Ananias— to plant a settlement in America. It had been a grand scheme, combining an ambition to exploit the natural bounty of the land with the imperial quest to stake a claim to the New World—an English America that would serve as a counter to the power of Spain. In time, a city would arise on the shore of the Chesapeake Bay, they would build harbors from which their ships could plunder the Spanish in the Caribbean and along the Main and attack treasure fleets that carried the wealth of the New World to the Old.

There were treasures, too, waiting to be found in the unexplored lands of the interior where no European had set foot. Rumors abounded of fabulous wealth in mountains known only to Indians. With the English firmly established in America, Spain's influence in the Indies would gradually wane; England would grow strong and eventually supplant the Spanish as lords of the world.

Perhaps, White pondered, he had allowed his enthusiasm for Virginia to get the better of his judgment. He recalled the exotic beauty of the land that had taken his breath away at first sight, the endless forests and wild profusion of trees, broad waterways and rivers teeming with life, strange animals and plants, and Indian peoples who had received the English in friendship and whose trust they had betrayed. The limitless potential of the New World that seemed within their grasp had somehow eluded them. Their attempt to found a great city had come to nothing. Perhaps the vision of an English America that he and Ralegh shared would never be more than a fantasy, a pipe dream.

And yet the men and women he had led to America were real enough. What of them? Despite his tireless efforts, he had taken not six months but three years to get back to Roanoke Island. By then they were gone. Unable to reach them, he would go to his grave bearing the guilt of his failure. His only comfort (small though it was) was his belief that the settlers were still alive on Croatoan Island with his Indian friend Manteo, or possibly in the interior, where they may have found a home with other peoples.

Sitting down to write a letter he had put off too long to his friend Richard Hakluyt, he reflected on his last voyage to Roanoke in 1590. He wrote about the hard-eyed mariners who cared nothing for him or the colony but only for profit, of months wasted in the West Indies while the privateers searched for valuable Spanish ships to plunder, and the foul weather that eventually forced his ship off the coast.

The voyage had been "luckless" and his hopes crushed. He could conclude only with an appeal to God's grace: "committing the relief of my . . . company the planters in Virginia, to the merciful help of the Almighty, whom I most humbly beseech to help & comfort them, according to his most holy will & their good desire." It was his final good-bye, an admission to himself that, exhausted in body and purse, he could no longer continue the search for them. Others might succeed where he had failed, but he could do no more.[1]

He laid down his pen and returned to the window, looked into the fading light, and asked himself for the thousandth time: Why had he listened to them? Why had he left? Why was he not with them still, wherever they were?

1

To "Annoy the King of Spain"

[W]hat an honorable thing
Both to the realm and to the king
To have had his dominion extending
There into so far a ground.

—John Rastell

In early September 1583 two small ships battled through mountainous seas in the mid-Atlantic. They were all that remained of a fleet commanded by Sir Humphrey Gilbert that had set out three months earlier from Plymouth, England, to take possession of North America in the name of Queen Elizabeth.

The storm had come on quickly: the ocean rising and falling, Edward Hayes, captain of the *Golden Hind*, later recalled, like "hills and dales upon the land." But Gilbert, brave and reckless, paid little heed. Seated at the stern of the tiny frigate *Squirrel*, he read calmly from a book, as if to defy the elements raging around him. Sailing as close as he dared, Hayes called to Gilbert to join him on the *Hind*, the larger of the two ships, but Gilbert refused, saying he would not forsake his men, with whom he had endured so many perils.

As the storm worsened the *Squirrel* was repeatedly swamped by huge waves. Several times Hayes thought her lost, yet somehow each time she recovered. Gilbert signaled that all was well and cried out repeatedly above the howling wind the old adage: "We are as near to heaven by sea as by land." Then, about midnight on Monday September 9, the lights of the frigate suddenly went out. The lookout of the *Hind*, peering into the darkness ahead, shouted that the frigate was cast away, which Hayes in his account of the voyage remarked was true, for in that instant the *Squirrel* and her crew were "devoured and swallowed up of the Sea." England's first attempt to establish a colony in North America had ended in failure.[1]

WALTER RALEGH was likely at Durham House, his magnificent London residence on the banks of the River Thames, when he learned of Gilbert's death. The news was of more than passing interest. He had invested heavily in the venture, but of greater importance to him was the fact that Gilbert was his half-brother and close business partner.

Ralegh was born in 1554 at Hayes Barton in the parish of East Budleigh, Devon, a small village in rolling countryside a few miles from the coast. His father (also named Walter) was a prosperous gentleman farmer who was related to a number of prominent merchant and seafaring families of the region, including the Drakes of Plymouth. In the late 1540s he wed Katherine Champernoun (Walter's mother), who had previously been married to Otho Gilbert and had three sons by him, John, Humphrey, and Adrian. The match was a step up the social ladder for the Raleghs and brought the family into the highest circles of county society. But more significant in the long run was the role the Gilberts would play in Walter's life.[2]

Humphrey Gilbert was a towering influence on the young Ralegh. Walter, who was seventeen years younger, had grown up hearing about his half-brother's exploits at the dazzling court of the young Queen Elizabeth. While still in his teens, he had followed in Gilbert's footsteps, fighting for Protestant Huguenots in France in the wars of religion and later in Munster (southern Ireland) against Irish rebels. He shared Gilbert's fierce Protestant convictions, his hatred of Catholic Spain, his delight in learning, and his unquenchable thirst for knowledge of faraway lands.

Ralegh's fascination with America may also be attributed to his half-brother's influence. Gilbert had been among the earliest and most vocal proponents of western voyaging and the expansion of England's commercial empire. In 1566 he had written "A discourse of a discovery for a new passage to Cataia [Cathay]," which argued for the existence of a sea route to the Far East along the north coast of America and called upon the English to take the lead in finding it. A "General Map" attached to the "discourse," adapted from a world map produced two years earlier by the expert Flemish cartographer Abraham Ortelius, showed the route clearly and how England was ideally placed to take advantage of it.

According to Gilbert, not only was the distance to Cathay (China) via the Northwest Passage considerably shorter than a northeastern route to Asia around the top of the Russia, but much of the sea passage was below the Arctic Circle and therefore free of ice. Ships leaving London or Bristol would head to approximately 60 degrees north, around "Cape Fredo" on the easternmost extremity of Labrador and then continue westward

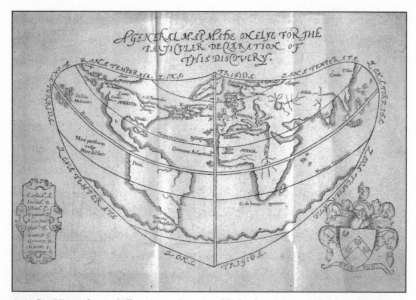

1.1 Sir Humphrey Gilbert's map was published in 1576 with his *A discourse of a discovery for a new passage to Cataia*. The map clearly shows a navigable Northwest Passage to the Orient along the top of America.

along the northern edge of the North American continent to the broad straits of "Anian," which opened into the Pacific Ocean. Once through the straits it would be only a short journey to Japan, China, the Moluccas, and the untold wealth to be found there in precious spices and silks. If England secured such a route, she would establish herself as a major commercial power and eventually come to rival Spain's rapidly growing overseas empire.[3]

Gilbert was unable to raise sufficient interest or money from merchants and wealthy gentry for a voyage to discover a Northwest Passage, but he remained enthusiastic about prospects for an expedition to the New World. In the mid-1570s, against the background of escalating raids on Spanish America by English privateers, he started to develop a daring new project that combined colonization with a large-scale assault on Spain's possessions in the West Indies.[4]

About this time Ralegh became involved in his half-brother's plans. After returning to England from the battlefields of France and spending several years at Oriel College, Oxford, he had moved to London in 1575. The following year he registered at the Middle Temple, one of the prestigious Inns of Court, located in spacious grounds just to the west of the old walls of the City of London (that part of the capital within its ancient walls). The Inns of Court provided young gentlemen with an introduction to common law, which was considered an indispensable part of their education, and offered a respectable position in London society. Ralegh was not interested in a career in law and had already set his sights on finding preferment at Queen Elizabeth's court.[5]

It is probable that shortly after Ralegh arrived in the city, Gilbert introduced him to Richard Hakluyt, the lawyer and elder of two Richard Hakluyts (they were cousins). Both were among the foremost promoters in England of overseas ventures. Hakluyt the lawyer, also a resident of Middle Temple, was an expert on geography and in regular contact with other leading authorities of the age. One can easily imagine Gilbert, Ralegh, Hakluyt, and others of Gilbert's circle gathered in the lawyer's rooms, poring over maps and books, talking long into the night about prospects for discoveries in the New World.[6]

In Hakluyt's chambers Ralegh would have had ready access to books of cosmography (general descriptions of the world),

1.2 Abraham Ortelius, *Typus Orbis Terrarum*, 1570. Walter Ralegh may have studied this map at the lodgings of Richard Hakluyt, the lawyer, of the Middle Temple, London. The map reveals a sea passage to the East along the top of America and was the inspiration for Sir Humphrey Gilbert's map.

including one of the most influential works of the period, Sebastian Münster's *Cosmographia Universalis*, a vast compendium of information about the world that had been republished many times since its appearance thirty years earlier.

Yet it might have been Hakluyt's sumptuously colored world map that depicted the Americas in detail that fired Ralegh's imagination. Obvious to the eye above a detailed depiction of the Americas was a sea passage that ran from Greenland to the Bering Straits. Looking more closely, Ralegh may have picked out the course of the St. Lawrence River, shown as penetrating far into the heart of the continent and separated by a narrow mountain range from a great river flowing to the west coast. Was this a route through the landmass that might provide a means of reaching the Pacific, should the Northwest Passage prove impossible to navigate?

Perhaps the most striking aspect of the map, however, which Ralegh could not have failed to notice, was that whereas New France and New Spain were prominently displayed, a "New England" was nowhere to be seen. As Ralegh and Gilbert were painfully aware, the English had fallen far behind Spain and France in exploring and colonizing the New World.[7]

In the late fifteenth and early sixteenth centuries, the English had been among the pioneers of Atlantic exploration, but during the long reign of Henry VIII (Queen Elizabeth's father) merchants and mariners had turned away from distant horizons and focused instead on opportunities nearer to home, trading with Europe and countries bordering the Mediterranean Sea. Other than the seasonal ebb and flow of shipping to the Newfoundland fishing banks and occasional illegal trading ventures to Brazil and the West Indies, the English showed little interest in America through the 1550s.

Spanish possessions in the New World, by contrast, had expanded enormously. The colonization of major Caribbean islands in the first decade of the sixteenth century was followed by the conquest of Mexico and Peru in the 1520s and 1530s, during which vast lands and numberless people came under the jurisdiction of the Castilian crown. The increase in Spanish populations in the West Indies and Central and South America had led to an enormous growth in Atlantic trade, enriching Spain and bringing about a decisive shift in the balance of power in Europe. Gold and silver plundered from Indian peoples and extracted from American mines had financed the buildup of Spain's formidable armies and expanding territories. When Elizabeth I ascended the throne in 1558 the Spanish king, Philip II, ruled an empire that stretched halfway across the globe, from the Mediterranean to the Americas. The English, on the other hand, had recently lost Calais to the French, the last vestige of once extensive lands in France, and their only overseas possession apart from some eastern counties of Ireland.[8]

The New World had emerged as an important theater of war by the middle decades of the sixteenth century, not only because of deep-rooted dynastic rivalries among the major powers, but also owing to the hostilities between Catholics and Protestants that had split Europe in two. Spain's claim to possess the Americas was based on discovery, conquest, and settlement, but even more important, it was founded on the sacred enterprise of extending the Catholic faith to (in Spanish eyes) "barbarous" native peoples. America was Spain's by virtue of the responsibility placed on Spanish monarchs by successive popes to convert Indians to Christianity. Philip believed the Lord had reserved for him the holy work of creating a universal Catholic monarchy that would reunite Christendom and eventually all peoples under one ruler, one faith, and one sword.[9]

That Philip took his role seriously can be seen in his efforts to ensure that Protestants—"heretics"—were kept out of America. In the early 1560s the king was especially concerned about the efforts of French Huguenots to take possession of Florida. Jean Ribault, a veteran privateer, had set out from Le Havre, France, in February 1562 to reconnoiter the southeastern coast of North America, where he established a small garrison named Charlesfort, on the border of modern-day Georgia and South Carolina. He had then returned to France to plan a larger privateering base in the area, from which attacks on the Spanish shipping in the West Indies would be launched.

Charlesfort did not last long; the men left behind soon abandoned their post. But a couple of years later Ribault and his lieutenant, René de Laudonnière, were back on the Florida coast with more than a thousand Huguenot settlers. This time they chose to establish a colony a hundred miles or so to the south of their first settlement, where they believed prospects were better, which they called Fort Caroline. The heavily armed warships, cannons, firearms, pikes, and lances they brought with them left little doubt in Philip's mind that the French were intent on establishing a harbor for privateers.

To counter the French threat, the king ordered Pedro Menéndez de Avilés, the recently appointed governor of Tierra Florida, to destroy the new settlement and safeguard the region from Protestant interlopers by creating a line of forts along Florida's coast. In the late summer of 1565 Menéndez led a large force of soldiers and Indian allies to Fort Caroline and in a surprise attack put the entire garrison to the sword, granting mercy only to some women and children. Hundreds of settlers perished at the fort and in subsequent reprisals, news of which sent shock waves reverberating throughout Europe.[10]

The English were at peace with Spain during these years and had not attempted to plant settlements in America or mount privateering expeditions. In 1562 John Hawkins, a wealthy merchant of Plymouth, had begun transporting slaves to the West Indies, which Spanish planters were eager to buy. Yet in spite of local demand, Hawkins's trade was tantamount to smuggling in the eyes of the Spanish crown. Foreigners were not allowed to trade in Spanish America without permission from authorities in the islands, which Hawkins did not obtain.

Hawkins enjoyed two lucrative voyages to the West Indies, but his third was a disaster. In 1568, at San Juan de Ulúa, the port town of Vera Cruz, Mexico, Hawkins's fleet was treacherously cut to pieces, or so the English claimed, by shore batteries and Spanish warships after negotiating a truce to carry out repairs. Hawkins lost five of his seven ships during the battle and limped back to England with only a fraction of his original force. The loss of several hundred of Hawkins's men inflamed anti-Spanish feelings in England, while for those who had taken part in the "sorrowful voyage" (including Hawkins's cousin, Francis Drake) the Spanish betrayal would be long remembered.

The attack at San Juan de Ulúa and deteriorating relations between England and Spain caused by commercial disputes and allegations of cruelties inflicted on English sailors by the Spanish encouraged growing numbers of privateers to descend on Spanish America in the 1570s. The queen and her ministers turned a blind eye to Francis Drake and others who raided shipping and towns in the West Indies and along the Spanish Main (the coast of South America).

Drake was one of the most successful privateers (the Spanish called them pirates). In 1573 he and his men joined forces with local *cimarrones* (bands of runaway slaves hostile to the Spanish) and a group of French privateers to ambush a mule train laden with Peruvian silver near Nombre de Dios, on the Panama Isthmus, amassing a small fortune in booty.

Philip II's struggle against pirates and heretics swiftly evolved into a sea war fought in the Atlantic, Caribbean, and Pacific. On the strength of their successes in the West Indies, Drake and a number of West Country (Dorset, Somerset, Devon, and Cornwall) privateers, including Richard Grenville and John Hawkins, began drawing up ambitious plans to plant colonies south of the River Plate (near present-day Buenos Aires). They aimed to establish bases from which they could plunder treasure ships off the coast of Peru after entering the Pacific through the Straits of Magellan. Elizabeth would not permit the establishment of colonies in South America, which she considered unrealistic, but she was persuaded to permit an expedition led by Drake to reconnoiter the west coasts of North and South America.[11]

It was against this background of raids on Spanish America that Sir Humphrey Gilbert, recently knighted for his services in Ireland put forward his own grand strategy to undermine Philip II's power. To what extent Ralegh was involved is uncertain, but given his close association with Gilbert at the time and his subsequent involvement in the venture, it is likely he played an important role in the planning.

Sir Humphrey presented his proposal to the queen in early November 1577. War with Spain was inevitable, he argued, because Philip was wholly addicted to Catholicism and would sooner or later declare war on England, the last major obstacle in his struggle to eradicate heresy. Elizabeth was the leading Protestant monarch in Europe and, as she and her ministers knew well, Spain represented the greatest threat to the security of her realm. How could she withstand so great a prince? Gilbert insisted that it would be necessary to preempt Spanish aggression by striking a blow so damaging that Philip would quickly sue for peace.

Gilbert's plan called for an assault on two fronts. First, to protect the crown from diplomatic reprisals, Gilbert would fit out a fleet and sail to the Newfoundland fishing banks where, under the cloak of piracy, he would capture French, Spanish, and Portuguese ships. He would carry off the best as prizes to the Netherlands or England, and burn the rest. The raid would devastate the Spanish cod fishery off Newfoundland, which was an extremely valuable component of Spain's trade in the North Atlantic.

The profits from selling the captured ships and fish would be used to finance the second part of the plan, in which the English would occupy Cuba and Hispaniola, the two largest islands in the Caribbean. Gilbert believed this could be easily done because both were sparsely populated. Once the English were in possession of the islands, they would entrench themselves so effectively that no power would be able to remove them. They would draw upon the natural wealth of the islands and develop heavily fortified bases from which to harass Spanish treasure fleets on their way through the Caribbean to the Atlantic and Spain. The smallest loss to King Philip II in the Indies, Gilbert assured the queen, would be "more grievous to him than any loss that can happen to him elsewhere."[12]

The following summer Elizabeth gave Gilbert formal permission to proceed. In the vague language of the royal grant she awarded him in June 1578, he was given exclusive rights to explore and to plant a colony somewhere in North America unclaimed by other European powers. Should he discover and possess new lands, he could hold them forever, but he was required to make a discovery within six years, or he would forfeit all rights to the grant.[13]

Gilbert wasted little time in organizing an expedition and by September 1578 was ready to depart from Dartmouth, with a fleet of eleven ships carrying some 500 men. Ralegh was given command of the royal ship *Falcon*, a token of the queen's blessing of the voyage. The fleet's destination was kept a close secret. It was too late in the year to sail to Newfoundland, and Gilbert likely decided to make for the Caribbean, possibly to plunder Spanish shipping, possibly to plant a colony somewhere on the southern mainland of North America, or both.

Whatever Gilbert's intentions, the expedition was a fiasco. Bickering between Gilbert's captains and bad weather sapped morale and led to three of the ships of deserting the expedition even before the fleet set out for America. Gilbert eventually managed to leave port in mid-November with the remainder of his fleet and headed for Ireland to take on extra supplies. He may have spent a couple of months on the Irish coast before adverse winds finally forced him back to England early in the new year. Ralegh did not return, however, and left Gilbert's fleet to head southward, apparently intending to make his own voyage to the West Indies. A few months later, after suffering heavy casualties in a sea fight with the Spanish off the Cape Verde Islands near the coast of Africa, his ship limped back to Plymouth in May 1579, battered and bloody.[14]

The ignominious outcome was a severe blow to Gilbert's prestige and purse. He had invested much of his (and his wife's) personal fortune in the voyage and struggled over the next few years to pay off his debts. For his part, Ralegh had set out with high hopes, expecting to distinguish himself in fighting and ransacking Spanish shipping, just as his cousin Francis Drake had done in his raids on the Caribbean and Spanish Main. Ralegh might have anticipated taking a prize or two and returning home a rich man. As it was, he returned to London and spent the next couple of years on the fringes of Elizabeth's court, competing for the queen's attention among a crowd of other young hopefuls. Services to Sir Francis Walsingham, Elizabeth's leading advisor on foreign and domestic affairs, earned him the relatively minor position of Esquire of the Body Extraordinary, but that was not enough for Ralegh, who like Gilbert a decade before, decided to leave the city and seek his fortune soldiering in Ireland.

Ralegh arrived in Ireland in the summer of 1580 and spent eighteen months in Munster. He participated in the brutal suppression of a rebellion against English rule and took part in the slaughter at Smerwick Fort of hundreds of Italian and Spanish mercenaries sent by the papacy and Spain to invade Ireland. But he soon tired of the war and, highly critical of his superiors, who he thought were too lenient in dealing with the rebels, returned to Elizabeth's court in the winter of 1581–1582 to offer advice in person on how to subdue the Irish. His purpose was probably little more than to leverage his expert knowledge in the hope that he be given a diplomatic mission or perhaps a position in Walsingham's service.[15]

Ralegh was twenty-eight when he arrived back at court and quickly attracted Elizabeth's attention. He was in the prime of his life and presented a striking figure. A contemporary de-

1.3 This portrait shows Sir Walter Ralegh as Captain of the Guard, responsible for Queen Elizabeth's safety. He was appointed to the office in April 1587, five years after he first came to her attention following his return from Ireland.

scribed him as a "handsome and well compacted person, a strong natural wit and a better judgment, with a bold and plausible tongue." He stood six feet tall, a head taller than most men, and was of slim and muscular build. A high forehead framed by curly auburn hair gave him an imperious look, while his eyes revealed a keen intelligence.

It was not only Ralegh's good looks that attracted the queen. His acute analysis of complex issues and forceful opinions, tempered by deference to his superiors, made an instant impression on her. She enjoyed listening to his carefully reasoned answers to questions, delivered in his thick Devonshire accent, and paid close attention to his opinions because it was said she "took him for a kind of oracle." Some at court, especially his rivals, viewed him as little more than the queen's latest flirtation, but he took his role seriously and saw himself as a trusted advisor as well as a close companion.[16]

Ralegh was the ideal courtier. "What is our life?" he wrote, but "[t]he play of passion." As befitted his station, he was scrupulously courteous and by turns serious and playful. He extolled Elizabeth's eyes, her hair, and "those dainty hands which conquered my desire," and raised adoration of the queen to new heights:

Praised be Diana's fair and harmless light,
Praised be the dews, wherewith she moists the ground,
Praised be her beams, the glory of the night,
Praised be her power, by which all powers abound.

She was a perfect foil to his earnestness, calling him "Water" (close to how he pronounced his name) and claiming she died of thirst whenever he left her presence. The word games they played—his love poems slipped discreetly into her hands, secret riddles passed between them—were a testament to the mutual respect they had for each other's intelligence. "'Fain would I climb, yet I fear to fall," Ralegh was said to have scratched upon a lattice window pane one day with a diamond ring, to which she replied archly using the same ring, "If thy heart fails thee, climb not at all."[17]

But perhaps the most important factor in their relationship was timing. In the spring of 1582 Ralegh and Elizabeth were at a crossroads in their lives, at a point when both were looking for a fresh beginning. The previous few years had been a disappointment to him: his half-brother's New World venture had fallen through, his initial forays into court life had brought only limited returns, and though he had risen to senior command in Munster, little tangible reward had come from it.

The queen was approaching fifty when he came to her notice. She continued to enjoy the company of handsome young men, all of whom were expected to be hopelessly in love with her. They served as an adoring chorus, who would sing her praises but whose love would never be requited. She was their virgin goddess, Diana or Cynthia, the chaste deity renowned for her strength, beauty, and hunting prowess. Yet the charade was beginning to wear thin. Although she remained a good-looking woman and carried herself well, the advancing years had taken their toll. Lines around her eyes and mouth had deepened, her nose was sharper, and she relied increasingly on cosmetics to hide the inevitable imperfections of age.

As she grew older, Elizabeth probably realized that it was increasingly unlikely she would marry. Ever since ascending the throne as a young woman of twenty-five, she had used her sex and the prospect of marriage to keep her political enemies abroad off balance and her admirers at home enamored. Her recent courtship of the Duke of Anjou, brother of the French king, Henry III, and heir presumptive to the French throne, whom she had fawned over for a couple of years and lovingly dubbed her "frog," was her final wooing. He was hardly a great catch—he was very short and was described by contemporaries as having a large nose and a face scarred by pockmarks—but the queen was more interested in a union that would tie France to her side and end England's diplomatic isolation. When the serious possibility of a match arose in early 1579, there was even talk of Elizabeth producing an heir. Contrary to the expectations of her ministers, Elizabeth appeared to blossom in the company of the youthful Anjou and was bitterly disappointed when negotiations eventually broke off and he left England in February 1582, never to return. "I grieve and dare not show my discontent," she wrote upon his departure.[18]

The queen was strongly attracted to Ralegh's good looks and unswerving loyalty. As she had with Anjou, Elizabeth came alive in Ralegh's company, but unlike the French prince, Ralegh was careful not to press his attentions too hard. In the aftermath of her affair with Anjou, Ralegh was an ideal companion, attentive and devoted, someone who would perhaps stand by her as she looked to a future without a husband or family of her own.

To Ralegh, the queen's favor offered a world of possibilities: wealth and power and a means of fulfilling his boundless ambition. No one had risen so quickly in her favor since the early years of her reign, when she had been inseparable from Robert Dudley, the Earl of Leicester, who was rumored to be her lover and, his rivals had feared, would soon come to rule all. Elizabeth had eventually put Leicester in his place, telling him she would not be ruled by any man. But as Ralegh's fortunes rose, he may have wondered whether he would not only supplant the queen's other favorites but also become an important figure in her governing councils. Ralegh aimed to make his mark and play a leading role in the direction of policy.[19]

Ralegh benefited greatly from Elizabeth's generosity. He was showered with gifts, offices, and honors, which transformed him within a few months from a mere country gentleman into an

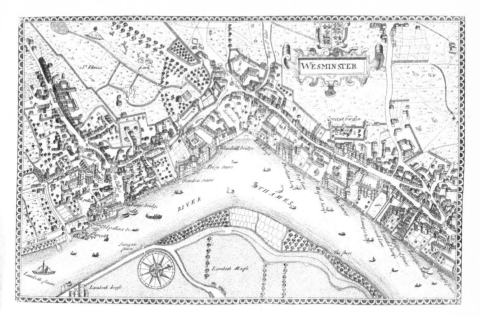

1.4 Durham House, to the right of center, was Ralegh's residence in London for twenty years. The mansion was situated on the Strand, the main thoroughfare leading to Fleet Street and the ancient City of London.

enormously wealthy grandee. The queen rewarded him with lucrative estates in Kent and Hampshire and a license to charge every vintner in England £1 a year for the right to sell wine, which brought him £700 annually (approximately $150,000–$200,000 in present-day value). As befitted his new status, he dressed lavishly in the high fashion of the day. His clothes and footwear were strewn with gems and pearls, he wore a great lace ruff at his neck and a jeweled dagger at his side, and he perfumed his long hair with musk. One of his hatbands alone was worth more than a common laborer was likely to earn in several years. He was insufferably proud and had few qualms about flaunting his newfound wealth and position whenever the opportunity arose.[20]

Early in 1583 Elizabeth granted Ralegh the use of Durham House, a "noble palace" on the Thames, formerly the London residence of the bishops of Durham. Dating to the reign of Edward I, the house had been rebuilt in the fourteenth century and was among the oldest of grand mansions that fronted the river between the City of London and Westminster. It included gardens, an orchard, two courtyards with outbuildings that accommodated up to forty servants, stables on the Strand, and a water gate, which gave Ralegh easy access by boat to Elizabeth's London residence at Whitehall. He was now at the epicenter of power, close to the royal palace and residences of the principal officers of state.

He adored Durham, soon known as Ralegh House, and renovated his quarters on the upper floors at huge expense. "I have heard it credibly reported," an observer who had visited the house on several occasions reported, "that Master Rawley hath spent within this half year above 3,000 pounds." His bed was covered with green velvet decorated with plumes of white feathers, his table was laid with silver engraved with his coat of arms, and he was attended by thirty men in expensive livery, some wearing chains of gold. For all the splendor of his newly furnished rooms, however, his favorite spot was his study, located in a small turret overlooking the Thames.[21]

From this vantage point he could see over the densely packed houses, shops, and churches far downriver to old St. Paul's Cathedral, still without a steeple (it had been destroyed by lightning twenty years earlier), and beyond to the fantastic Nonesuch

House, with its towers and cupolas built entirely of wood, sitting astride London Bridge. Upriver was Whitehall, adorned by a beautiful gatehouse, gallery, tennis courts, bowling alleys, and a cockpit built by Henry VIII. A little farther off was Westminster Hall, where the queen's courts were held, and the ancient abbey (founded in Saxon times) where English monarchs had been crowned from time immemorial. Across the Thames the open fields of Lambeth Marsh were clearly visible, and to the east were the thickly populated suburbs of Southwark; almost the size of a city and already notorious for their poverty and squalor.

Everywhere were the hustle and bustle of a great city: crowded streets and markets, animals and carts jostling for space along the busy thoroughfares, the raucous cries of men and women selling their wares, and the jests exchanged by watermen as they plied the Thames. Looking down from his little turret, Ralegh could have been forgiven for thinking all of London was at his feet.[22]

RALEGH'S DRAMATIC change in fortune gave him the opportunity once again to involve himself in his brother's schemes to establish a colony in North America. Following the disaster of the 1578 voyage, Gilbert had realized that another expedition would have to be planned more carefully. In March 1580 he had dispatched a small frigate on a reconnaissance mission to the North American coast under the command of an Azorean (Portuguese) master mariner, Simon Fernandes. After a swift crossing, Fernandes made landfall somewhere between New England and the mid-Atlantic seaboard, returning to England by the early summer. Although encouraged by the outcome, Gilbert was not in a position to finance and organize a full-scale expedition, and plans for another American voyage languished for the next two years.[23]

Ralegh's rising influence at court in 1582 was an important factor in the revival of Gilbert's plans. Sir Humphrey now had a powerful advocate close to the queen who could press the case for colonization with important ministers and investors. But Gilbert had to act quickly. If he failed to make a discovery and establish a settlement in America within the next two years, his 1578 grant would expire.

Throughout the summer Gilbert set about raising money by offering vast landed estates and commercial privileges to individuals and mercantile corporations. He granted rights to millions of acres in North America (at locations yet to be discovered) to groups of English Catholics led by Sir George Peckham and Sir Thomas Gerrard. The Catholics wanted to establish colonies where they could practice their faith free of the increasingly harsh penalties imposed on them in England. In response to Spanish and papal injunctions calling upon English Catholics to rebel against Queen Elizabeth, the government had recently introduced heavy fines for nonattendance at the established church. Gilbert's grants of lands to Catholics in North America, supported by the queen, provided a means by which they could escape the new penalties and create a distant refuge for themselves and their coreligionists.[24]

Sir Humphrey's plan was of necessity different than that of five years earlier. Because his personal finances were still fragile, he could not risk further heavy losses. To raise money for ships and men and to meet the terms of his royal grant, he was forced to focus on the establishment of colonies in North America rather than on plundering Spanish possessions in the West Indies. First he intended to locate a base for a year somewhere along the Norumbega (New England) coast, from which he would explore the interior and adjacent islands. Then, leaving behind a small garrison, he would return to England to drum up support for additional investment and to make specific allocations of lands to those who had already subscribed.

The colony in Norumbega would be virtually autonomous from England, organized as a series of independent settlements. It would be a rigidly hierarchical society of great and lesser landlords ruling over their tenants, with Gilbert having overall authority as the colony's chief lord and governor. In addition to rents, the exploitation of natural products and commercial rights granted to merchant groups would provide additional income, creating a flow of revenue that Gilbert could use to finance the second part of his plan: setting up a privateering base farther south, near Spanish Florida.

Gilbert had originally intended to leave England in the fall of 1582, but bad weather and delays in his preparations compelled him to postpone his departure until the following summer. The holdup had the important advantage of allowing Ralegh sufficient time to raise £2,000 for the *Bark Ralegh*, a swift, well-armed vessel, which he contributed with the expectation of commanding her on the expedition. In this he was to be frustrated. The queen refused him permission to go, considering the voyage far too hazardous; this was the first of many such disappointments.[25]

A fleet of five ships eventually got underway from Plymouth in June 1583. The largest was the *Bark Ralegh*, of 200 tons, followed by Gilbert's flagship, the *Delight*, of 120 tons, the *Golden*

Hind and *Swallow*, each of 40 tons, and tiny *Squirrel*, of 8 tons. A couple of days out the *Bark Ralegh* turned back, possibly because of disease among the crew or fears about the ship's seaworthiness. Gilbert was furious, but had little choice other than to press on, heading northwest for Newfoundland. The choice of destination was dictated by the need to take on more provisions, but Gilbert likely also had in mind his 1578 plan, which had involved raiding shipping off the Newfoundland fishing banks.

Gilbert arrived at St. John's Harbor, the largest port on the island, late the following month. There he found three dozen French, Spanish, Portuguese, and English ships peacefully plying their trade. Newfoundland was a miniature international community, in which the captains of the fishing vessels took turns regulating local affairs in the harbor and onshore, banding together to protect themselves from pirates. The fishermen were at first alarmed by the arrival of Gilbert's ships, thinking that they were another group of marauders. Following reassurances from Gilbert that he had not come to plunder, however, he was allowed to enter the harbor. A few days later he had a large tent erected on the shore, and the fishermen's captains were called together to attend him. His royal commission was read out, and in a formal ceremony Gilbert annexed St. John's and the surrounding region in the queen's name. The fishermen were told that their lands now belonged to England, and by virtue of his grant, to Gilbert, whom the queen had authorized to possess and enjoy them.

Had she known about it, Elizabeth would not have approved of Gilbert's high-handed declaration. His grant had expressly prohibited him from claiming territories in America that were occupied by other Europeans, a requirement included to avoid possible reprisals. She would not have wanted to disrupt the harmonious relations among the various nationalities involved in the Newfoundland fishing industry or to jeopardize the highly profitable trade. Fortunately for the queen, Gilbert's actions had little practical effect. The hardheaded fishermen tolerated his assertion of English overlordship and the imposition of levies and rents on their lands and trade because they knew that once Gilbert left, they could simply ignore his claims.

After several weeks of prospecting for minerals and surveying the area around St. John's, Gilbert was ready to move on. He was encouraged by the natural riches of the region and was especially pleased by the discovery of ore that might contain silver. He confided to his "mineral man," Daniel (a specialist in metals from Germany), that for himself he desired to go no farther. In high summer, the land appeared fruitful, the seas provided abundant fish, and Daniel's discovery suggested the existence of precious minerals. Gilbert claimed a huge swath of land at least 300 miles in each direction from his landing place at St. John's and probably had in mind offering much of it to settlers and speculators. Satisfied with the potential of the region, he could have returned to England with the good news, but the lure of the North American mainland and his desire to bring Norumbega within the compass of his royal grant persuaded him to continue the voyage.

Despite Gilbert's rosy assessment, the expedition was rapidly falling apart. His men were succumbing to disease that had spread throughout his crews, causing sickness and death. Some were too ill to work; others deserted or took up plundering fishing vessels along the coast. He dispatched the *Swallow* back to England with the sick and unruly and left St. John's on August 20 with his remaining three ships, heading southwest toward Cape Breton and the American coast.

Tragedy struck shortly after. The *Delight* ran aground in thick fog off Sable Island (Nova Scotia) at the end of the month and quickly broke up, consigning more than eighty men to the deep along with Gilbert's precious notes and maps of his explorations in Newfoundland. With supplies running low and his men refusing to continue the voyage, Gilbert had no choice but to set course for England. Although he continued to talk of bright prospects and the queen loaning him £10,000 for another voyage, his fortune was lost with his flagship as she slipped beneath the waves. He would be a laughing stock in London, hounded by creditors and scorned at court. Perhaps it was the enormity of the disaster that finally overwhelmed him and brought about a final act of folly: his stubborn refusal to abandon the *Squirrel* in the midst of a furious storm. He was, as Elizabeth commented dryly, "a man noted of not good hap [fortune] by sea."[26]

Voyages of exploration were highly dangerous, particularly those charting the cold waters of the North Atlantic. Ralegh's last communication with his half-brother had been an affectionate letter sent in March 1583, a few weeks before Gilbert left port, in which he had relayed Elizabeth's good wishes for the voyage and a token of her esteem. The token was a small jewel of rubies and diamonds depicting a queen on the back of an anchor, which carried the inscription "we are safe under the sacred anchor."

The irony would not have been lost on Ralegh as he reflected on Sir Humphrey's death. But beyond his personal loss, the failure of Gilbert's venture had left a gaping hole in his plans for an English America.

IN THE FALL of 1583, Ralegh made the momentous decision to assume the role of chief promoter of English colonies in America, formerly held by his half-brother. He was determined to be in the forefront of England's struggle to resist growing Spanish dominance in Europe and was convinced (as Gilbert had been) that the most effective means of undermining Philip II's power was by attacking his American possessions. The queen, he believed, should boldly assert English claims to North America forthwith by supporting the establishment of colonies. By carving out a vast realm in America where no other Europeans had settled, England would in time supplant Spain as the major New World power.

Between the fall and spring of 1583–1584 Ralegh turned his quarters at Durham House into a school for scholars and mariners. Among those who visited Durham House or consulted with Ralegh regularly were the two Richard Hakluyts, John Dee, and Fernandes, whom he already knew from his involvement in his half-brother's schemes; others, like Thomas Hariot, John White, Jacques Le Moyne de Morgues, Philip Amadas, and Arthur Barlowe, he recruited as his plans evolved.[27]

They were among the most remarkable men of their generation and would put forward the case for colonization, provide instruction on navigation and mathematics, collect and draft maps, identify Atlantic routes, and undertake Ralegh's voyages. The two Hakluyts served as his propagandists and would advance a range of arguments in favor of colonization to attract political and financial support. John Dee, a renowned scholar, was an expert on

English claims to the New World and on American geography. He would instruct Ralegh's mariners in navigation and help to draw up charts and maps for an initial reconnaissance voyage that Ralegh had already begun to plan. Simon Fernandes, the master pilot, would guide Ralegh's ships across the Atlantic to their destination on the coast of North America.[28]

Two men were especially important to Ralegh's plans: Thomas Hariot, a scientist, and John White, an artist. Ralegh knew Elizabeth would forbid him to go to America, and therefore he needed reliable and skilled men to record what they saw. Hariot would make a detailed record of the New World in writing, and White would undertake a series of illustrations and paintings. Together they would be Ralegh's ears and eyes in America.

Hariot had studied mathematics and astronomy at St. Mary's Hall, Oxford. After graduating in 1580 he went to London, where over the next couple of years he applied his learning to "Cosmography, and the art of Navigation." Hariot became well known in the city and, possibly on the recommendation of Dee, Ralegh took him into his household to help train his men. At first Ralegh may have thought to employ him solely for his expertise with mathematics and navigation, but it quickly became apparent that Hariot was a scholar of exceptional ability who would be an asset to the enterprise in other ways. His rigorous scientific methods and careful recording of information persuaded Ralegh that he should accompany the expeditions to North America and keep detailed notes on the topography, climate, peoples, fauna, and flora of the lands they discovered.[29]

Little is known about John White before he joined Ralegh's circle. He was descended from an old gentry family of Truro,

Cornwall, and may have moved from the provinces to London when a young man. Alternatively, he may have been born and bred in the city. In 1566 he married Thomasine Cooper in the "new built" church of St. Martin Ludgate, a stone's throw from St. Paul's Cathedral, and maintained his ties with the area for the next twenty-five years. He was an educated man and may have attended one of the universities or Inns of Court, but more likely he served an apprenticeship during the 1560s with a London master to learn the skill of a limner (miniature painter). Of modest means, he might have earned his living from decorative painting for London's rich and fashionable classes as well as from occasional work farther afield.[30]

White had taken part in an Atlantic voyage a few years earlier. In 1577 he had accompanied an expedition led by Martin Frobisher to Baffin Island (off the east coast of Canada), which had set out to find gold. There he had painted exquisitely detailed pictures of a Nugumuit Inuit man, called Kalicho, and his wife and child, as well as illustrating a brief but bitter encounter with a group of Inuit that occurred at a place the English called "Bloody Point." Ralegh may have seen the paintings and recruited him on the strength of them.

The artist drew on his experience on Baffin Island to prepare for the task of illustrating Indian peoples of North America, but he also probably took advice from a Huguenot artist, Jacques Le Moyne de Morgues, who lived near White's residence in the City of London. Le Moyne was one of the few survivors of the French colony at Fort Caroline who had somehow made his way back to France after the destruction of the fort. In the 1570s he had left his homeland and settled with his wife in Blackfriars, where some years later he became known to Ralegh, who took him into his service in 1582 or 1583. Le Moyne kept a collection of his paintings at his house, and White may have visited him many times to study the Timucuan Indians of Florida and landscapes the Frenchman had painted two decades earlier. In Le Moyne's work, White discovered a treasure trove of information about America and its peoples that provided him with invaluable examples of how to approach his own paintings.[31]

HAVING ASSEMBLED the men who would plan and take part in his expeditions to America, Ralegh's next task was to determine where a colony should be located and what kind of settlement it would be. He may have initially considered adopting Sir Humphrey's plans to settle Newfoundland and to continue the search for the Northwest Passage, but if so, he quickly changed his mind. Turning away from the North Atlantic, he focused his attention instead on more southerly latitudes nearer to the West Indies, where he believed the greatest prizes and glory were to be won from plundering Spain's annual treasure fleets.

The potential returns from privateering were enormous. Every year treasure galleons from Panama and Mexico—carrying gold, silver, pearls, cochineal, hides, and cacao—sailed to Spain in convoys protected by a squadron of warships. They gathered at Havana, then headed north in late spring past the Florida Keys, through the Bahama Channel (or Florida Strait), which separated Florida from the Bahamas, and out into the Atlantic, where they would pick up prevailing westerly winds and ride the Gulf Stream back to the Guadalquivir River and Seville.

The sea lanes the fleets followed were well known to pirates. Attacks by the French had begun in the 1530s and escalated over the next couple of decades, while English privateers prayed on Spanish shipping in the early 1570s and early 1580s. Philip II had responded by organizing a convoy system and deploying warships to shepherd the treasure ships back to Spain. Even so, dangers remained. Without question, the most hazardous part of the journey was the Bahama Channel. Navigation was difficult owing to its reefs and shoals and hurricanes, and because the numerous islands of the Bahamas offered privateers limitless hideaways, where they could wait for stragglers to fall into their hands. Proximity to the Bahama Channel had persuaded Ribault and Laudonnière to establish Fort Caroline in Florida, and Ralegh was similarly influenced in his decision to plant a colony on the northern mainland within reach of the treasure ships' route.[32]

Ralegh believed the English needed a permanent privateering base on the coast of North America. Sporadic attacks on the West Indies and Spanish Main had brought substantial profits to individual privateers and their financial backers, but large-scale operations were hampered by the need to provision fleets and make repairs to ships, which for the most part could only be done safely in England. If Ralegh could establish a secure base in America, he could provision and repair his own ships on the American coast, collect payments from other privateers that called in at his colony, and attract investors who would be keen to share in the profits. He could harass Spanish shipping and at the same time lay claim to North America.

The question remained: where? Two main arguments inclined him toward the mid-Atlantic seaboard. Mindful of the destruction

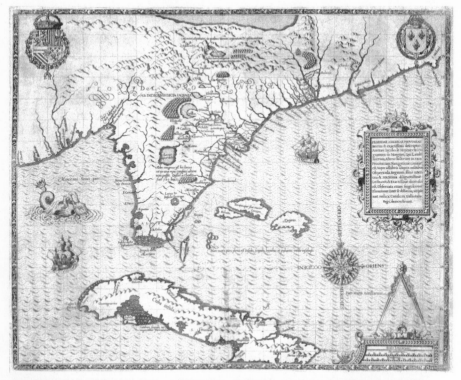

1.5 Jacques Le Moyne's Map of Florida, c. 1565 (engraving by Theodor de Bry, 1591), was highly influential in shaping Ralegh's ideas about the interior of Eastern America. Note the mountains at the top of the map where gold, silver, and copper were to be found. The shoreline of a great lake, or possibly the South Sea (Pacific), is also visible.

of Fort Caroline by the Spanish in 1565, Richard Hakluyt the younger recommended against a site too close to Spanish garrisons in Florida and the Caribbean, where it would be vulnerable to attack by warships. Ralegh therefore decided on a location somewhere to the north of Florida and turned to his most experienced mariner, Simon Fernandes, for advice. Fernandes recommended the coast of North Carolina, which he had visited many years before in the service of the Spanish governor, Pedro Menéndez de Avilés. The region was sufficiently remote from Spanish naval bases, and Fernandes was familiar with inshore waters along that part of the coast. Persuaded by Hakluyt and Fernandes, Ralegh chose North Carolina as his destination.[33]

But there may have been another reason why Ralegh was attracted to the region. Twenty years earlier Jacques Le Moyne had taken part in explorations of the area around the French settlement at Fort Caroline in search of gold and silver and a passage to the South Sea. The colony's leader, René de Laudonnière, had been disappointed by the failure to find riches or a passage, but he did learn from local Indians of mines to the north about 60 leagues (200 miles) up the St. Johns River in the Appalachian Mountains. Le Moyne depicted the promising news on a map of Florida that noted gold, silver, and copper in the mountains and a lake where "the natives find grains of silver." This area was a good way south of the location that Ralegh intended to explore, but if precious metals and a passage to the Pacific existed in the mountains inland from the Florida coast, perhaps gold and silver were to be found in the interior of North Carolina.[34]

⁂

By the spring of 1584 Ralegh's preparations were in their final hectic stages. Two ships were being readied in the Thames, provisions loaded, and the crews assembled. He had prepared meticulously for the voyage, recruiting experts in navigation and men with practical experience of seamanship so as to avoid the misfortunes that had befallen his half-brother. In mid-March Ralegh obtained the queen's official support for the voyage and by royal letters patent was given the same rights as those enjoyed by Gilbert to discover and possess unknown lands in America. A few weeks later, as his ships left the Thames to head for Plymouth, where they would take on a last round of supplies, Ralegh may well have wondered whether his dream of founding an English empire in America was at last becoming a reality.[35]

2

ROANOKE

In praise of those who have discovered new
parts of the world
The Portuguese subdued the tracts of China
And the stout Spaniard the fields of Mexico:
Florida once yielded to the noble French:
VIRGINIA now to thy scepter, Elizabeth!

—MARTIN BASANIER

THE TWO SHIPS that would carry Ralegh's first expedition to
the New World were ready to leave Plymouth by the end
of April 1584. The names of the ships are unknown, but the
larger of the two (the admiral) may have been the *Dorothy*, a 50-
ton ship owned by Ralegh. She probably carried about forty-five
soldiers and sailors as well as stores and armaments. The smaller
ship, a pinnace of about 30 to 40 tons, likely carried thirty men
and would be used for exploring rivers and shallow waters. The
inclusion of soldiers in the expedition suggests that Ralegh was
prepared to meet with force any hostile Indians his men encountered. In addition, he may have anticipated opportunities to

plunder Spanish shipping in the West Indies, which would help defray the cost of the voyage. Colonization and privateering were closely connected in his mind.[1]

Philip Amadas and Arthur Barlowe commanded the expedition. Amadas, captain of the larger ship, was a young man from a prominent Plymouth family of gentlemen-merchants who had entered Ralegh's service a few months before the voyage. Little is known of his background, but he had likely served in the army and may have had some experience at sea. Short in stature, he was sometimes referred to as "little Amadas" and was quick to lose his temper. Arthur Barlowe, who commanded the pinnace, had been in Ralegh's service longer and may have been an officer in the company commanded by Ralegh in Ireland. Again, little is known about him other than that he had possibly made a voyage to the eastern Mediterranean and was highly literate. The journal he kept of the voyage reveals him to be a sensitive and keen observer of the land and peoples the English discovered. He may have been a steadying influence on the aggressive and headstrong Amadas.

Simon Fernandes, who sailed with Amadas as master pilot, was a rough-hewn character with a checkered past. Variously known as Simon Fernando, Ferdinando, or Fernandes, he was born on Terceira in the Azores and trained in Portugal as a pilot. He served the Portuguese and Spanish before moving to England sometime after 1572, following which he took up plundering ships in the English Channel. After being sent to London in the spring of 1577 to answer charges of piracy, he came to the attention of Sir Francis Walsingham. The queen's minister had no time for pirates but considered that Fernandes's knowledge of Spanish American waters might prove useful, and he arranged his reprieve. Possibly on Walsingham's recommendation, Fernandes entered Gilbert's service later in 1577 and sailed with Ralegh on the *Falcon* the next year. Ralegh had been impressed by the Portuguese mariner and believed Fernandes would be important to the success of his plans to establish a colony in America. But Fernandes was first and foremost a pirate, not an explorer.[2]

Ralegh's instructions for the expedition have not survived, but it is likely that he ordered his two commanders to find a convenient route to the mid-Atlantic coast, reconnoiter the region, make contact with local Indian peoples (bringing back one or two to England if possible), and locate a suitable site for the colonists that Ralegh intended to send out the following year. He encouraged Amadas and Barlowe to trade with Indian peoples and to take careful note of the economic potential of the region. John White and Thomas Hariot were included in the expedition to get their first view of the American mainland and to report to Ralegh personally.

The voyage to the Americas was largely uneventful. The two ships left the west coast of England in fair weather on April 27, 1584, following the usual southerly route taken by privateers sailing to the West Indies, and reached the Canaries by early May. After a rapid Atlantic crossing, they arrived at Puerto Rico a month later and remained in the West Indies for nearly two weeks, taking on fresh water and provisions. Some of the men became ill during the layover, and it was with evident relief that Barlowe recorded in his journal their departure from the islands, heading for the North American mainland.

2.1 John White's *The Arrival of the English*, 1585–1586 (engraving by Theodor de Bry, 1590). Port Ferdinando, where Amadas and Barlow entered through the Outer Banks into Pamlico Sound is shown to the left at the north end of the Hatarask Island. The lands of the Secotans and Weapemeocs are shown as well as the Indian settlement on Roanoke Island where Granganimeo was the local chief.

The Englishmen followed the Florida coast for a little more than a week and arrived off the Outer Banks of North Carolina in early July. The Outer Banks are a line of narrow, sandy islands extending approximately 150 miles, from near the mouth of the Chesapeake Bay in the north to Cape Lookout in the south. Created by prevailing winds and currents, the islands act as a barrier between the Atlantic Ocean and the shallow waters of the sounds within: Currituck, Albemarle, and Pamlico. Fernandes had to skirt the Outer Banks for over a hundred miles before he found a passage between the islands that the ships were able to navigate, albeit with some difficulty. Entering Pamlico Sound, they dropped anchor about a mile from the island of Hatarask and gave thanks to God for their safe arrival.[3]

Amadas and Barlowe were aware of the significance of their arrival off the American shore. They would be the first Englishmen to set foot on mainland North America in the vanguard of an English New World colony. Accompanied by a group of soldiers, they rowed to Hatarask in their long boats and gathered together on the beach, where they took possession of the land in right of "the Queen's most excellent Majesty." The ceremony likely involved reading out a formal declaration of sovereignty and affixing some kind of permanent marker (a lead plaque engraved with the royal coat of arms for example) to a prominent tree. No Indians were present to witness the event by which the newcomers had asserted their ownership of the land, but as far as the English were concerned, the entire region extending for hundreds of miles in every direction was now part of the realm of England.

After the ceremony, the Englishmen set out to explore Hatarask Island. Great stands of red cedars, pines, cypress, and sassafras trees covered the land in such abundance, Barlowe commented in his journal, as was not to be found anywhere else in the world. Everywhere they found the woods teeming with deer, rabbits, and wild fowl, the latter in such numbers along the waterside that when they discharged their muskets, huge flocks of herons rose into the sky with a great cry, "as if an army of men had shouted all together." Amadas and Barlowe were delighted by their initial impressions; here was a rich, fertile land ready for exploitation.[4]

2.2 Indian Peoples of Ossomocomuck and Surrounding Regions. Drawn by Rebecca L. Wrenn.

The English had not seen any local peoples since arriving off the Outer Banks, but it is certain that the Indians had seen them. The two ships would not have taken the Indians entirely by surprise; they had seen such ships before. From the 1520s onward,

Europeans had occasionally sailed by the Carolina coast on their way to the Chesapeake Bay or farther north, and in 1558 some (probably Spanish or French) sailors had been shipwrecked on the Outer Banks. The men had remained a few weeks on the island of Wococon before putting out to sea in a makeshift boat and had perished soon after; Indians had found the remains of their boat washed up on the shore.

A Spanish ship had arrived off the coast some years later. The ship had been trying to reach the Bahia de Madre de Dios (Chesapeake Bay) to return an Indian convert called Paquiquineo, known as Don Luis to the Spanish, to his homeland. For reasons that are unclear, the Spanish had failed to find the entrance to the bay and while off the coast of Maryland were driven southward in a storm to the Outer Banks. After spending a few days exploring the islands the Spanish sailed away, leaving behind a cross made of branches to mark their discovery. The Spaniards did not make contact with local peoples, but the Indians had witnessed their coming and going and later recounted the story to Barlowe.

Besides their own experiences of Europeans, it is probable that the Indians had picked up news of other white men who had entered lands to the south and north of them. Information passed by word of mouth from one group to another across hundreds of miles, and peoples of the Carolina region may well have heard stories of the Spanish in Florida, who had built forts and made war on the peoples of those lands. They may also have heard that a small group of Spaniards had tried to build a settlement on the Chesapeake Bay but had been destroyed by the Indians there (in 1571). Following the murder of the white men, several ships had entered the bay, and the whites had killed many people. The question likely on the mind of the Indians who sighted the ships of Amadas and Barlowe was whether the strangers had come to trade, fight, or settle.[5]

Three major peoples inhabited the coastal lands called by the Indians Ossomocomuck: the Secotans, Weapemeocs, and Chowanocs. All were Algonquian-speaking peoples descended from ancestors who had moved into the mid-Atlantic coastal region from the west and north thousands of years earlier. They were made up of loose groupings of semiautonomous peoples rather than centralized political entities controlled by powerful rulers. No single people or paramount chief dominated the entire coastal region.

The Chowanocs, ruled by an old and wise chief, Menatonon, were the most numerous and powerful. They lived in towns and villages scattered along the western bank of the Chowan River and along the lower reaches of the Merherrin and Blackwater. The capital, Chowanoc, located on a bluff overlooking the Chowan, had been inhabited for centuries and was a large settlement of perhaps 2,500 people at the time the English arrived. The Chowanocs' influence over the region derived from the fertility of their lands and access to trade routes to the north and west that connected Ossomocomuck to the broader mid-Atlantic seaboard. Their role linking the interior to the coastal lands sometimes sparked hostilities with equally powerful peoples beyond the region, such as the Tuscaroras farther to the west and the Powhatans in Virginia.[6]

Lands from the eastern bank of the Chowan River to the coast were occupied by the Weapemeocs, who were led by a chief named Okisko. Most of their settlements bordered the lower reaches of the Chowan River and the northern shore of Albemarle Sound and its tributaries, but their territory extended at least as far north as the Great Dismal Swamp and possibly beyond to the area inhabited by the Chesapeakes. Okisko's relationship with the Chowanocs is uncertain, but it is known he was subject to Menatonon.

The area from Albemarle Sound to the Pamlico River was occupied by the Secotans. The capital (of the same name) was located on the northern bank of the Pamlico River and was one of the primary residences of their chief, Wingina. Occasionally the chief stayed at the fortified town of Pomeiooc, approximately forty miles to the east, and at Dasemunkepeuc, on the mainland across the water from the island of Roanoke, where his brother, Granganimeo, was the local ruler.

To the south of the Secotans' territory were peoples independent of and hostile to the three main groups. The Pamlicos, who occupied the peninsula south of the Pamlico River, and the Neuse and Coree of the Neuse River, were Iroquoian—of entirely different linguistic and cultural stock than the Algonquian peoples. The Pamlicos had formed an alliance against the Secotans, perhaps in league with Iroquoians who lived in the interior. Altogether, there may have been as many as 7,000 Algonquians and Iroquoians living in the coastal region in the late sixteenth century.[7]

Algonquian peoples had much in common. Allowing for local variations and dialects, they spoke the same language. Their towns usually consisted of between 50 and 150 people related by kinship and marriage, living in ten to twenty longhouses spread over several acres. They avoided exposed areas of the coast or sounds and favored inland locations near rivers, on sheltered necks, or along smaller estuaries and tributaries. Waterways offered abundant food and an efficient means of getting around and occasionally served as borders separating different (sometimes hostile) peoples. High ground close to the water was preferred, to avoid flooding and provide a vantage point for watching comings and goings along the river and inland approaches to the town or village.

The Indians enjoyed the bounty of the land and rivers. In fields around the towns they grew corn, pumpkins, squash, and beans, and from spring until fall an abundance of food was available through foraging, fishing, and hunting. When in season, several kinds of fruits and nuts such as mulberries, huckleberries, persimmons, acorns, and hazelnuts provided an important part of the diet. Beaten roots and wild grasses substituted for corn meal in the months before crops were ready to harvest.

Cultivating the crops was women and children's work; hunting and fishing was men's. Fish were taken by trapping in weirs, netting, and wading in shallow waters with spears; shellfish were gathered from convenient places along the shores and riverbanks. Fish and shellfish were usually roasted or boiled in a thick stew or smoked to preserve them. Deer were the major source of meat, supplemented by bears, squirrels, waterfowl, and turkeys.[8]

Indian society was not characterized by great inequalities in wealth or rigid social hierarchies. Common access to the natural produce of the land, rivers, and coastal waters ensured a relatively comfortable living for the majority of people, lessening social divisions. Local chiefs, priests, and councilors drawn from the people's elders and bravest warriors formed the pinnacle of

2.3 John White, *Indians Fishing*, 1585. White undertook a series of paintings of Indian peoples in the summer of 1585. The various methods the Indians employed to catch fish are clearly illustrated together with the variety of fish and shellfish available to them in the sounds.

Indian society and were distinguished from ordinary people by their more elaborate dress. But apart from chiefs, among whom the right to govern remained in the family, no elite hereditary upper class existed. High status was not a function of caste, wealth, or privilege but rather depended on the favor of the local ruler. In a political sense, the major division in Indian society was between chiefs and priests on the one hand and the rest of the people on the other, yet for the majority the most important social distinctions were determined not by civil status but by kinship, age, and gender. Indians found their place and role in society according to their family ties, how old they were, and of what sex.[9]

Religious and spiritual beliefs were fundamental to making sense of daily experiences, serving to provide glimpses of the future and explain the mysteries of the cosmos. Indians across the region believed in a pantheon of greater and lesser gods. The Indians' chief god was Ahone, who had existed since the beginning of time. He had created the universe, the world, and petty gods, and was the author of everything good. But he had withdrawn himself from human affairs and was beyond the peoples' reach. Lesser gods, such as the sun, moon, and stars, had carried out his creation and governed thereafter. Some took human form and inhabited the waters; woods; skies; and everything around, visible and invisible, not separate from but very much part of the real world. They reflected the Indians' reverence for the natural world and the forces that shaped it.

Another deity, Kiwasa, was the most influential in the Indians' everyday lives. He was responsible for all the harm and misfortune in the world, and brought with him suffering, disease, blighted crops, bad weather, hunger, and defeat in war. Ordinary people sought to appease Kiwasa through worship and offerings, whereas priests prayed daily in temples, more out of fear than love. Nevertheless, despite their efforts, the unpredictable and mischievous god remained a source of chronic insecurity in peoples' lives.

Ritual and ceremony were vital to Indian society. Large towns had spaces set aside for public ceremonies in which the people celebrated success in war and good harvests and called upon the gods to maintain the fertility of their fields. Great fires were lit, and men and women gathered to rejoice long into the night. Prayers and rituals were performed in the temples and in public places to reduce the likelihood of disaster and maintain harmony between the natural and spiritual forces that struggled for mastery over the world.[10]

Ossomocomuck was an unpredictable place. Shortly before the English arrived a brief but vicious war between the Secotans and Pamlicos had left Wingina badly wounded. The most powerful people to the west, the Iroquoian Tuscaroras, pressed on the borders of the Chowanocs and Secotans. Numbering many thousands, the Tuscaroras occupied a huge region inland from the Neuse to the Roanoke River. The English referred to them as Mangoaks or Mangoags, a name adopted from the Secotan meaning treacherous or crafty. To the north in Virginia, Wahunsonacock, paramount chief of a powerful Algonquian people, the Powhatans, was forging alliances and extending his influence among peoples of the fertile James River Valley and surrounding area. Finally, despite the intercession of priests, Kiwasa flailed the land with a severe drought that withered crops and forced game into the interior. Such was the uncertain world encountered by the English in the summer of 1584.[11]

First contact occurred three days after the English dropped anchor off Hatarask. Curious about the new arrivals, three Indians approached the ships in a boat and landed on the island. Amadas, Barlowe, and Fernandes went to meet them, and with their consent took one of the Indians back to their ship, where they gave him a shirt, hat, and some other things that "he liked very well."

The next day several boats, bearing forty to fifty Indians, came to the island, including the chief, Granganimeo, and waited for the Englishmen to come meet them. Barlowe described the Indians as a very handsome and "goodly people" of a yellowish hue with black hair. The chief seated himself on a mat with four of his councilors next to him and the rest of his men standing some way off. When Amadas, Barlowe, and their armed guard arrived, the chief beckoned them over and invited them to sit. He welcomed them, striking his head and chest and smiling to let them know his joy at their arrival. After Granganimeo delivered a long speech, the Englishmen returned his welcome and gave him gifts to signify trade and their peaceful intentions.

Both sides were interested in trading. The English acquired deer and bison skins and the Indians various metal goods. Granganimeo was particularly delighted with a bright tin dish given to him, which he pierced at the brim and wore around his neck, "making signs, that it would defend him against his enemies' arrows." With an eye to attracting support from merchants for future ventures, Barlowe mentioned that they received twenty skins worth £5 for the tin dish and fifty skins worth £12.10s. for a copper kettle. Hatchets, knives, and axes also brought good returns.[12]

2.4 John White, *One of the Wives of Wingina*, 1585. The painting may have been done when White visited the town of Secotan. He renders naturalistically the woman's body paint and tattoos. Her apron-skirt is made of deer skin and her jewelry of pearls and painted bone. The wife of Granganimeo, who greeted Amadas and Barlow on Roanoke Island in 1584, was dressed similarly in a short leather skirt and wore pearls and coral around her neck.

Relations with the Indians were friendly and relaxed during the first few weeks. One of Granganimeo's wives and three or four of his children visited the ships often. His wife was described as a good-looking woman of small stature and "bashful [modest]" demeanor. She wore a leather cloak over a short deerskin skirt, a band of white coral around her head, pearl earrings, bracelets, and a long necklace down to her waist that was made of pearls as large as peas. Granganimeo's apparel was similar to his wife's, but he wore a large plate of copper on his head as well as pendants in his ears. He and his wife were accompanied by forty attendants when they visited the English. No people in the world pay more respect to their chiefs than these people, Barlowe observed; their behavior was as "mannerly and civil as any of Europe."[13]

When exploring the sounds and lands adjoining, however, the English received a very different reception. Barlowe and seven men, including Thomas Hariot, made their way to Roanoke Island, where Granganimeo lived. According to Hariot, "as soon as they saw us [the Indians] began to make a great and horrible cry, as people who never before had seen men appareled like us, and came away making out cries like wild beasts or men out of their wits." The English called them back and showed them their trade goods—glass beads, knives, dolls, "and other trifles"—which, according to Hariot, they delighted in. Realizing the strangers were no threat, the Indians took them to their town, where the English were entertained. The incident may have been a misunderstanding; Hariot possibly misinterpreted the Indians' behavior. But another possibility is that Hariot's account is a more accurate description of how the English were initially viewed by the Indians, compared to the rosy version provided by Barlowe for readers in England.[14]

Worse was to befall Amadas and Fernandes, who had taken the pinnace to lands bordering the northern shore of Albemarle Sound. Details are sketchy, but it seems that a number of the English were killed in a skirmish with Indian warriors, forcing Amadas's men to withdraw quickly and return to Roanoke, where they joined Barlowe. No explanation for the attack was given, but Amadas had likely stumbled into the middle of hostilities between the Secotans (Granganimeo's people) and the

Weapemeocs. The attack was a clear message to Amadas that not all peoples of the region welcomed the arrival of the English. Relations between the colonists and various Indian groups would likely be more complicated than he may have first assumed.[15]

By mid-August Amadas and Barlowe were ready to leave Roanoke Island. They had arranged to take two Indians back to England—Manteo, the son of the chief of the Croatoans, and a Secotan named Wanchese—and in return left two of their own men with the Indians. White, Hariot, and the two Indians sailed on board the pinnace and made a rapid crossing, arriving in Plymouth a month later. Amadas and Fernandes went cruising for Spanish prizes off the Bermudas and Azores and returned to England empty-handed in early November.

Amadas and Barlowe had good reason to be pleased with the outcome of their voyage. They had successfully navigated a route to America and discovered a bountiful land, larger than England, bordered by a mighty sea (the sounds) that enclosed scores of islands of different sizes. One island in particular might turn out to be a suitable location for the first English colony: Roanoke, ten miles long and two and a half wide, described by Barlowe as "a most pleasant and fertile ground" inhabited by peaceful Indians, the Secotans, the Englishmen's friends and allies. Manteo and Wanchese, from whom Thomas Hariot had begun learning Algonquian on the return voyage, provided more information about the peoples of the coastal lands and to the west, including a people who inhabited a great city called Skicóak.

Most important of all, if a Spanish report of a couple of years later is to be credited, the English had picked up news from the Indians of gold and silver to be found in the interior as well as a passage to the South Sea that lay at the head of a large river called Occam. The coastal region was rich in natural resources, but possibly greater treasures beckoned inland.[16]

WHILE AMADAS and Barlowe had been exploring the coast of North Carolina, in London the court was aflame with talk of war with Spain. Relations with Madrid had deteriorated alarmingly over the past four years as the Catholic powers appeared to be in the ascendant once more. Early in 1580 old Cardinal Henry, king of Portugal, had died, and by the following spring Philip II, who had a strong dynastic claim to the throne, succeeded him. Spain had thereby gained control not only of strategically important Atlantic ports such as Lisbon but also of Portuguese possessions in Africa, the Far East, the Atlantic, and Brazil. Philip's already vast empire was translated into truly global proportions, the first on which the sun never set.

Elizabeth's ministers were also deeply concerned by developments nearer to home. In France, Henry III and his Catholic supporters were growing in strength and drawing closer to Spain. In Ireland, rebellion against English rule was spreading. And in Scotland, the overthrow of the pro-English regent, James Douglas, Earl of Morton, opened the door to the possibility of the young Scottish king, James VI (the future James I of England), falling under Catholic influence.[17]

But the major threat to England's security, as well as the epicenter of conflict between Catholics and Protestants in Europe, was the Spanish Netherlands. Ever since the late 1560s, when Philip's leading general, Don Fernando Alvarez de Toledo, third duke of Alba, had crushed opposition to Spanish rule and unleashed a reign of terror to bludgeon Protestant rebels into submission, the presence of a massive army of seasoned veterans just across the English Channel had been a constant source of concern to Elizabeth and her advisors. The Dutch had fallen victim to Spanish tyranny; the English might be next.[18]

During the early 1580s the crisis intensified. In 1581 Dutch Protestants rose again and declared Philip II deposed, taking as their sovereign ruler the Duke of Anjou (Elizabeth's amorous "frog"), who was given the title "Prince and Lord" of the Netherlands. In response, the new Spanish governor-general of the Netherlands, Alexander Farnese, Duke of Parma, led a brilliantly successful military campaign that pushed through the southern Dutch provinces, seizing the key Flemish ports of Dunkirk and Nieuport in 1583, and Bruges and Ghent the next year. Then in July 1584 the rebel cause suffered a catastrophic blow with the murder of its charismatic leader, William of Orange, by a French assassin.

The manner of William's death and Parma's praise of his killer, whose "heroic action," he wrote, was "an example to the whole world," would not have been lost on Elizabeth's ministers. Only the year before, the queen's spymaster, Sir Francis Walsingham, had unmasked a plot to assassinate Elizabeth and place the queen's Catholic cousin and heir, Mary, Queen of Scots, on the English throne. Orchestrated by the Spanish ambassador in London, Don Bernardino de Mendoza, with the aid of the French ambassador and an English Catholic gentleman, the plot was uncovered early and never came close to succeeding. Yet the fear of assassination lingered, and the cold-blooded murder of William, one of Europe's foremost Protestant leaders, was another reminder of how vulnerable the English queen was. Elizabeth had escaped this time, but how long would it be before she too fell victim to an assassin's knife or bullet?[19]

England and Spain were moving inexorably toward open confrontation. The quasi-war that had been fought in American waters for the last fifteen years was coming to an end. In August 1583 Philip II's preeminent naval commander, the Marquis of Santa Cruz, had advised the king to launch a seaborne invasion directly from Spain, overthrow the "heretic woman," and take the English throne for himself. With England in Spanish hands, Santa Cruz reasoned, the king could finally subdue the Dutch. Philip was thinking along similar lines and wrote to Parma shortly afterward to sound him out. Parma believed the king could not rely solely on English Catholics to rise in support of a force sent from Spain and argued that a powerful army of at least 34,000 men should be sent from the Netherlands. This could only be accomplished, however, after the Dutch rebels had been reduced to submission.

Philip thought both proposals had merit, and so the plan was conceived for the "enterprise of England" that combined the two: a Spanish armada would sail from Spain, secure the English Channel, and escort battalions of Parma's army in the Netherlands to England. Elizabeth would then be deposed, and a Catholic nominee favorable to Spain would take her place. All the king had to do was be patient and wait for an opportune moment to strike.[20]

As the threat of a massive Spanish attack on England loomed larger in 1584, Elizabeth's councilors urged her to take action. Diplomatic relations with Spain were severed and Mendoza was expelled early in the year. London authorities called out local militias for drill, and 4,000 men mustered before the queen at Greenwich in May. And in the fall, a Bond of Association circulated throughout the country that bound signatories by oath to put to death anyone seeking to gain the throne by harming Elizabeth. If Elizabeth was murdered by a Catholic assassin, in other words, Mary, Queen of Scots, would be put to death.

Thousands signed in an outpouring of popular sentiment for the queen that reflected a determination not to submit to a Catholic successor should she be killed. Yet whatever the strength of domestic support for Elizabeth, England had no allies in Europe other than the Dutch rebels. She remained dangerously isolated. Lord Burghley, the lord treasurer, remarked bleakly that in confronting Spain, the queen could look to "no help but her own."[21]

Rather than wait to be attacked, during the winter of 1584–1585 the queen and her ministers began to formulate a strategy to take the initiative. Convinced there could be no more prevarication in providing aid to the Dutch, Elizabeth's government entered into negotiations with the Protestant rebels to send an English army to the Netherlands. At the same time, Sir Francis Walsingham dusted off proposals put forward by Gilbert and Ralegh several years before that involved harassing Spanish and Portuguese fishing fleets off Newfoundland, dispatching a large fleet to the West Indies, and the establishment of a colony on the North American mainland.

Along with Walsingham and the Earl of Leicester, Walter Ralegh counted himself foremost among the war party at court. Although he did not hold a formal office and was excluded from the high councils of state, his privileged position close to the queen enabled him to remain fully informed about the approaching war with Spain, a war in which he expected to play a major part. This was the moment to marry his personal ambitions with Elizabeth's foreign policy, and as the queen's ministers developed plans to mount a major assault on Spanish America, his proposal to plant a colony north of Florida took on greater significance.

The double-edged attack was planned on a grand scale. Sir Francis Drake would command a powerful fleet that would ransack the West Indies and Spanish Main, delivering an immediate and shattering blow to Spanish America. Ralegh would organize (but not lead) a large expedition to establish a harbor on Roanoke Island, from which English privateers could harass Spanish shipping in the Caribbean and western Atlantic, establishing a long-term English presence in the New World that would in time fatally undermine Spain's empire.[22]

SINCE THE RETURN of Amadas and Barlowe to England in the fall of 1584, Ralegh had been working feverishly on arrangements to establish a colony. Recognizing that the two Indians brought back to London could play an important role in his efforts to stimulate interest in the voyage, in October he presented Manteo and Wanchese to the court along with a copy of Barlowe's account of "Wingandacon" (as the English initially called coastal North Carolina) to Elizabeth. The Indians had been living at Durham House since their arrival, where they were taught English by Thomas Hariot. Hariot, in turn, had been able to master sufficient Algonquian to have simple conversations with them.

A traveler from Pomerania, Leopold von Wedel, visited Durham House at the end of October and painted an unflattering portrait of the two Indians: "In face and figure they were like white Moors. Normally they wear no shirt, just a wild animal skin across the shoulders and a piece of fur over the privies, but now they were dressed in brown taffeta [a silky fabric]. No one," he continued, "could understand what they said, and altogether they looked very childish and uncouth." Manteo and Wanchese proved extremely valuable, however, in providing information about the newfound land and in raising public awareness of Ralegh's venture.[23]

Given the enormous expense of the undertaking, Ralegh's first priority was to raise as much financial support as possible from Elizabeth, the court, and London's mercantile community. Promotional pieces by Richard Hakluyt (the lawyer) and his younger cousin of the same name explained the many benefits of American colonies to the nation and individual investors. Ralegh's emphasis on trade was not entirely mercenary. He, like John Dee and the two Richard Hakluyts, viewed commerce as indispensable to England's ambition to rival Spain: "This was Themistocles' opinion long since, and it is true," Ralegh later wrote, "that he that commands the sea, commands the trade, and he that is Lord of the Trade of the world is lord of the wealth of the world."[24]

The younger Hakluyt played a vital role in Ralegh's propaganda efforts. His "Discourse on Western Planting," completed in 1584, brought together a huge amount of current information about America. Shaped into a forceful and urgent appeal for English action, the "Discourse" was intended for the queen's and her councilors' eyes only. Authoritative and persuasive, the "Discourse" was highly influential in government circles in summarizing opinions about how to undermine Spanish power in America and advocating the benefits of English colonization.

A recurrent theme of Hakluyt's argument was the importance of colonies to the expansion of commerce. America, Hakluyt promised, "will yield to us all the commodities of Europe, Africa and Asia." The New World offered a cornucopia of goods—fish, furs, hides, fruits, dyestuffs, precious minerals, timber, and naval supplies—which would supplant England's traditional reliance on the Mediterranean and Baltic for imports. But to produce these goods, large numbers of English colonists would have to settle in America. For Hakluyt, the demand for laborers in the colonies was an advantage in its own right: the able-bodied poor, unemployed, and idle, an "altogether unprofitable" drain on the English economy, could be profitably put to work in the New World. England would gain doubly from the growing volume of colonial goods that could be sold in Europe and the export of home-produced goods to her American colonies.

Developing colonial trade was not the only motivation for establishing colonies. Planting English settlements in North America, Hakluyt believed, would promote the "godly and Christian work" of converting millions of Indian peoples to the "glorious gospel of Christ." Spanish conversion of Indians showed that they could be redeemed, and he looked forward to the establishment of the Anglican Church in North America, which would serve as a counterbalance to the expansion of Catholicism in Spain's possessions. North America would become a stronghold of Protestantism and provide a bulwark against Catholicism in the West Indies and South America.

English colonization and the erosion of Spanish power in America went hand in hand, in Hakluyt's view. Cutting off the flow of American treasure was critical. "If you touch him in the Indies, you touch the apple of his eye," he wrote of Philip II. By attacking the source of the king's wealth in the New World, his armies in Europe would wither, his strength would be "diminished, his pride abated, and his tyranny utterly suppressed."[25]

But perhaps the greatest prize of all for English colonists would be the discovery of fabulous wealth in North America, riches to rival or surpass those of Mexico and Peru: gold and silver mines and a passage through the continent to the Pacific Ocean. Breaking Spain's monopoly over the New World would open up untapped riches to the English. Hakluyt wrote that the River May (St. Johns) in Florida, where Jean Ribault and the French Huguenots first settled in 1562, penetrated through the landmass to the Pacific, "from whence great plenty of Treasure is brought thither." Indians had informed Ribault that the South Sea (Pacific) was only about twenty days away by boat. Hakluyt believed that the evidence pointing to the existence of a passage made the case for English colonization even more compelling. He therefore urged the queen to support her most willing "and forward" subjects (such as Ralegh) in planting colonies and exploring the continent.[26]

The arguments of the younger Hakluyt and his elder cousin had their desired effect—the queen backed Ralegh's venture. In December 1584 Ralegh, now a member of Parliament for Devon, introduced a private bill to confirm the royal patent granted to him earlier in the year by the queen for the establishment of a colony in America. His intention was likely to associate the queen more closely with his project and bring his plans to the attention of important members of the Commons and Lords who might be influential in helping him to raise money.

Ralegh gained the support of the Commons for the bill but not that of the Lords, whose members did not see the necessity for an additional measure beyond the queen's original grant. Nevertheless, he had achieved his main objectives in bringing in the bill. His plans had been discussed among those associates—Walsingham, Sir Francis Drake, and Sir Richard Grenville—whose support he particularly desired. And the bill had been something of a promotional coup in emphasizing Elizabeth's explicit wish that her people benefit from the establishment of colonies and her hope that a rich unknown land would be discovered.[27]

Throughout the winter and into the new year, Ralegh continued to lobby the queen and to enjoy her special favor. During a banquet at Greenwich Palace late in December, von Wedel described how she flirted with Ralegh, pointing to his face and saying there was some dirt on it. She went to wipe it off with her handkerchief, "but before she could he wiped it off himself. She was said to love this gentleman above all others," he remarked, "and this may be true, because two years ago he could scarcely keep a servant, and now with her bounty he can keep five hundred." On January 6, 1585, amid the splendor and spectacle that marked the twelfth day of Christmas, Elizabeth knighted Ralegh at Greenwich and shortly after granted him permission to name the new land he had discovered in her honor (she was popularly known as the virgin queen); he then assumed the title "Lord and Governor of Virginia."[28]

PREPARATIONS FOR the expedition to Roanoke were completed a few months later. Bernardino de Mendoza wrote to Philip II from

2.5 This portrait of Sir Richard Grenville in 1571 at the age of 29 shows him fourteen years before he commanded the first major expedition to Roanoke. Grenville played a leading role in Ralegh's Roanoke ventures from 1585 to 1588.

Paris in February that Elizabeth had contributed one of her own ships, the *Tiger* (160 tons), and that Ralegh had bought four other ships and was building four pinnaces. Mendoza reported that altogether sixteen vessels were being prepared (which was a gross exaggeration) and would sail with Drake's fleet as soon as they were fitted out (also a mistake; Drake would not leave until September). He expressed surprise, considering "the King of Spain was shortly to take possession of England, [that] Sir Walter Ralegh . . . does nevertheless undertake voyages to seek to hinder the Spaniards."[29] Ralegh was determined to lead his expedition, but the queen adamantly refused to let him go, so he turned to his cousin, Sir Richard Grenville, to take charge.

Twelve years older than Ralegh, from an old Cornish family related to the Drakes and Gilberts, Grenville had seen fighting in Hungary against the Turks and in Munster in the late 1560s. Several years later he had taken an interest in Gilbert's American schemes and had petitioned the queen to lead a voyage around the world. She ignored him, favoring Drake instead. In the spring of 1585 his close friendship with Ralegh, together with his military background and high political standing, made him an obvious choice to take charge of the voyage. But his arrogance and refusal to listen to advice would sorely try the patience of his subordinates.

The expedition was composed of five ships and two pinnaces, carrying approximately 600 men. Among Grenville's chief officers was Colonel Ralph Lane, a longtime servant of the queen, recently made sheriff of County Kerry, Ireland. He was known as an experienced military man and an authority on fortifications. Philip Amadas was chosen as "admiral of Virginia," responsible for organizing the colony's defenses; his partner in the earlier reconnaissance mission, Arthur Barlowe, likely commanded the *Dorothy*. Other officers included George Raymond, captain of the *Lion* (100 tons), a leading privateer, and John Clark, one of Ralegh's men, who commanded the *Roebuck* (140 tons). Thomas Cavendish, captain of the *Elizabeth* (50 tons), was a wealthy young man from Suffolk who would serve as high marshal or judicial officer of the expedition. Simon Fernandes was appointed chief pilot, and John White and Thomas Hariot were to carry out a thorough survey of the region, aided by Manteo and Wanchese.[30]

About half of the rank and file were sailors and the remainder soldiers and artisans. No women or families were included. Instead, the colony had the character of a military expedition. Some of the soldiers had previously served in Ireland with Ralegh or other leaders; some were young gentlemen who had staked their own money on the voyage in the hope of getting rich quick. The artisans included smiths, carpenters, coopers, shoemakers, cooks, and store masters in charge of provisions, essential to the task of building the settlement and feeding the colonists. Also included were laborers and common watermen, such as John Stile of London, who made a living on the Thames, and some, like Irishman Darby Glande (Glavin), who had been pressed into service.

There was at least one Anglican minister on the voyage to tend to the spiritual needs of the men. He would also carry the gospel to the Indians to ensure that ignorance and superstition were quickly banished from the queen's new dominion. Finally, the expedition included a number of mineral specialists from Germany, such as Joachim Gans, a Jewish expert from Prague, who had been employed by the Society of the Mines Royal in England for several years to improve output from the Society's copper works. The dozen or so miners and mineralogists of the expedition, led by Gans and Daniel Höchstetter (also associated with the Society of the Mines Royal) were responsible for the important task of testing metals acquired from local Indians and prospecting for iron, copper, silver, and gold.[31]

Ralegh's strategy was to send Grenville with the first wave of colonists to Roanoke Island to establish a beachhead. Shortly after, Bernard Drake and Amias Preston, two experienced mariners, were to follow with a second group of about 200 men to strengthen their position. Further supplies and settlers would then be sent over as the colony grew. In the meantime, Grenville was to conduct a reconnaissance of the Outer Banks, establish the initial settlement, and depending on circumstances, either stay with the colony or return to England (after cruising the Atlantic for prizes). An assessment of the region's wealth and its potential as a privateering base was a major objective and if it were favorable, would be an important argument in raising support for future voyages.

Leaving Plymouth on April 9, 1585, Grenville's squadron was one of the most powerful English fleets to set sail for American waters. The voyage began badly when, after only a week at sea, a fierce storm arose off the coast of Portugal that caused the loss of one of the pinnaces and scattered the rest of the fleet. Grenville, in the flagship *Tiger*, lost sight of the other ships and was forced to make the Atlantic crossing alone. Nearly a month later he arrived at a prearranged rendezvous in Puerto Rico (which the English called St. John's), on May 11.

Waiting for the rest of his fleet to appear, Grenville established a fortified camp at Mosquetal (Guayanilla Bay), named by the Spanish for its swarms of biting mosquitoes. After Cavendish's *Elizabeth* joined him on May 19, Grenville spent a couple of weeks building a pinnace to replace the one lost in the storm, and then decided to set sail for Hispaniola, where he hoped to trade for supplies. En route he captured a small Spanish frigate and a larger ship laden with cloth and other goods. The plunder was quickly sold to locals on one of the smaller islands for provisions, cattle, horses, and swine as well as plantains and sugar cane for Virginia. Grenville's fleet, now made up of the *Tiger*, the *Elizabeth*, the new-built pinnace, and two captured Spanish vessels crewed by his own men, moved quickly on to Isabella, on the

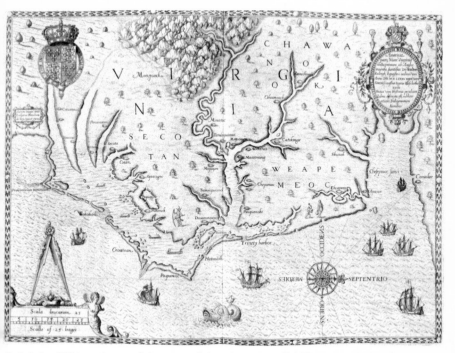

2.6 John White, *A map of that part of America, now called Virginia*, 1585–1586 (engraving by Theodor de Bry, 1590). White depicts the entire region from Cape Lookout to the Chesapeake Bay, showing the lands of the Secotans, Chowanocs, and Weapemeocs, together with the Mangoaks in the interior. Wococon inlet, where the *Tiger* went aground, is shown to the left. As Grenville quickly learned, ocean-going ships had to remain off the Outer Banks in deeper waters; only the pinnaces and ships' boats were able to navigate the shallow waters of the Sounds.

north coast of Hispaniola. There the English established friendly relations with the mayor and purchased more cattle, horses, hogs, and sheep as well as hides, ginger, tobacco, and pearls for sale in England.[32]

In early June Grenville led his ships from the Caribbean northward through the Bahamas Channel and along the Florida

The towne of Pomeiock and true forme of their howses, covered and enclosed some with matts, and some with barcks of trees. All compassed abowt with smale poles stock thick together in stedd of a wall.

2.7 John White, *Pomeiooc*, 1585. A large expedition led by Grenville visited Pomeiooc in July 1585. The house to the right with the pointed roof may have been a temple, and the large longhouse to the left was likely the chief's residence.

coast, reaching the Outer Banks three weeks later. On June 29 he suffered a major setback. While attempting to enter the Outer Banks through an inlet off Wococon Island, the *Tiger* ran aground on a sandbank and was battered for two hours in the surf, seriously damaging the ship and ruining much of the food stores. Sir Richard was furious and liberally berated the pilot,

Simon Fernandes, for his "unskilfulness." Fortunately his men were eventually able to float her off and beach her so that repairs could be made, but it was obvious that the larger ships could not navigate the inlets leading into the sounds and would therefore be unable to play a major role in the exploration of the region.[33]

Grenville's mood brightened considerably over the next week. He had sent a couple of men (and possibly Wanchese) to greet Wingina, who was at Roanoke Island. The English commander wanted to alert the Secotan chief of his arrival at Wococon and to find out if any of the ships separated from him off Portugal had arrived. He was delighted when his men reported that the *Roebuck* and *Dorothy* had made their way safely across the Atlantic and were on their way from Hatarask (recently named by the English Port Ferdinando) to join him.

Grenville could now turn his attention to locating a suitable site for the settlement. On July 11 he led a party of sixty men, guided by Manteo, from Wococon Island across Pamlico Sound to the mainland, where they spent a week exploring and visiting several Secotan towns. The expedition produced mixed results. Soundings taken during the crossing confirmed that even if the English discovered an entrance for large ships through the barrier islands, the shallow waters of the sounds could not possibly serve as a harbor for oceangoing ships. Only the fleet's long boats and pinnaces were able to move about freely.

Ashore, the English were welcomed at Pomeiooc, where John White undertook a series of careful drawings and watercolors of the settlement and people. Situated near Pamlico Sound, the town was made up of eighteen longhouses encompassed by a sturdy palisade. The houses skirted the inside perimeter, leaving a large open space in the middle of the settlement where people gathered for public celebrations and ceremonies. Beyond the town, Grenville and his men marched several miles inland to visit a great lake called Paquype (Lake Mattamuskeet) and then returned to their boats at Wyesocking Bay. There they spent the night before sailing to the Pamlico River the next day.

At Aquascocock on the Pungo River, a tributary of the Pamlico, the reception from the Indians appears to have been less friendly. White made no paintings, and the English alleged that some of their goods, including a small silver cup, were stolen. The cup and perhaps pieces of copper were shown to the Secotans as the soldiers traveled from town to town in the hope of hearing news of like metals (silver, copper, and gold) in the region, just as Fernandes had picked up similar information the year before. Grenville opted to quickly move on.

The English rejoined the Pamlico River and sailed westward to the capital town of Secotan. The town consisted of a dozen houses scattered among the trees and along a main thoroughfare near open fields, where tobacco, several types of corn, and garden vegetables grew. Here the English were well entertained. The people had laid out food and drink on mats in readiness for a feast that would last long into the night, lit by the flames of "great fires to avoid darkness, and to testify their Joy." John White observed a group of men and women singing and dancing in a circle of beaten earth marked by wooden posts with carved faces, while in a smaller adjoining plot some people had assembled to pray. Quite likely he painted Wingina at Secotan, standing with simple dignity, arms crossed over his chest, wearing a leather skirt about his waist and a copper plaque and pearls

2.8 John White, *Secotan*, 1585. Grenville's company visited the capital town of Secotan a few days after Pomeiooc. Houses are dispersed throughout the surrounding woods and grouped along a central open space that runs through the town. In the foreground is the tomb of the Secotans' chiefs and two sacred places where the Indians prayed and danced in religious rituals. The cornfields are carefully laid out in order of planting.

2.9 John White, *Indians Dancing*, 1585. White depicts a festive ritual at Secotan involving a group of Indians dancing within a circle of posts with carved faces. Three "fair virgins" are shown in the center and 14 men and women dance around them. The ritual may have been a celebration of the harvest.

around his neck to symbolize his authority. The chief, an older man, appears fit and lean, like most of the Secotans whom White illustrated.[34]

After leaving Secotan, Grenville sent Captain Amadas with eleven men back to Aquascocock to retrieve the stolen silver cup. When the cup was not returned, the soldiers burned the town and corn fields nearby; the people having fled in advance. Grenville intended to leave no doubt in the Indians' minds of the dire consequences of disobeying the English, but what the Indians thought of the aggressive and heavy-handed act can be easily imagined. Word must have traveled quickly about the strangers' erratic and violent behavior.[35]

On July 18 Grenville and his men returned to the fleet anchored off Wococon. The exploration of the Pamlico region had probably been a disappointment to the English commander. None of the towns they had visited had revealed any signs of wealth, and the Englishmen had learned nothing from the Indians to suggest that gold or other treasures might be found in the interior.

Three days later the fleet sailed north and moored off Port Ferdinando in preparation for the establishment of a settlement on Roanoke Island. Shortly after their arrival, Granganimeo and Manteo visited Grenville on board the *Tiger* to seal the accord by which the English were permitted to settle near his village at the north end of the island.

By now Grenville had made up his mind to return to England the next month and leave a garrison of slightly more than a hundred men on the island under the command of Ralph Lane. The loss of a good part of the *Tiger*'s stores while stranded on the sand bar at the entrance to Pamlico Sound made provisioning a larger garrison impossible. But Grenville probably reasoned that Drake and Preston's fleet bringing the second wave of settlers and fresh supplies would arrive shortly, perhaps even before he left. He had no way of knowing that Drake and Preston's fleet had been stayed by the queen and diverted to Newfoundland to harass Spanish shipping.

Over the next few weeks Grenville and Lane put their men to work transporting their gear through Port Ferdinando to Roanoke Island and clearing ground for their settlement, located close to the shore on the northeastern side of the island. On a

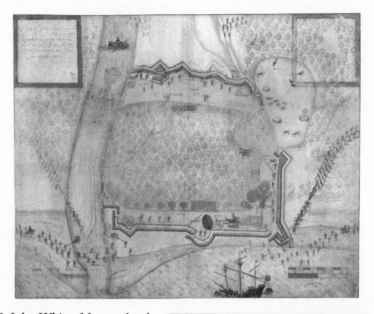

2.10 John White, *Mosquetal* and *Cape Rojo*, 1585. Mosquetal, on Tallaboa Bay, Puerto Rico, was built in May 1585 when Grenville's ship put in at the island for two weeks. Ralph Lane's fortifications and earthworks at *Mosquetal* and *Cape Rojo* may suggest how he approached constructing the fort on Roanoke Island.

small inlet nearby, Lane built a jetty to offload equipment and stores from the pinnace and boats going back and forth from ships anchored off Port Ferdinando. No records have survived that reveal how Lane designed and constructed the fort. At Mosquetal, Lane had laid out the fortified encampment on the shore, approximately 120 by 100 yards square, bounded by the sea and a river on two sides and earthworks on the others. It had been large enough to accommodate the 160 men of the *Tiger*, and its light defensive works were more than adequate to deter attacks from local Spanish forces. A couple of weeks later at Cape Rojo, Puerto Rico, Lane had further honed his skills when he constructed elaborate entrenchments made of sand to give his men a modicum of protection should the Spanish attempt a raid while they laded salt into one of the pinnaces.

On Roanoke Island Lane probably adopted for a similar approach: a fortified enclosure, possibly triangular or an irregular four-sided form, constructed primarily of ditches, earthworks, and palisades. The enclosure was meant to be simple and flexible so that it could be expanded when the next group of settlers arrived. Given that Granganimeo's people were allies and posed no obvious threat, and a large-scale assault by Spanish warships was unlikely (if the English could not get their great ships into the sounds, then neither could the Spanish), Lane believed that stronger defenses were unnecessary. But mindful of the fate of the French Huguenots at Fort Caroline, wiped out by a small Spanish force in a surprise attack from the landward side of the fort, Lane built several large bastions where a couple of dozen men could be stationed and artillery mounted on specially constructed gun platforms to protect the major approaches to the settlement.

The settlement was likely made up of a storehouse, magazine, and barracks for the men; a rudimentary chapel for daily services; and small single-unit houses for Grenville and the officers. There were probably also a forge, a cooper's workshop, a kitchen, and a garden plot where the men could experiment with local crops as well as with roots and seeds brought from the West Indies. The livestock would have been penned in enclosures near the settlement to prevent the cattle and hogs from destroying the crops. Farther off, where noxious fumes would not poison them, the colonists constructed a small building approximately ten feet square for Joachim Gans and Thomas Hariot's laboratory for testing metals. Gans and Hariot may also have had a house nearby.[36]

WHILE LANE was busy overseeing the construction of the fort and settlement, Grenville dispatched Amadas and about twenty men to reconnoiter Albemarle Sound, once again in the hope of discovering signs of wealth in the interior. Fernandes may have gone as well; he had been with Amadas the year before when they learned of the mighty river "Occam," which they believed to be the Albemarle. By European standards, Albemarle Sound is massive, some twelve miles wide at its mouth and fifty-five miles long. Earlier explorations of the Pamlico Sound region by Grenville had failed to reveal a waterway anywhere near as large, which persuaded the English that the Albemarle was likely to be the best means of moving men and supplies inland should the need arise.

The expedition may also have been punitive. Richard Butler, who was with the expedition, later recounted that the Englishmen killed about twenty Weapemeocs in a skirmish and captured some women, whom they gave "to the other savages" (the Secotans). The English had been attacked themselves the year before when they had scouted the northern bank of the Albemarle. What better way to exact revenge and at the same time demonstrate the benefits of an alliance with the English to Wingina than by destroying several Weapemeoc towns and carrying off captives?

Amadas and his party traveled about fifty miles inland and discovered the entrances to the Chowan and Moratuc (Roanoke) Rivers. Halfway along the sound they found fresh water and plenty of fish, and on the northern bank in the lands of the Weapemeocs an abundance of red grapes. But the best news by far was the strength of the current of the Roanoke River, which Butler described as strong enough to make headway nearly impossible. Ralph Lane provided a more detailed account eight months later:

> And whereas the River of Choanoak [Chowan] and all the other sounds, and Bays, salt and fresh, show no current in the world in calm weather, but are moved altogether with the wind: This River of Morotico [Roanoke] has so violent a current from the West and Southwest, that it made me almost of [the] opinion that with oars it would scarce be navigable.

A strong current, which Lane reckoned was comparable to that of the River Thames at London Bridge during an ebb tide, suggested that the Roanoke River rose from a place far away. If so, perhaps the river would lead the English to the mountains where precious minerals or a passage to the South Sea might be found.[37]

By EARLY AUGUST 1585 Grenville considered he had sufficient good news to warrant sending a ship back to England to inform Ralegh and the court of the voyage's success. John Arundell was given the happy task and set sail on the fifth, followed a week or so later by some of the other ships. Grenville himself departed with the *Tiger* on August 25. Only John Clark (with the *Roebuck*) remained, and he too would leave shortly.

Now in charge of the fledgling settlement, Ralph Lane must have been in good spirits as he watched the flagship slip away from the Outer Banks, doubtless relieved to be rid of his haughty commander. His men were secure behind their fortifications, and he could expect reinforcements to arrive at any moment. He sent letters brimming with enthusiasm to his patrons, Sir Francis Walsingham and Sir Philip Sidney, extolling the natural bounty of Virginia and even making a virtue of the difficulties of navigation along the Outer Banks in providing protection from a Spanish attack.

Writing in an optimistic vein to his friend Richard Hakluyt the elder, Lane claimed the mainland to be "the goodliest soil under the cope of heaven" and assured him that all sorts of commodities imported from Spain, France, Italy, and "the East parts" would in time be produced or cultivated in Virginia. The region, he wrote, was the

> most pleasing territory of the world (for the soil [continent] is of a huge unknown greatness, and very well peopled and towned, though savagely) and the climate so wholesome, that we have not had one sick, since we touched land here. To conclude, if Virginia had but Horses and Kine in some rea-

sonable proportion, I dare assure myself being inhabited with English, no realm in Christendom were comparable to it.[38]

Amadas's expedition to the head of Albemarle Sound had promised much, and Lane was already planning to probe farther into the interior: to the north toward the city of Skicóak and the Chesapeake Bay, and west up the Chowan and Roanoke Rivers into the mountains, following the lure of riches.

⟨∽∞∽⟩

"Being inhabited with English" was a phrase hardly likely to have reassured Granganimeo and Wingina had it come to their ears. But in any event, the chiefs had already begun to have doubts about English intentions by the fall of 1585. Manteo and Wanchese had returned from their voyage to England with extraordinary stories about what they had seen on the other side of the ocean: a city of stone that stretched as far as the eye could see, buildings that pressed in on all sides, rivers full of tall ships, and streets teeming with men and women, too many to count. The stink of the city (and its people) was overpowering on the crowded streets and by the river at low tide. They had stayed in a large house belonging to a powerful lord and met many important people, including one they called the queen, who was the greatest among them.

Manteo and Wanchese differed in their attitudes toward the English. Manteo reported that the two of them had been well treated and believed the English were their friends. Wanchese disagreed; he had been unable to discover why the strangers wanted to come to their lands and was suspicious of their intentions. The incident at Aquascocock, he believed, confirmed the men were dangerous and unpredictable.[39]

Wingina was undecided, at least for the time being. Manteo might be right that the newcomers were friendly and could become valuable allies. The English might prove useful in supplying precious trade goods and support in wars against his enemies. But if Wanchese's opinion turned out to be nearer the mark, Wingina would have to move swiftly to kill or expel the strangers from his land.

3

"Chaunis Temoatan"

To get the pearl and gold,
And ours to hold,
Virginia,
Earth's only paradise.

—Michael Drayton

Sir Richard Grenville found the riches he was looking for, but not in Virginia. Ten days out from Port Ferdinando, he spotted a sail on the horizon off the Bermudas and gave chase. She was the *Santa Maria de San Vicente*, a large Spanish merchantman, struggling to catch up with a convoy of thirty ships carrying sugar, hides, and other goods from Vera Cruz to Seville. As soon as she was in range the *Tiger* opened fire, sending shot into her rigging and holing her along the waterline. With one man dead and several injured, the captain, Alonzo Cornieles, surrendered to avoid further casualties.

Grenville had left his longboat back in Virginia with Ralph Lane, so he fashioned a makeshift boat by lashing together some old sea chests. Accompanied by thirty well-armed men, he then gingerly made his way to the *Santa Maria*, in a crossing that turned out to be rather more hazardous than he had anticipated. The waterlogged tub sank ever lower in the water as the Englishmen rowed frantically toward the ship, and it disappeared beneath the waves just as they clambered up the *Santa Maria*'s sides.

Once on board, Grenville wasted no time getting down to business. He and his men quickly relieved the *Santa Maria*'s passengers of their valuables, then Grenville demanded the cargo of gold, silver, and pearls worth 40,000 ducats (£12,500) be delivered to him personally. Besides sugar and hides, the *Santa Maria* also carried ginger, cochineal, and ivory worth another 80,000 ducats. As soon as the Spanish ship was in order Grenville set a course for England, opting to remain on board to keep a close eye on his prize. He stopped off briefly in the Azores for fresh supplies and reached Plymouth in mid-October, where he was met by Ralegh, anxious to hear his news.[1]

At the house of old William Hawkins, one of Plymouth's leading privateers, Ralegh and Grenville discussed the latter's dashing improvisations, which had transformed the expedition from near disaster into a brilliant success. Grenville had survived storms and mishaps to reach the coast of America, carrying out an exploration of the Outer Banks, developing good relations with local peoples, establishing a garrison on Roanoke Island, and taking a rich merchantman on the way home sufficient to return investors a handsome profit.

News of the capture of the *Santa Maria* spread like wildfire in London. A report in November 1585 put the value of the cargo and treasure at a million ducats (more than £300,000). Henry Talbot, writing to his kinsman the Earl of Shrewsbury a couple of weeks earlier, mentioned that the prize had made Ralegh a rich man.

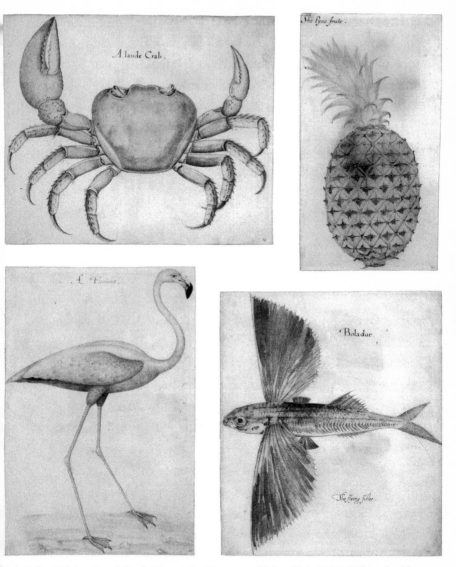

3.1 John White, *Land Crab, Pineapple, Flamingo, Flying Fish*, 1585. White had been instructed by Sir Walter Ralegh to make a careful record of the flora and fauna he saw on the voyage. These paintings were likely undertaken at Mosquetal and during the *Tiger*'s voyage through the West Indies and Bahamas.

Grenville's bold action captivated Elizabeth's court and seemed a good omen for England's effort to establish colonies in America and for the coming war with Spain. All the talk, commented Talbot, was "of killing the Spaniards, both at sea and land."[2]

With the fanfare surrounding Grenville's return, the arrival of other members of the expedition went largely unnoticed. John White, who had sailed on the *Tiger*, quickly made his way to London to see his family and report to Ralegh. He brought his wonderfully detailed paintings of the flora and fauna of the West Indies and the peoples of Virginia, the first images of Indians of the region and (apart from his own paintings of the Inuit made during Frobisher's second voyage and Jacques Le Moyne's paintings of Florida Indians) the first accurate illustrations of North American peoples seen in England. At Durham House he presented his watercolors of land crabs, herons, and ducks he had spotted near the encampment at Mosquetal in Puerto Rico; the pineapple and plantains taken from the West Indies to Roanoke Island; the iguana, frigate bird, and flamingo he had seen in the Bahamas; the many varieties of fish he had observed throughout the voyage; and most important, the startlingly naturalistic pictures of men, women, and children of the Secotan people.[3]

Little is known of White's movements in London, but it is not too fanciful to imagine him spending long hours in animated conversation with his recently married daughter, Eleanor, and her husband, Ananias Dare, during which he tried to convey the strangeness of the New World—its vivid colors, different peoples, and exotic creatures. Following the reconnaissance of the year before, Arthur Barlowe had described the Outer Banks as a Garden of Eden where the people "lived after the manner of the golden age" and the "earth brings forth all things in abundance, as in the first creation, without toil of labor." White knew better. Virginia was not a land of milk and honey. He had seen the hardships the people endured, the daily struggle to provide food for themselves in the midst of drought, and the scars of war worn proudly by their warriors. But if not paradise, Virginia was nevertheless an enchanting land, and White was captivated.[4]

ON ROANOKE ISLAND, as fall turned to winter, Ralph Lane's men grew restless. They had given up hope of being joined by Bernard Drake and Amias Preston's fleet, which they had expected soon after Grenville's departure, and had no idea when reinforcements would eventually appear. Lane had tried to keep his men busy around the settlement and made regular visits to neighboring Secotan towns to trade for provisions, skins, and local pearls, but as the weeks dragged by the men became increasingly bored and irritable. He decided the time was right, therefore, to send an expedition north to the Chesapeake Bay. Earlier explorations had scouted regions as far south as the principal town of Secotan and west up the Albemarle to the mouth of the Chowan, but lands north of the Weapemeocs had not been investigated.

The expedition left the island in late October or early November 1585 and sailed up Currituck Sound, out through an opening in the Outer Banks to the ocean, along the coast for approximately thirty miles until they reached Cape Henry, unnamed on John White's map, and into the Chesapeake Bay. Philip Amadas, who had stayed behind with Lane rather than return to England, was most likely the leader of the expedition and

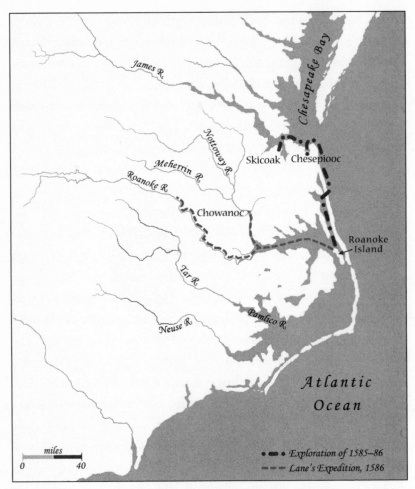

3.2 Explorations of 1585–1586. Drawn by Rebecca L. Wrenn.

decided first to explore Lynnhaven Bay, near the mouth of the
Chesapeake Bay. They visited the town of "Chesepiooc," but did
not stay long before continuing along the southern shore of the
bay to the Elizabeth River, where about fifteen miles inland they
discovered Skicóak, the capital of the Chesapeakes.

The town may have been a disappointment. Barlowe, in his account of the previous year, had described Skicóak as the region's largest city, "which this people [the Secotans] affirm to be very great." Amadas may have hoped that the capital would be comparable in size and wealth to towns the Spanish had conquered in Mexico and Peru. What they discovered was not a metropolis but rather a cluster of longhouses and few signs of wealth.

If the town was a disappointment, the Englishmen were nonetheless impressed by the country around Skicóak. The land "of the Chesepians," they subsequently reported to Lane, "for pleasantness of seat [location], for temperature of Climate, for fertility of soil, and for the commodity of the Sea . . . [is] not to be excelled by any other whatsoever," including (presumably) the Roanoke area. They camped outside the town for a couple of months, during which they explored the lower reaches of the James-York peninsula and possibly crossed the bay to the Eastern Shore. They then returned to Roanoke in late February or early March 1586.[5]

RELATIONS BETWEEN the English and Secotans had deteriorated rapidly during the three or four months that Amadas's expedition was away. Tensions arose owing to the continuing dependence of the colonists on the Indians for food, which during the winter months was increasingly difficult to supply. Yet the most important reason for the souring of relations was the terrible toll inflicted on the Secotan population by European diseases since the beginning of the fall. Epidemics, perhaps smallpox or influenza, swept through the region and claimed many lives.

3.3 John White, detail from *A map of that part of America, now called Virginia*, 1585–1586 (engraving by Theodor de Bry, 1590), showing the Mouth of the Chesapeake Bay. The extent of Amadas' exploration of the lands of the Chesapeakes and neighboring peoples is indicated in this detail. The towns of Chesepiooc and Skicóak are located (on the Lynnhaven and Elizabeth Rivers), and the entrances to the James and York Rivers are suggested at the top of the map.

Thomas Hariot later reported in his account to Ralegh the deadly impact of the outbreak. As the English moved from town to town, "the people began to die very fast, and many in short space; in some towns about twenty, in some forty, in some sixty, and in one six score, which in truth was very many in respect of their numbers." With no natural immunity to the diseases and no means of curing them, Indian priests could do little other than pray to their gods for relief and hope the sickness would pass.

How the strange mortality had come about and what it portended were issues hotly debated by Wingina's people. Some Secotan elders believed the English were dead men who had returned to the world and were immortal. They prophesied that "there were more of our generation [the English] yet to come, to kill theirs and take their places." Others believed the trail of death left by the colonists was not caused by disease but by "invisible bullets" fired by soldiers from many miles away to punish those who affronted them. Ensenore, described by Lane as one of the chief's closest advisors, warned Wingina that the English were "the servants of God" and could not be harmed and that any who sought the colonists' destruction would only "find their own." The sighting of a comet in the night skies the previous fall had coincided with the onset of the sickness brought by the English and seemed an ominous sign.[6]

With the deaths of Ensenore and Granganimeo in early 1586, Wingina finally made up his mind. He did not believe that the English were immortal, although he recognized the intruders' power. He had come to understand that the English, no more than his priests, were able to end the drought or treat the diseases that afflicted his people. The colonists were just as vulnerable to

3.4 John White, *Wingina*, 1585. Wingina, chief of the Secotans, played a highly significant role in the events of the first colony. White likely painted him during his visit to the town of Secotan in July 1585, when relations between the English and Indians were cordial.

food shortages as Indians, and throughout the winter and spring had been utterly dependent on his people for provisions. He eventually came to the same conclusion as Wanchese: the English were too violent and unreliable to be allies. They had brought death and disease to his people, and he must get rid of them as soon as possible.

Wingina took a new name, Pemisapan, in the spring, which may have meant something like "he who watches closely." The change of name signaled the end of his efforts to help the colonists and the beginning of a strategy aimed at their destruction. Under the cover of his continuing friendship, Pemisapan planned to orchestrate a large-scale attack on the English in conjunction with other peoples of the region. The first part of the plan was to lure Lane and some of his men away from the fort by informing them of a "general assembly" of Indians to be held by Menatonon, chief of the Chowanocs, at his capital on the Chowan River. Pemisapan told Lane that Menatonon intended to forge an alliance between the Chowanocs and Mangoaks, as well as other peoples, to attack the English. The chief advised the English commander to take a strong force to Chowanoc as soon as possible and launch a preemptive attack on the Indians gathered there. Privately, Pemisapan calculated that by this means Lane and his men would become embroiled in hostilities with the Chowanocs and their allies and be cut off. The remaining English on Roanoke Island would be starved into submission or killed as they attempted to escape the fort in search of food.

Pemisapan played his role well and convinced Lane of the necessity to act swiftly. How much Lane knew about the Chowanocs and Mangoaks is uncertain. He had been intending for some weeks to explore the Chowan and Roanoke Rivers, and once Amadas and his men were safely back at the fort, Lane took the pinnace and two boats and set out in March with fifty or sixty men (including Manteo and three other Indians) to engage the Chowanocs. An expedition that had been planned initially as a friendly visit now took on a more deadly purpose.[7]

The Englishmen moved rapidly up Albemarle Sound and entered the broad waters of the Chowan River, where they found a fertile land, well watered with "goodly" corn fields. They sailed past "Ohaunoock," the blind town, as Lane called it because it could not be seen from their boats, and shortly afterward arrived at Chowanoc. Muskets at the ready, Lane and his men stormed into the capital and seized the aged and "impotent" (infirm) chief Menatonon. As Pemisapan had foretold, an assembly of the principal men of the Chowanocs, Mangoaks, Weapemeocs, and Moratucs was in progress, but the Indians were not plotting an attack on the English. Taken completely by surprise, they offered no resistance and sought instead to negotiate.

Menatonon told Lane that it was Pemisapan, not he, who conspired to stir up trouble between the colonists and local Indians. Pemisapan, the old chief explained, had sent word that the English were fully bent on destroying his people and had dispatched similar messages to the Moratucs and Mangoaks along the Roanoke River. Menatonon had therefore called together his chiefs and allies to assess the threat. The Secotans, he emphasized, were the colonists' enemy, not the Chowanocs or Mangoaks, who had no reason to attack the English other than in self-defense. But who was Lane to believe, Pemisapan, who had been a reliable ally during the previous nine months, or Menatonon?[8]

The English commander decided to reserve judgment and entered into lengthy talks with the Chowanoc chief. During the two days they conferred, he learned more about the region than he had in all the explorations and conversations with other peoples up to that time. The old chief told him that three days up the Chowan River by canoe and another four days overland to the northeast lay a province bordering the sea, ruled by a powerful king whose seat was on an island in a bay. This king had such great quantities of pearls that he adorned not only himself with them, but also his chief men and followers, and his "beds and houses are garnished with them . . . that it is a wonder to see." The king traded with white men, but Menatonon advised Lane to go only with a large force and plenty of provisions, because the king was reluctant to allow strangers to enter into his country or "to meddle with the fishing of any Pearl there." Menatonon said that the king was able to take a great many men into battle who fought very well.[9]

This was the first time the English had heard of Wahunsonacock (Powhatan), the formidable chief of the Powhatans, who ruled over approximately a dozen tribes along the James and York Rivers in Virginia. Undaunted by the fierce reputation of the Powhatan chief, Lane resolved to organize a major expedition to the Chesapeake Bay by land and sea once reinforcements arrived from England. Attracted by riches in pearls and the fertile country around Skicóak, he believed that the Chesapeake might offer the English a better location for a settlement than the Outer Banks.

For the time being, however, Lane's interest remained focused on lands to the west. A few months earlier he had picked up rumors from Indians living at the mouth of the Roanoke River of "strange things" at the head of the river, thirty to forty days away. They say, Lane wrote, that the river issued forth from a great rock that bordered a sea. When winds blew off the sea, the upper waters of the river became salty and brackish. Menatonon confirmed the rumors, prompting Lane to wonder whether there might be a water passage through the mountains that led to the Pacific.

Menatonon's son, Skiko, offered even more valuable information about the interior. He told Lane that the Mangoaks often

3.5 Indians Panning for Gold in a Mountain Stream (engraving by Theodor de Bry, 1590). Jacques Le Moyne's map of Florida noted the existence of a great lake in the Appalachians where Indians gathered silver from a river flowing from the mountains. Skiko told Ralph Lane in 1586 that the Indians of Chaunis Temoatan panned for gold in a swift running river in the mountains.

journeyed up the Roanoke River to a distant province, where they traded for a "marvelous and most strange Mineral." The famed province was called "Chaunis Temoatan" and was more than twenty days from the land of the Mangoaks. The Indians' name for the mineral was "wassador," which meant copper. But Lane noted in his report to Ralegh that *wassador* could refer to any metal, and Skiko, who had learned of the metal when held captive by the Mangoaks, had described it as very soft and pale. To Lane's ears this suggested gold, and according to Skiko, the region was full of it. Although he had not been to Chaunis Temoatan himself, Skiko had learned that Indians of the country panned for *wassador* in a swift-running river that came down from the mountains. He reported that the Mangoaks had such vast quantities of the metal "they beautify their houses with great plates" of it.[10]

Skiko's sensational news was a turning point for Lane. Here at last was specific information that might lead him to gold in the mountains and perhaps other riches beyond. His course of action was clear. He would have to make contact with the Mangoaks, find out more about the mysterious metal *wassador*, and follow their trading route inland to Chaunis Temoatan.

After receiving a ransom for the release of Menatonon, Lane left the Chowanoc capital and sailed back downriver to the head of Albemarle Sound, where he dispatched the pinnace with Skiko on board to Roanoke Island. He had taken the precaution of holding Skiko hostage in case the Chowanocs should be tempted to turn against him. But Lane saw to it that Skiko was treated well, since he had no wish to antagonize the Indians unnecessarily.

Lane then set out with forty men to explore the Roanoke River. He hoped to be supplied with food by local peoples en route, but Pemisapan's messages to those along the river warning them that the English intended to attack anyone they encountered had had their desired effect. Lane reported that they did not see a single Indian for three days, nor was an ear of corn to be had in any of the towns they passed.

The decisive encounter took place about a hundred miles upriver. Near the falls of the Roanoke, the English were suddenly set upon by a party of warriors (probably Mangoaks) hidden along the river bank, who let fly a volley of arrows at one of the boats as it passed by. None of the English were injured, but in Lane's mind the attack confirmed that far from helping him in his quest to find Chaunis Temoatan, the Mangoaks would likely be a significant hindrance.

Only a much larger and better equipped expedition would have any chance of penetrating far into the interior, and Lane therefore reluctantly decided to return to the fort. After a difficult journey back, during which they ran out of supplies and were reduced to eating the two mastiffs they had brought with them for the assault on Chowanoc, the half-starved men arrived at Roanoke Island on Easter Monday, exhausted but grateful to be alive.[11]

The expedition's outcome had been frustrating, like so much else about the colony's first nine months. Lane was convinced he was on the brink of a great discovery and yet could not find the certain proof he needed to send to England. The fleet that he had thought would arrive by the spring had still not appeared, and now he had the added worry of being attacked by the Secotans and their allies at any moment. Lane's one comfort was his growing regard for the Chowanocs and their chief, Menatonon, who had been faithful in their promises and had stated their wish for a firm alliance with the English.

That Lane's expedition had survived took Pemisapan by surprise. He had not expected the Englishmen to return, believing they would surely perish in the interior. But the chief knew that the best means of fatally weakening the colonists was through their stomachs, and in the late spring he moved to cut off all food supplies. Lane had not considered the possibility that his men would have to cultivate their own food; his men were soldiers, not farmers. Other than a small garden plot used for experiments with plants brought from the West Indies, the English had made no effort to raise their own crops. They assumed they would either have sufficient stores from England or would be able to barter with local peoples for supplies. Pemisapan's refusal to provide food therefore gave Lane little choice but to divide his men into small bands and send them out to live off the country as best they could. Groups of about twenty were sent to Croatoan, Hatarask, and the mainland opposite Roanoke Island.

Lane's decision to divide his men into small groups made the English far more vulnerable to attack. Pemisapan's warriors could now pick off the colonists piecemeal. Lane and his principal officers would be killed first, the chief planned, which would be the signal for a general uprising to dispatch the rest of the colonists. Pemisapan had spent the previous couple of months trying to recruit Mangoaks, Moratucs, and Weapemeocs to join him by promising large quantities of copper and shares in the spoils and had called for a council to meet on June 10, 1586. A council would confirm whether or not others were prepared to support him and provide an opportunity to plan the attack.

How successful Pemisapan was in recruiting support for the attack is unclear, because the council never took place. In late May Lane received advance warning of the Secotans' intentions from Skiko, who had befriended the English, and quickly devised a counterstrategy. Lane sent a messenger to inform Pemisapan that he had heard news of the arrival of an English fleet and was going south to Croatoan Island to meet it. With Pemisapan under the impression that he had left the fort, Lane organized a surprise attack on the Secotans living on Roanoke Island and destroyed their settlement.

Quickly following up, on June 1 Lane crossed to the mainland with twenty-six men, including Manteo. On entering Dasemunkepeuc Lane saw that the Secotan chief was accompanied only by a small group of his principal followers and seized the opportunity to attack. Shouting "Christ our victory," the prearranged watchword, he led his men toward the startled Indians surrounding the chief. Philip Amadas shot Pemisapan, who fell to the ground, and the English began killing all those assembled, except some of Manteo's friends who happened to be in the town.

In the midst of the fighting, the English were amazed to see Pemisapan, whom the soldiers had thought dead, suddenly leap to his feet and sprint into the woods nearby. Although badly wounded, he had kept his wits about him and had feigned death while waiting for an opportunity to escape the slaughter. One of Lane's men, Edward Nugent, went off in hot pursuit and after a long chase emerged from the woods, holding up the severed head of the chief for all to see. Pemisapan's death ended the fighting and soon afterward the English returned across the water to Roanoke Island in triumph.[12]

THE HOSTILITIES between the Secotans and English that led to the murder of Pemisapan transformed Anglo–Indian relations in the region. The Secotans on Roanoke Island and the mainland had been routed by the English and seriously depleted by disease. The killing of their chief made the likelihood of any future renewal of good relations with the English extremely remote. The Weapemeocs, who until recently had been enemies of the Secotans, had split over whether to join the attack to expel the English. Okisko's people who were loyal to Menatonon had refused to take part, whereas other Weapemeoc peoples who lived in the eastern part of their territory near the coast (and closer to the English) probably joined Pemisapan. The Chowanocs had aligned themselves with the English, perhaps in the expectation that the newcomers would aid them against the Mangoaks, or other Iroquoian peoples in the interior, who might try to invade their territories. For Menatonon, the threat from the west was more pressing than that posed by the English in the east. Finally, Manteo had remained loyal to the English throughout the hostilities, which suggests that his people, the Croatoans, were also willing to support the English rather than the Secotans.[13]

There was no general uprising of the Secotans and Weapemeocs following Lane's murderous attack on Dasemunkepeuc, which no doubt led Lane to assume that he had foiled Pemisapan's plans. The English likely plundered the town for stored provisions that would help them get through June and July, by which time the Secotans' ripening corn would be ready for harvesting. If the Indians' supplies were not enough to last his men through the summer until a relief expedition arrived from England, Lane probably reasoned they had every justification to attack other Secotan towns for food and compel local peoples to supply them. Nevertheless, Lane remained anxious about the possibility of reprisals by the Secotans and Weapemeocs and must have realized that the colonists' occupation of Roanoke

Island was in the long run untenable. His assessment reinforced his growing belief that the English should relocate their colony to the southern shore of the Chesapeake Bay as soon as possible.

ONLY A WEEK after the killing of Pemisapan, Lane was suddenly confronted by a potentially far more dangerous threat. Captain Edward Stafford, stationed at the southern end of Hatarask Island, had spotted a great fleet, "but whether they were friends or foes, he could not yet discern." Either help was at hand at long last, or the Spanish had learned of their location and sent a fleet of warships from Havana to destroy them.[14]

The fleet was friendly. But the ships that lined the horizon off the Outer Banks were not those anticipated by the English commander. Instead of the expedition headed by Bernard Drake and Amias Preston, the fleet sighted by Captain Stafford belonged to Sir Francis Drake, newly arrived from the West Indies and Florida coast.

The strategy devised by the queen and her ministers the previous year to undermine Spanish power in America had had two major components. The first was a large-scale attack on the West Indies and Spanish Main, the second the establishment of a colony and privateering base on the mainland of North America.

In September 1585 Sir Francis Drake had left Plymouth with a fleet of twenty-five ships (two of them the queen's own galleons) and eight pinnaces, carrying approximately 900 mariners and 1,000 soldiers, the greatest force yet sent by the English to Spanish America. The plan called for Drake first to harass shipping off the Spanish coast, possibly capturing one of the annual treasure fleets arriving from New Spain. He was then to proceed to the West Indies, where he would occupy Cartagena or Nombre de Dios as a preliminary to crossing the isthmus to attack Panama and disrupt the flow of Peruvian silver and other valuable commodities. If all went well, he might attempt to establish a garrison in the region with the aid of escaped slaves and local Indians, who, it was anticipated, would join the English out of hatred for their Spanish overlords.

Drake's fleet had arrived in the West Indies in mid-December. During the winter he pillaged Santo Domingo, Hispaniola, and Cartagena, but failed in the critical objective of establishing a beachhead on one of the islands or the mainland from which to attack Panama. Since their arrival, disease had ravaged the fleet, and Spanish authorities reported that the English had secretly buried "boatloads" of dead. The amount of booty taken from the Spanish did not remotely approach the expectations of those participating in the voyage, leading to widespread grumbling and disputes among Drake's men. Drake realized by April 1586 that he had neither the manpower nor the support of his officers for an assault on Panama, and after considering an attack on Havana, Cuba, dismissed the idea for the same reasons. Instead, he left the West Indies the following month and set a course for Roanoke.

The Virginia leg of Drake's expedition had been integral to plans for the voyage from the beginning. After ravaging the West Indies, Drake was to send part of his fleet north to Virginia to reinforce Ralegh's colony on Roanoke Island. Drake probably made the decision to clear the Florida coast of Spanish garrisons en route to Roanoke Island after picking up rumors of an imminent attack on the English colony. By the 1580s only a couple of small garrisons remained, Santa Elena to the north and the main settlement, St. Augustine, farther south, which was the Florida governor's seat.

Drake arrived at St. Augustine toward the end of May and landed his men unopposed near a small wooden fort that the governor, Pedro Menéndez Marqués, had hastily thrown up. With only seventy or eighty soldiers to confront the English, Marqués opted to withdraw and join the townspeople hiding in the surrounding woods, leaving the English to loot and burn at will. The town was systematically stripped of any items—artillery, tools, furniture, and hardware—that would be useful to the colonists at Roanoke before it was completely destroyed. An eyewitness reported that of the 250 houses, not one was left standing.[15]

Continuing north, the English considered attacking the small garrison at Santa Elena on Port Royal Sound but could not find an entry to the harbor. After refilling their water barrels a few miles farther up the coast, the fleet moved on and arrived at Hatarask Island on June 8. A day later the fleet reached Port Ferdinando, where Ralph Lane, accompanied by some of his officers, hastened to meet "the Generall," as he called Drake.

To Lane's weary eyes the fleet must have been a magnificent sight. Twenty-three ships, including Drake's royal flagship, the huge *Elizabeth Bonaventure* (600 tons), the *Primrose* (400 tons), and the *Galleon Leicester* (400 tons), rode bravely at anchor a couple of miles out to sea, serviced by a flotilla of small boats hurrying back and forth between them. At that moment, as Lane surveyed the great fleet strung out along the coast, the ships' pennants fluttering in the brisk wind, the promise of an English

North America must have finally seemed a reality. For the first time, an English fleet in American waters had put in at an English colony.[16]

Drake had learned something of Lane's desperate situation on Roanoke Island from a pilot he had taken on board at Hatarask. After consulting with his captains, he offered the colonists as much help as he could. Lane explained that he needed a vessel to search for a harbor more suitable for shipping than the Outer Banks, as well as small boats for exploring rivers and shallow waters. In addition, he desperately needed provisions, arms, powder and shot, clothing, and men to replace the weak and unfit he proposed to send back to England. Drake obliged and gave Lane a bark of 70 tons, the *Francis*, two pinnaces, and four small boats, with equipment and supplies sufficient for a hundred men for four months. Lane had in mind sailing to the Chesapeake Bay to find a site on one of the deep water rivers discovered the previous winter, which would be a good location for a colony. He would then leave a small garrison behind and return with his men to England in August to report to Ralegh.

Disaster struck even as preparations for Lane's expedition began. Winds from the south began to strengthen, and lookouts on the larger ships could see storm clouds massing along the horizon. Within twenty-four hours a hurricane came roaring up the coast from the Caribbean, striking the fleet with such ferocity that anchor cables broke, masts snapped, and many of the smaller ships, including the *Francis*, were driven far out to sea or lost. The massive storm raged for three days, during which hailstones as big as hens eggs battered the fleet, lightning played continuously across the sky, and great water spouts were sucked up high into the air, "as though heaven & [earth] would have met." For those men who had never witnessed a hurricane, the experience was terrifying and confirmed Lane's opinion that the unprotected anchorage offshore was far too dangerous for shipping.[17]

Lane's plans were in disarray. Drake offered him another ship, the *Bark Bonner*, but she was much too large to pass through Port Ferdinando into the sounds for lading and possibly too large to enter Chesapeake Bay. In any case, the colonists were thoroughly disheartened by the storm and the loss of the *Francis* and their comrades onboard and would not countenance the voyage north. The "very hand of God as it seemed," Lane wrote, "stretched out to take us from thence." He did not expect another relief expedition to arrive until the following year, and given recent hostilities with the Secotans, he could not risk leaving a small garrison on Roanoke Island to wait for reinforcements, even if he could have persuaded a group of men to stay, which is doubtful. Lane therefore decided to abandon the settlement and return directly to England with Drake.

A final setback occurred as the sailors sent to Roanoke Island to gather the colonists' baggage and equipment struggled to navigate their boats through the shoals. Several boats ran aground in rough weather, and to refloat them the sailors threw most of the settlers' possessions overboard. Into the choppy waters of the sound went papers, maps, books, a chain of black pearls given to Lane by Menatonon, and many of the samples of ore and specimens gathered by Thomas Hariot and Joachim Gans, an incalculable loss to Ralegh and posterity.

Because the weather continued to be blustery in the wake of the hurricane, Drake was anxious to get away, and the colonists were quickly dispersed among the ships. Lane sailed with Drake on the flagship, along with Manteo and another Indian, named Towaye. The English weighed anchor on June 18 and with strong winds behind them quickly left the American shore behind, a little short of one year after they had arrived. Most of the colonists were probably glad to be going home. They had not made any spectacular discoveries of Indian wealth, and during the last few months they had been short of provisions and in continual danger of attack by local peoples.

Lane may have shared some of his men's frustrations. He had been disappointed by the region, which had few natural resources other than timber and had serious limitations as a privateering base. But he saw greater potential in a settlement farther north on the Chesapeake Bay and remained convinced that riches were to be found somewhere to the west in the mountains. As the coast passed out of view, Lane was likely already preparing to persuade Ralegh that it was essential to mount another expedition.[18]

DRAKE'S RETURN was greeted with rejoicing in England. Shortly after the fleet docked in Portsmouth at the end of July 1586 a contemporary remarked that Drake had brought back great riches and honor and had so "inflamed the whole country with a desire to adventure unto the seas in hope of the like good success that a great number prepared ships mariners and soldiers and travelled every place at the seas where any profit might be had." The sacking of Santo Domingo and Cartagena, it was said, had exposed the weakness of Philip II's American empire, just as Richard Hakluyt the younger and Ralph Lane had predicted. An agent of Sir Francis Walsingham in Germany argued that one year of war in the West Indies "will cost the Spaniards more than two or three in the Low Countries."

Yet for all the public acclaim, Drake, as well as the queen and her ministers, had hoped for a better outcome. The plunder brought back to England amounted to only £67,000, which after expenses for the cost of the expedition were deducted represented a significant loss. More than 750 men had perished during the voyage, most from a pestilent fever that had dogged the fleet from the Cape Verde Islands to the Caribbean. But most important, the English had failed to deliver a decisive blow. They had not achieved their major objective of taking Panama, thereby disrupting the flow of treasure to Spain, or their secondary goal of maintaining a garrison in the region. Philip had been inconvenienced and would have to divert precious resources from Europe to strengthen fortifications in America, but he had not been appreciably weakened.[19]

For Ralegh, the abandonment of Roanoke Island was infuriating. Drake was supposed to have reinforced the colony, not evacuated it. During the spring Ralegh had sent a ship with provisions to tide over the colonists while he fitted out a larger expedition that would bolster the colonists' numbers. Little is known about the voyage other than that the ship reached Roanoke Island shortly after Lane had left. The second, larger expedition of six ships carrying approximately 200 colonists, once again commanded by Grenville, arrived off the Outer Banks in July. After making his way to Roanoke Island, Grenville was baffled to find no sign of the colonists or the earlier supply ship, and after a few weeks of exploration decided to return to England. "Unwilling to lose the possession of the Country, which," Richard Hakluyt the younger wrote with a touch of exaggeration, "Englishmen had for so long held," Grenville installed a small garrison of fifteen men with provisions for a year, then departed.[20]

Given the highly optimistic reports about Roanoke of a year before, Ralegh was mystified by Lane's decision to abandon the island. After everything the English had achieved by discovering the region and establishing a settlement, why had he given up?

Lane explained that he was forced to leave because of the failure to supply the colony in a timely fashion. The fleet he had expected to arrive by Easter had not appeared, and his men could not endure on Roanoke Island any longer. More important than the rights or wrongs of his decision to return with Drake, Lane believed, was the discovery of information from his explorations and discussions with Indians that provided proof of the greater region's potential. This information might well unlock the wealth of Virginia and eventually fulfill Ralegh's dream of a prosperous and powerful English America. Lane had returned to England to deliver the good news in person.

The key to Lane's thinking, as he laid out in his explanations to Ralegh, was his conception of a Virginia that linked the Chesapeake Bay to the Roanoke region and beyond. There was no longer any doubt that the Outer Banks were ill-suited for large ships, but the "good harbor" found by Amadas and his men on the southern shore of the Chesapeake the previous winter was a different matter. Lane argued that a settlement established on the large river system (Elizabeth River) near Skicóak could easily accommodate the volume and size of ships that Ralegh had intended for Roanoke.

From information provided by Menatonon, Lane had learned that the Chowanocs' territories were just a few days to the south of Skicóak and that an additional day's travel overland would bring the English to the first town of the Mangoaks on the Roanoke River. This "river of Moratico [Roanoke] promises great things," he wrote in his account, adding that Thomas Hariot had heard from local peoples that the head of the river rose from the Bay of Mexico, which opened into the South Sea. Somewhere beyond his own navigation of the Roanoke to the rapids, Lane believed the river turned south toward the Gulf of Mexico and a passage to the Pacific Ocean.

The possibility that the Roanoke River's headwaters were in mountains far to the south was a crucial piece of news. From a deep-water port on the Elizabeth River, Lane advised, sconces (light earthworks) could be raised to protect an overland route to the Roanoke River, and boats could be left along the way. By this means, he explained, "you shall gain within four days travel into the heart of the main 200 miles at the least, and so pass your discovery into that most notable and to the likeliest parts of the mainland." Colonists would be able to travel easily along the Roanoke River far inland to the province of Chaunis Temoatan and perhaps find the passage to the South Sea nearby. The interior to the southwest, not the coastal area, offered the brightest prospects of a spectacular discovery, and he had found the most convenient way of getting there.[21]

Lane had given Ralegh much to consider. But there was a further step to be taken. In the months following Lane's return, Ralegh and his advisors at Durham House—principally Lane, Hariot, and possibly Jacques Le Moyne—pieced together a new theory of the geography of eastern North America. If the mines of Chaunis Temoatan were somewhere in the vicinity of the headwaters of the Roanoke River twenty days—perhaps 250–300 miles—from the lands of the Mangoaks, and if Lane and Hariot were correct in their assumption that the Roanoke River originated in the mountains far to the south, then perhaps Chaunis Temoatan was one and the same as the "Montes Apalatci" depicted by Le Moyne at the top of his Florida map. The fit was not perfect; Le Moyne's Appalachian Mountains, where gold, silver, and copper were mined by local Indians, lay near the shore of a huge lake (or the South Sea) that was to the north rather than close to the Gulf of Mexico. Nevertheless, Ralegh believed that sufficient evidence existed to merit further investigation.

Support for the theory that Chaunis Temoatan and the Montes Apalatci were the same came from an unexpected source. During Drake's raid on St. Augustine the English had captured two men—Pedro Morales, a Spanish deserter, and Nicholas Burgoignon, a Frenchman seized by the Spanish on the coast of Florida six years before—who returned with the fleet to Portsmouth and were subsequently interrogated by Richard Hakluyt the younger and Hariot. Morales claimed that sixty leagues (about 150 miles) northwest of the Spanish garrison of Santa Elena were mountains full of gold and crystal mines, named "Apalatci." He claimed to have seen a great diamond that was brought from the mountains to the west. These mountains, he believed, were possibly "the hills of Chaunis Temoatam, which Master Lane had advertisement of [learned of]."

Burgoignon confirmed Morales's story and embellished it with astonishing details. In the mountains, he said, there were great quantities of crystal, gold, rubies, and diamonds that gleamed so bright in places that during the day the Indians "cannot behold them, and therefore they travel to them by night." Fifty leagues from Santa Elena, he continued, the Spanish had encountered Indians wearing gold rings in their nostrils and ears.[22]

The hearsay that Morales and Burgoignon had picked up derived not from recent information but from a Spanish expedition of twenty years earlier. In 1566 Captain Juan Pardo had been instructed by the then governor of Florida, Pedro Menéndez de Avilés, to journey inland from Santa Elena to search for precious minerals and a possible route to the great silver mines of Zacatecas, Mexico, which the governor supposed were no more than a few hundred leagues away. In two expeditions, in 1566–1567 and 1567–1568, Pardo and his men had headed northwest from Santa Elena as far as North Carolina (and possibly to the extreme southwestern tip of Virginia), then west across the Blue Ridge Mountains to the chiefdom of Chiaha in Tennessee, ending up on the western slopes of the Great Smoky Mountains. Sometime after the expedition, one of the principal officers reported that forty leagues (100 miles) from the coast they had discovered "a crystal mountain" made of diamonds. Another account stated that Pardo and his men had found gold and silver mines and also a river that they followed from the coast into the interior, which ultimately led to Canada and a passage through to the South Sea and China.[23]

Putting all the information together, Ralegh now had three independent reports of riches in the Appalachian Mountains inland from the Florida coast—Le Moyne's, Lane and Hariot's, and the testimony of Morales and Burgoignon. The evidence he pored over for several months at Durham House all seemed to point in the same direction: gold, silver, copper, gems, and a passage to the Pacific all existed in the mountains several hundred miles to the southwest, and the Roanoke River was the key to getting there. The proximity of Spanish garrisons at Santa Elena and St. Augustine prevented him from planting a settlement on the Florida coast south of Cape Fear, but what if he could chart a route through the backcountry from the Chesapeake Bay to Chaunis Temoatan, the Montes Apalatci?

To help him visualize the various regions, Ralegh instructed John White to draft two maps, one of the Roanoke area based on the discoveries of 1585–1586 and a second that combined Le Moyne's rendering of Florida with the new Roanoke map. Drawing upon his own experiences as well as measurements made by Thomas Hariot and observations of other colonists, notably Ralph Lane, White began working first on the Roanoke map. He detailed the major natural features of the area—the sounds, Outer Banks, rivers, ports (or entrances), and shoals—together with major Indian towns such as Secotan, Dasemunkepeuc, several Weapemeoc communities, and Chowanoc. The progress of Grenville's *Tiger* is shown rounding Cape Lookout, anchored off Wococon and near Port Ferdinando, while smaller boats and canoes ply the shallow waters of the Sounds and rivers. At the top of the map is the striking presence of the Chesapeake Bay, on the southern shore of which, inland upon a river, is the Chesapeake Indians' capital town of Skicóak. White placed Roanoke Island prominently at the center of the map, which allowed him to clearly show Lane's recommended route to the Chesapeake Bay: up the Albemarle Sound and Chowan River to Chowanoc and then overland about fifty or sixty miles to Skicóak.[24]

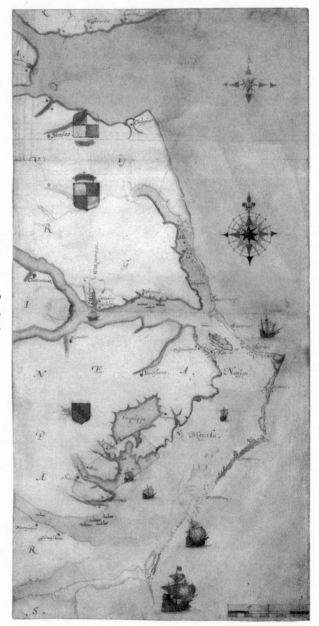

3.6
John White,
Roanoke, 1586.

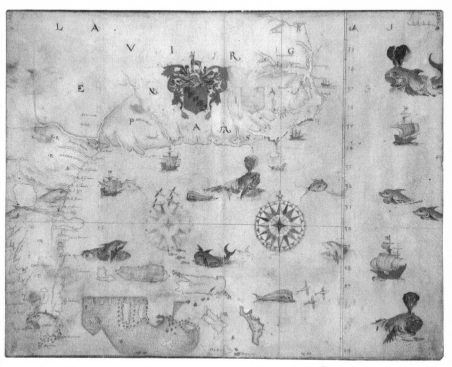

3.7 John White, Map of the East Coast of America, 1586.

White then combined his Virginia map with Le Moyne's Florida map. This was the first detailed map of the entire region from Florida to the Chesapeake Bay, but more important, it was the first English map to suggest the promise of the interior. White depicted a large river flowing from Port Royal to the shadowy outline of a great lake or the South Sea and showed Le Moyne's Montes Apalatci inland from the St. Johns River. He made no attempt to link the Roanoke River to the gold- and silver-bearing mountains to the south by tracing its inland course. There may have been no need; a cursory glance at the map would have persuaded Ralegh that the English simply had to follow a southwesterly route from the Roanoke River (or from the southern shore of the Chesapeake Bay) to reach the mines and the Pacific.[25]

At the same time that White was working on the maps, Thomas Hariot was busily writing up his notes for Ralegh about the natural products of the Roanoke region that might prove of interest to merchants and investors. The English had found silk grass like that grown in Persia, which could be cultivated to great profit because of the demand in England and abroad. They had discovered silkworms as large as walnuts, and if they introduced mulberry trees they would be able to develop a trade as great as that promoted by the Persians, Turks, Spanish, and Italians. There were all kinds of trees that could be used to produce pitch, tar, and turpentine; cedar for furniture and other timber products; sassafras "of most rare virtues in physic for the cure of many diseases"; flax and hemp; alum, used in various manufacturing processes; oils from nuts, berries, and bear fat; dyestuffs; wine; furs; copper; iron ore; and pearls. The colonists' efforts to grow sugar cane brought from the West Indies had been unsuccessful, but Hariot was optimistic that they would succeed eventually because cane was cultivated in southern Spain and Barbary, which were on the same latitude as Virginia.

Explorations up the rivers had convinced Hariot that Virginia's interior, which stretched westward hundreds of leagues, held even greater promise. Inland, the soil was richer, trees were larger, there was a greater variety of animals, and the country was more densely populated. Pasture was as good as any in England, and the mountains promised mineral wealth.

Just as the Spanish had discovered riches on the mainland in the Indies, so the English could hope for greater plenty from the "inner parts" of the country. And because the climate of Virginia, Hariot believed, was similar to those of Japan, China, and countries of the Levant and Mediterranean, any number of commodities traded from those places might be produced in the English colony. Not only were precious minerals to be found in "the main," as Lane speculated, but also a rich and fertile land ripe for development.[26]

⚭

Only the discovery of a good mine or a passage to the South Sea, Lane had told Ralegh, could justify the expense of establishing a colony in America, and only then would the country's natural produce "be worth the fetching." Ralegh agreed. Despite Hariot's enthusiastic account, Sir Walter was uninterested in establishing a colony devoted solely to harvesting the natural produce of the land. Cultivating natural products would encourage self-sufficiency and perhaps attract investment from merchants, but cultivation alone would not cover the costs of establishing a colony and did not conform to Ralegh's expansive vision of an English America. Instead, he continued to favor the idea of a settlement that would serve as a harbor for English privateers and a base for explorations into the interior in search of gold, silver, and a route to the Orient. Virginia would play a major role in the war against Spain in America, and from discoveries inland might return treasures to rival those of Spanish conquests.[27]

Roanoke had proved unsuitable as a location for a colony, and Lane's search for the distant province of Chaunis Temoatan in the spring of 1586 had been inconclusive. By the fall of 1586, Ralegh was convinced that another attempt to establish a settlement should be made, but this time to the north, on the Chesapeake Bay. The stakes were too high not to try again.

4

A CITY ON THE BAY

*No history hitherto set forth has more affinity,
resemblance or conformity with yours of Virginia, than this of Florida.*

— RICHARD HAKLUYT THE YOUNGER

B Y CHRISTMAS 1586 Ralegh's plans for the new colony were
well advanced. Following conversations with Ralph Lane
and Thomas Hariot, he had concluded that a major failing of the
first colony was not only its location on the Outer Banks but also
the caliber of its settlers. Lane described the soldiers he had
commanded as wild men, unruly and difficult to control. Hariot
criticized them for being too aggressive and quick to resort to violence. They killed the local people, he wrote, "upon causes that
on our part, might easily enough have been borne." Many of the
men had been unsuited to the hardships of life in a fledgling
colony and continually complained about the lack of comfortable
lodgings, dainty food, and soft beds of down or feathers. And
when they failed to discover the gold and silver they expected to
find, they became discouraged and miserable.

Ralegh had therefore decided that the new colony would be a civilian settlement rather than another military garrison, made up of men and women committed to the venture who had an interest in its outcome. The colony would be located on the Chesapeake Bay, as recommended by Lane and Richard Hakluyt the younger. In December Hakluyt had written an enthusiastic letter from Paris, urging Sir Walter to go forward with his "enterprise of Virginia." There could be little doubt about the legitimacy of England's right to settle the region, he argued. Even Spanish chroniclers acknowledged that the Chesapeake was first discovered by the English, referring to the explorations of Sebastian Cabot along the North American coast in the early years of the sixteenth century. To further encourage Ralegh, Hakluyt emphasized the discovery of silver mines by Antonio de Espejo in 1582 on the same latitude, to the west in New Mexico (information that turned out to be highly exaggerated), hinting that Ralegh might find similar riches in Virginia.[1]

Sir Walter's most pressing task was to decide upon the new colony's leader, who would take on responsibility for day-to-day preparations as soon as possible. This was especially important given that his own involvement in the arrangements would be limited by commitments elsewhere. Earlier in the year Elizabeth had granted him 12,000 acres in Munster and appointed him one of the principal sponsors from Devon, Somerset, and Dorset to oversee the peopling of the region by English immigrants. As a consequence, Ralegh had become involved in planning the establishment of English communities in southern Ireland at the same time he was advancing plans for the settlement of America.[2]

Few obvious candidates presented themselves. Ralph Lane may have wanted to return to Virginia to complete his discoveries, but Ralegh ruled him out because he and the queen were angry that Lane had abandoned Roanoke Island. Sir Richard Grenville was not in England during the fall and probably would not have relished going back to America so soon after his abortive voyage to the Outer Banks that year. Hariot was busy preparing his account of the Roanoke region for publication, which Sir Walter viewed as a major work on the New World and an important promotional piece. That left only John White of Ralegh's inner circle.[3]

SINCE THE SUMMER, White had been hard at work at Durham House preparing the maps Ralegh had requested of Virginia and the broader mid-Atlantic coastal region. Besides possibly helping to attract investors, the maps would be useful to the colonists in their preliminary explorations of the Chesapeake Bay region. Following Ralegh's decision to put him in charge of the colony, White spent a great deal of time meeting with family and friends, trying to persuade them to join the voyage on which he had decided to stake his life and fortune.

White had lived in London for at least two decades, most likely in the parish of St. Martin's, close by Ludgate and St. Paul's Cathedral. During those years the city had changed dramatically. Bursting at the seams, its population doubled in the second half of the sixteenth century, fueled by enormous numbers of migrants, who streamed through its gates from all parts of the realm or settled in the sprawling suburbs that had grown up around its ancient walls. By the 1580s London's population exceeded 100,000

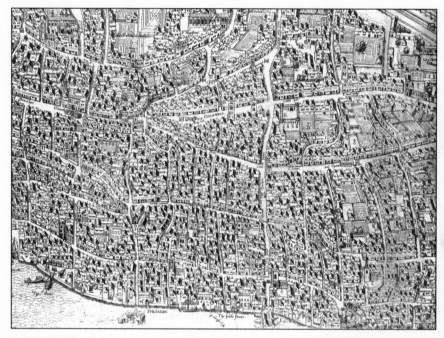

4.1 Detail from the Copperplate Map of London, showing Cheapside, ca. 1559. The map illustrates the density of housing in the central part of the walled City of London, about a quarter of a mile east of St. Paul's Cathedral. The streets and markets of Cheapside would have been familiar to John White and many of the settlers from the City.

people, crammed together in a patchwork of densely populated neighborhoods.

Everywhere the effects of rapid growth were evident: in the slums, which each year spread farther into surrounding fields like a canker on the countryside; in the belching chimneys of brick and lime kilns clearly visible north of the city near the small village of Islington; in the magnificent pile of the Royal Exchange (the new commercial center erected in 1566), which had required the demolition of scores of poor tenements on Cornhill to make

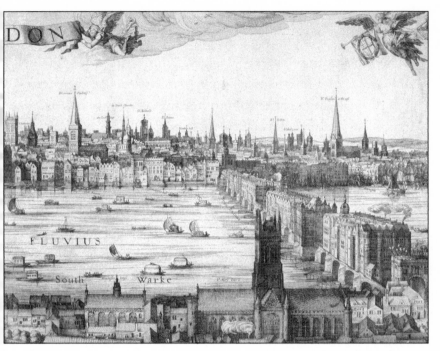

4.2 Claes Visscher, detail from a panoramic view of London, showing London Bridge, 1616. The engraving illustrates the busy water traffic along the river and riverside housing of those involved in maritime trades. Large ships could only navigate as far as London Bridge, hence the many small boats beyond.

way for its elegant shops and colonnades; and in the wretched faces of countless men, women, and children who had moved to London hoping to find work but instead found themselves out of luck and on the streets.

Trade was the lifeblood of the city. Such was the influence of its merchants by the 1580s that contemporaries complained London had wholly "eaten up" the commerce of the rest of the country's towns and ports, which could no longer compete. During the thirty years of Elizabeth's reign, England had emerged from the margins of the European commercial system to occupy a central role, and London merchants had benefited enormously. They replaced foreigners ("strangers") who had formerly controlled lucrative international trade routes, expanded their activities throughout Europe, and profited from a massive increase in imports of luxury and manufactured goods.

Riverfront parishes were alive with activity from dawn to dusk, full of the noise, bustle, and smells of docks and shipping above and below London Bridge. So many ships lay tied up, loading and off-loading their cargoes, that the antiquary William Camden commented the river appeared "a very wood of trees" like a forest glade, shaded with masts and sails. The names of specialized wharves, such as Vintry, Timberhithe, Fish, Salt, and Hay, represented the commodities brought and stored there from all over the country, but many more quays along the River Thames dealt in all sorts of finished goods and raw materials. Large numbers of mariners, lightermen, fishermen, shipwrights, ropemakers, and sailmakers, as well as victuallers, millers, and brewers lived along both sides of the river.

Away from the Thames, the majority of the population worked in the clothing industry, building trades, or as merchants and petty traders. The numerous halls of the companies (guilds) that regulated production, apprenticeship, and entry into London's political life testified to their important role in the city. Great companies such as the Mercers, Merchant Taylors, Haberdashers, and Goldsmiths were the wealthiest and most influential, but there were also scores of lesser companies such as the Butchers, Bakers, Bricklayers, Chandlers, and John White's own Painters and Stainers. Blackwell Hall, the country's premier cloth market, regulated the sale of cloth, "broad and narrow"; just outside the city's walls Smithfield was a major market for livestock and hides. Trades connected with the ebb and flow of commerce along the river—building and manufactures, wholesaling, provisioning, and local markets—provided economic vitality to an increasingly prosperous middle class.[4]

It was to this rising, middling group of people that Ralegh and White appealed for support of their venture to America. Sir Walter had designed terms to attract men and women of modest means, who would invest their own resources to support themselves and establish the colony on a profitable footing. To encourage settlers to join the enterprise, he granted each individual 500 acres and families proportionally more, a huge amount of land by the standards of the day. The approach may have been modeled on the short-lived French Huguenot settlement at Fort Caroline in the 1560s, which had included farmers and artisans in family groups as well as soldiers and single men.

The colony was to be established as the City of Ralegh. Ultimately, Sir Walter hoped that the settlement might eventually come to rival major English ports such as Plymouth and Bristol or even London itself. The colony would be governed by John White, aided by twelve "assistants." They would provide the core leadership and undertake the vital tasks of founding the settlement and preparing for the arrival of more colonists, who would follow once the colony became profitable. Three of the assistants were to remain in London to represent the colony's commercial interests among City merchants and lobby for additional financial support. Ralegh would continue to exercise overall authority, but the establishment of his colony as a corporation ruled by "one

Body politic" was an acknowledgment on his part that those on the spot needed sufficient independence to manage local affairs in their best interests.

Most of the colony's ruling group came from respectable middle-class backgrounds. White had a distant claim to gentility from his family's Cornish origins, but his profession as a working artist suggests a humbler status. Dyonis Harvie (Harvey) was possibly a relative of Sir James Harvey, a former Lord Mayor of London and ironmonger. Ananias Dare, married to White's daughter, Eleanor, was a member of the Tilers and Bricklayers Company and may have been reasonably well off. Simon Fernandes, on the other hand, came from rough and ready seafaring stock, although he was well connected through his service to Ralegh and Sir Francis Walsingham. About the remaining nine assistants—Roger Bailie (Bailey), Christopher Cooper, Thomas Stevens, John Sampson, Roger Pratt, George Howe (all of whom went to Virginia), and William Fulwood, John Nichols, and James Plat (who did not)—we can only speculate that they were likely related to other colonists, resided in or near London, and had important ties with City merchants and mariners.

Whatever their backgrounds, the social rank of White and his assistants was about to change radically. In a characteristically flamboyant gesture, Ralegh arranged a coat of arms for his new city, which combined the red cross of St. George with his own symbol of the roebuck. In January 1587 White and his assistants were also elevated to gentry status and each awarded the privilege of his own coat of arms. Besides providing an additional incentive for those contemplating joining White's colony as one of its leaders, the creation of a minor aristocracy

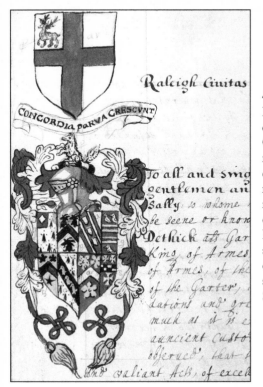

4.3 Coat of arms of the City of Ralegh and those of John White, copy, post-1660. The arms of the City of Ralegh consisted of the red cross of St. George, which emphasized that the colony remained within the English realm; and a roebuck in the first quarter, the badge of Sir Walter Ralegh. John White's coat of arms indicates his Cornish origins and connections with several gentry families of the Southwest of England.

to govern in Virginia was a clear signal of the colony's importance in Ralegh's eyes. The perilous international situation and financial losses associated with Sir Richard Grenville's recent voyage to Roanoke prevented him from dispatching a large-scale expedition, but he could nevertheless underscore the venture's status.[5]

Grenville arrived back in England shortly before Christmas 1586 to help with the recruitment of settlers, but White probably continued to shoulder the main burden. During the winter and spring of 1586–1587, ninety-two men, seventeen women, and nine children joined the venture, together with the pilot, Fernandes, and two Indians, Manteo and Towaye.

The colonists were a young group. Only White, Fernandes, and possibly a couple of others were in their forties; the majority of men were in their twenties and early- to mid-thirties, and most of the women in their late teens and twenties. All nine children were boys, aged between three and twelve. Ten or eleven couples joined the voyage, four accompanied by (or expecting) a child. Another thirty were either married or had been, including men who had opted to leave their wives behind and several recently widowed women.

White recruited most of the settlers in London. They came from communities scattered across the city, from Westminster to Deptford, but two parishes, St. Clement Danes and St. Dunstan's, in Stepney, contributed more than any others. St. Clement Danes was the center of the recruitment effort and home of Ananias and Eleanor Dare. They probably played a major role in the recruitment of fellow parishioners such as Thomas Ellis and his son Robert, Joan Peers (Pierce or Pearce), and Charles Flurrie (Flory), just seventeen years old when he joined the voyage. Christopher Cooper, who likely played a similarly active role in recruiting settlers from his local community, may have resided in St. Dunstan's, Stepney, a large parish to the east of the City.

Within the City's walls, Arnold and Joyce Archard were from the riverside parish of St. Mary-at-Hill, not far from London Bridge; young William Wythers was from St. Michael, Cornhill, near the Stocks, where London's fishmongers and butchers had their stalls; and Thomas and Audrey Tappan were from All Hallows, Lombard Street, close by. James Hynde was born just out-

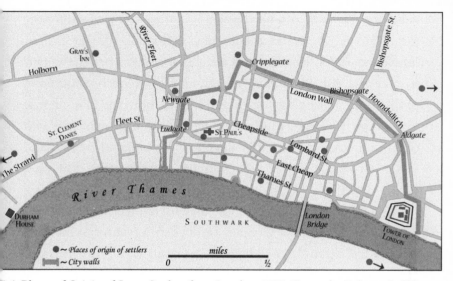

4.4 Places of Origin of Some Settlers from London, 1587. Drawn by Rebecca L. Wrenn.

side the walls, in St. Giles Cripplegate; John and William Wyles (Willes) were twins from Christ Church Greyfriars, Newgate; and across the Thames, downriver in Deptford, Edward and Winifred Powell had married on January 10, 1585.[6]

What persuaded a seemingly unremarkable group of middling and working-class men and women to leave their homes, friends, and familiar surroundings and set out for an unknown land thousands of miles across the ocean? There are no obvious answers—no diaries or letters (or any other records) shed light on what must have been for many the most difficult decision of their lives and for all of them the most consequential. But a handful of clues suggest some possible explanations.

Family connections were important. White himself went to his own family to recruit settlers. He may have gone first to his daughter, Eleanor, and her husband Ananias to discuss the venture. Married three and a half years, the couple already had an infant son and a daughter and initially may have been reluctant to take the risk of moving the family. They likely solved the problem by arranging for the children, John and Thomasine (named for Eleanor's mother), to be cared for by relatives. Two other couples, Ambrose and Elizabeth Viccars and Arnold and Joyce Archard, possibly made similar arrangements, but each took a young son with them.

After visiting the Dares, White may have traveled across London to see Christopher Cooper, quite likely a relative of his wife. Cooper had three children under five as well as two teenage sons. His wife, if she was still alive, did not go with him and probably stayed at home to look after the children. Similarly, George Howe, gentleman, John Sampson, Thomas Ellis, and Roger Pratt all traveled with young sons but without their wives. They most likely planned to wait until the colony was firmly established before risking bringing over their families.[7]

At least a third of the settlers were related to other members of the group. Henry and Richard Berrye, John and William Wyles (Willes), Robert and Peter Little, and John and Thomas Chevan (or Phevan) of London were possibly brothers or cousins. Some of the colonists probably had relatives among the men who had been involved in previous voyages or were in Ralegh's service. Alice Chapman could have been the wife of the (Robert?) Chapman left on Roanoke Island with a small holding party by Grenville in the summer of 1586; she was also quite possibly related to John Chapman of the 1587 settlers. John Gibbes may have been related to two Lane colonists as well as to Lewes Wotton of White's group, and Anthony Cage, gentleman, was likely a relative of John Cage, who had also accompanied Lane.[8]

Other connections among the colonists are more tenuous. St. Matthews, Friday Street, where John Chapman may have lived, was the parish of Valentine Beale and John Chandler, both of whom had been with Lane's colony. Edward Powell was possibly the same man who sailed to the West Indies and Roanoke Island with Sir Francis Drake's fleet on board the *Tiger* in the service of Christopher Carleill. He may have been the brother of Captain Anthony Powell, also with Drake, who was killed in action at St. Augustine and was described as "an honest wise Gentleman, and a soldier of good experience, and of great courage as any man might be." A John Sampson, another of Drake's land captains, fought alongside Powell.[9]

There is a strong possibility that some of the London colonists were Puritans. London was at the heart of the English Puritan movement after the restoration of the Protestant church in 1558. Puritans (or reformers) were dissatisfied with the changes introduced under Elizabeth's religious settlement, which they argued had not gone far enough in ridding the new Church of England of the trappings of Catholic ceremony and belief. With Elizabeth's accession to the throne, Puritans had anticipated that England would take the lead in the European Protestant Reformation and were frustrated by the queen's conservative approach to religious change. They opposed what they saw as the persistence of popish remnants such as clerical dress and kneeling during communion. Giving primacy to the word of God as revealed in the Bible, which spoke directly to individual conscience, they bridled at the prescribed liturgy and ritual of the

Church of England and resisted the rule of bishops, whose authority they believed had no basis in scripture. "You preach Christ to be priest and prophet," a group of London Puritans told Bishop Edmund Grindal forthrightly in 1567, "but you preach Him not to be king."

The religious conflict of the Reformation had been particularly intense and disruptive in London. The city witnessed the reformers' early salvos in the 1530s in the long struggle to establish a Christian commonwealth and bring the faithful into the light. Puritan congregations thrived throughout London, in St. Martin's in the Fields, Smithfield, Cripplegate, St. Matthew Friday Street, St. Michael Cornhill, Aldgate, Holborn, Southwark, and parishes to the east of the City walls, such as Stepney.

John White might have remembered from his boyhood days the widespread destruction of popish statues and images of saints in parish churches that occurred shortly after the accession of Edward VI (Elizabeth's younger brother). Altars had been removed by zealous Protestants, who associated them with the Catholic Mass and idolatry. About the time White was married, the altar had been pulled down in his church at St. Martin Ludgate, and in some of the colonists' churches walls were whitewashed so that the Ten Commandments could be written on them.[10]

During the 1570s and early 1580s the Church of England's efforts to enforce orthodoxy gained momentum. In London the clergy were commanded to wear their clerical robes and confirm their commitment to Church doctrine. Those who refused were removed from their parishes or arrested. In St. Clement Danes, the radical preacher Robert Johnson was thrown into prison in 1574 for his "puritan practices," where he died a few months later of jail fever. Meetings of clerics and lay people to discuss the scriptures were suppressed, and prominent Puritan sympathizers, including a number of leading Presbyterians, were imprisoned or forced into exile. Elizabeth's appointment of John Whitgift, a strict disciplinarian, as Archbishop of Canterbury in 1583 provided further proof that the queen and her bishops were determined to stamp out Puritanism in London and elsewhere.[11]

By the time White's colonists left England, religious radicals were coming to realize that there was to be no thoroughgoing reformation of the Anglican Church. London would not be another Geneva (where the reformed religion flourished), and efforts to thoroughly purge the Church of England of popish practices had largely failed. The opportunity to worship according to their own beliefs in America may have been a major incentive for some settlers to join White's venture.

Ralegh may have encouraged the recruitment of Puritans. He was known by contemporaries to be well disposed toward Puritanism and aligned himself with those at court, such as Leicester and Walsingham, who favored further church reform. Ralegh's father had been a zealous Protestant, and he himself had fought for the Huguenot cause in France. He had taken the Huguenot artist Jacques Le Moyne into his service and possibly looked to the Huguenot settlement at Fort Caroline as a model for his own colony. Strong religious convictions among the settlers might help to bind the expedition together.

Ralegh was strongly attracted by the prospect of planting the seed of the Anglican Church in North America, which in time would flower into a redoubtable Protestant bulwark and secure the northern continent against the Spanish and spread of Catholicism.

The Huguenots had been driven out of Florida in the 1560s, but he would establish the Protestant faith in Virginia. His vision of the Church incorporated both settlers and Indian peoples. What could be more pleasing to God, the pious lawyer John Hooker pointed out in a dedication to Ralegh, than to bring the knowledge of the gospel "to a lost people [the Indians]"? Who would perform the godly work of saving the souls of millions of Indians, Richard Hakluyt the younger asked, to bring "them from darkness to light, from falsehood to truth, from dumb idols to the living God, from the deep pit of hell to the highest heaven"? His appeal had been directed at Elizabeth, but by the spring of 1587 he was convinced that Ralegh was God's instrument. The conversion of Indians to Christianity was integral to Sir Walter's plans for an English America in which colonists and local peoples would live together in Christian fellowship.[12]

THE LATE WINTER and early spring of 1587 were exceptionally busy as the settlers prepared for the voyage. They gathered their personal possessions, sorted out arrangements with family and friends to look after the children and take care of their affairs while they were away, and spent time with loved ones. Meanwhile, White was fully occupied in bartering with local victuallers and overseeing the outfitting of the three ships provided by Ralegh, moored just below London Bridge: the flagship *Lion* (120 tons), on which White, Fernandes, and probably about fifty settlers would sail; an unnamed flyboat (100 tons) commanded by Edward Spicer, which would carry about forty-five or fifty passengers as well as the colony's bulk cargo; and a pinnace (30 tons) under the command of Captain Edward Stafford, who had been with Lane's colony, which had room for about twenty settlers. In total, the three ships would transport approximately 150 passengers and crew.

Throughout much of February and March, mariners loaded stores, provisions, and equipment. Tools and hardware were needed to build the settlement and for planting crops; glass beads and copper would be used as trade goods; cloth, blankets, and ticking for clothes and bedding; books, devotional works, cards, and toys for recreation and tending to spiritual needs; medical supplies, cooking pots, and kettles for domestic use; and firearms, pikes, and armor in case the Spanish discovered them or they encountered hostile Indian peoples.[13]

White's preparations were interrupted on February 19 by the sound of church bells ringing out across the city. Londoners lit bonfires, drank to the health of Elizabeth, and celebrated the news of the death of the Catholic Mary, Queen of Scots. Mary had fled from Scotland nearly twenty years earlier after factions of the Scottish nobility had forced her to abdicate the throne in 1567 in favor of her infant son, James VI. The nobles had been determined to rid themselves of their Catholic queen and to raise the young King James as a Protestant. Mary had gone to England in the hope that her cousin, Elizabeth, would help her to regain her throne. But Elizabeth had chosen not to become embroiled in Scotland's internal affairs and kept Mary under house arrest. The arrangement was not to the liking of Elizabeth's ministers, who understood that Mary's presence in England was a serious threat to the queen's security. She would be a rallying point for Catholics in England and for foreign agents who conspired to kill or depose Elizabeth. Mary was the legitimate heir, who would succeed to the

English throne if Elizabeth died, which would mean that once again England would be ruled by a Catholic monarch.

The Scottish queen had been suspected of involvement in two earlier Catholic plots, of 1571 and 1583, but Elizabeth had refused to bring her to trial. Then in 1586 a conspiracy to assassinate Elizabeth, led by a Catholic gentleman, Anthony Babbington, had been uncovered. Walsingham had thwarted the plot, and Babbington and his co-conspirators suffered the grisly death of traitors on a scaffold erected at St. Giles in the Fields, where they had met to plot Elizabeth's death. Mounting evidence had connected the exiled Scottish queen to the conspiracy, and when her complicity was proven beyond doubt, Elizabeth had little choice but to reluctantly consent to her councilors' demand for Mary's execution.

To Londoners who celebrated news of the Scottish queen's execution, Mary's death seemingly extinguished the likelihood of a return to Catholicism and religious upheaval. The serpent that had been poised to strike at the bosom of the realm had itself been cut off. Little wonder that people danced in the streets as if, a contemporary remarked, "they believed a new era had begun in which all men would live in peace."[14]

Yet while her subjects rejoiced, Elizabeth wept in the solitude of her private quarters at Greenwich. She was troubled by the possible consequences of Mary's execution. In consenting to the death of a fellow queen she had diminished herself. Monarchs were anointed by God, she believed, and to interfere with divine will was to court disaster.

Elizabeth's mind was also occupied with political considerations. Would news of Mary's execution stir up trouble in Scotland, where her son, James VI, ruled, potentially bringing down the fury of the Scots upon the English borderlands? Would there be diplomatic repercussions in France, where Mary's brother-in-law, Henry III, was king? And most worrying of all, how would Philip II react? A popular prophecy that circulated in 1586 warned that if harm befell Mary, England would be invaded by the Spanish, Elizabeth would be deposed, and an army of peasants with "clubs and clouted shoes" would rise to overthrow those who had oppressed them—a mélange of calamities that had haunted the Tudor state since the unsettled times of the mid-sixteenth century.[15]

In one sense at least, the prophecy appeared likely to come true. In mid-March news of Mary's death reached Philip at the great government complex and monastery of San Lorenzo de El Escorial, in the form of a letter from the Spanish ambassador in Paris. Don Bernardino de Mendoza was an astute observer of the political scene and erstwhile ambassador to Elizabeth's court (he had been expelled in January 1584 in response to allegations that he was involved in a plot to bring down the queen). Mary's execution offered Mendoza a perfect opportunity to persuade the king that now was the time to let the sword fall. "I pray that your Majesty will hasten the Enterprise of England to the earliest possible date," he wrote to Philip, "for it would seem to be God's obvious design to bestow upon Your Majesty the crowns of these two kingdoms [England and Scotland]."

Mendoza's urging was well received. Perhaps Philip did indeed believe that the horrible crime committed against Mary was an unmistakable sign from God prompting him to act, but Mary's death also removed the possibility of her becoming queen of England and possibly entering into a treaty with France. A cardinal principle of Habsburg statecraft ever since his father, Charles V's, time had been the prevention of an Anglo–French alliance that would prove a powerful counterweight to Spanish interests in Europe. Now that Mary had gone to a martyr's grave and there was no risk of French intervention, Philip decided to take on the mantle of Catholic king of the English and Scots himself and set in motion plans for the invasion.

The "enterprise of England" was to be put into effect. Philip shed his usual plodding caution and embraced plans for a combined land-sea attack with an alacrity that must have stunned his ministers. A massive armada would sail from Spain early the following year, immobilize the English navy, and take up station off the coast of Kent to provide protection for the Duke of Parma's army as it crossed the channel from Flanders. Parma's superb army of battle-hardened veterans would then march on London and take control of the capital. As the king's commanders set in motion arrangements for the invasion, neither Ralegh nor White could possibly have foreseen the impact of Philip's decision on their efforts to establish a colony in America.[16]

BY THE END of March 1587 White and Ralegh had completed their plans for the voyage. It was agreed that the fleet would follow the route to America usually taken by English mariners. Fernandes would lead the ships to the Canaries, cross the Atlantic to the West Indies, and then move on to the North American coast. White was to go first to Roanoke Island, where he would make contact with the small garrison left earlier by Grenville. The garrison would continue to maintain an English presence in the area and provide a base for a larger settlement should Ralegh decide to expand activities there. White was to inquire about the condition of the country and Indian peoples, and may have had in mind learning whether the men had picked up any further news of mines in the interior. He would have been eager also to let the men know where he intended to locate his settlement to the north.

During his stay on Roanoke White was to return the two Indians, Towaye and Manteo, to their own peoples. Then the colonists were to move on to the Chesapeake Bay, find a site for the main colony, and begin building their settlement. At that point, Fernandes and Spicer would go back to England to inform Ralegh of the colony's safe arrival, leaving the pinnace behind for the settlers' use. White probably anticipated that once Ralegh heard the colony had been established, he would fit out another expedition to reinforce the colony as soon as possible.

The expedition was ready to sail in early April. Some of those who had agreed to join White could not bring themselves to go once confronted with the reality of leaving England, possibly forever. As many as two dozen settlers may have backed out at the last moment. For those who remained, the day of departure was a scene of tearful farewells to children and final instructions to friends and kin before they boarded their ships to catch the ebb tide that would carry them downriver past Gravesend and beyond to the North Sea.

One can imagine White and the colonists, as the crews worked busily casting off, taking their last look at London and waving to loved ones gathered in small knots along the dockside. Then the tide took hold of the ships, swinging them out into the river and setting all on course for the most momentous journey of their lives.

WITH FAIR WINDS it would have taken only a couple of days to make the journey south and west to Cowes, on the Isle of Wight, where White intended to meet Sir George Carey, commander of Carisbrooke Castle. But the weather was not fair, and the first leg of the voyage along the coast took a week or so longer than usual. After first putting in at Portsmouth, the fleet anchored in the Solent on April 26, where they remained for eight days, a welcome relief to the colonists, who had been tossed around like corks in a bucket in the dark, cramped, and stinking ships' holds. White used the time to call on Carey, who was organizing a privateering expedition to the West Indies. He carried letters from Ralegh that likely requested Carey's three ships call in at Roanoke and possibly the Chesapeake Bay after cruising the Caribbean. They may have agreed that Carey's ships would carry additional provisions or acquire them in the West Indies, and perhaps also bring a few settlers to the colony. White would have handed over detailed instructions about how to reach the bay and a map showing the projected location of the settlement.

White's fleet arrived at Plymouth in early May to take on water and last minute supplies. Then, with all his preparations completed, White noted briefly in his journal on May 8, "we weighed anchor at Plymouth, and departed thence for Virginia." Those ten plain words hardly captured the significance of the moment—the departure of a fleet that would lay the foundations of an English America—but fortunately for posterity, Richard

Hakluyt penned a more lyrical panegyric to Ralegh, which proclaimed the heroic proportions of the venture and promise of the New World:

> Reveal to us the courts of China and the unknown straits which still lie hid: throw back the portals which have been closed since the world's beginning at the dawn of time. There yet remain for you new lands, ample realms, unknown peoples; they wait yet, I say, to be discovered and subdued, quickly and easily, under the happy auspices of your arms and enterprise, and the scepter of our most serene Elizabeth, Empress— as even the Spaniard himself admits—of the Ocean.

Ralegh's colony would be the beachhead from which the English would ultimately find a way through the continent to the Pacific and beyond to Cathay, redeem a barbarous people from idolatry and convert them to the Protestant church, bring riches to their country, and confirm the queen's rightful position as sovereign of the seas.[17]

The crossing proved long and arduous. A major setback occurred a little more than a week after leaving Plymouth. The flyboat was separated from the *Lion* and pinnace during the night, possibly in bad weather, a misfortune uncannily similar to the one that had occurred at the start of the voyage White had made with Grenville two years earlier. Confronted with the problem of how they would establish the colony without the four dozen settlers, the stores, and the equipment left behind on the flyboat, White pushed on in the hope that Captain Spicer would avoid capture by hostile ships and eventually rejoin them at one of the agreed upon rendezvous points in the West Indies and Virginia.

From the Bay of Portugal, where they had lost sight of the flyboat, they continued on a southerly course for another thousand miles until they reached the Canary Islands off the west coast of Africa, where they perhaps called in briefly to refresh their water casks and give the colonists a chance to stretch their legs ashore.

The Canaries were the last landfall the colonists would enjoy for several weeks. The next stage was more than 3,000 miles across the vast expanse of the Atlantic Ocean, the two ships dropping from 25 degrees to 15 degrees north latitude, pushed along by the northeast trades and equatorial current. Experienced mariners such as Fernandes knew the winds and currents intimately, but no amount of experience could determine whether the crossing would be rough or smooth or how long a voyage would take. Seafarers understood the unpredictability of the weather and oceans and that their fate was governed by forces beyond their control. All they could do was commit themselves to the care of the Almighty and hope for fair winds and good fortune.[18]

At first the exhilaration of being underway may have outweighed some of the discomforts experienced by the colonists. In the early weeks of the voyage, the shared experience of adjusting to life at sea and crowded shipboard conditions would have encouraged the settlers to get to know each other. In fact, they could hardly avoid one another; there was little privacy in their living quarters below deck. Colonists from London and elsewhere may have met only occasionally during preparations but now had plenty of time to exchange stories and talk about their hopes for the future.

The excitement would soon have faded, however, as the *Lion*, followed by the pinnace, headed into the Atlantic and day after day passed in dull succession. Families occupied themselves looking after their children. The older boys—William Withers, who was thirteen, and Thomas Ellis, who was ten—probably spent days larking about on deck when the weather was fine and exploring below when it was not, but the younger ones would have been kept close to their parents for safety. A ship was a dangerous place for small children; little Ambrose Viccars was only three or four years old when his family left London.

Most settlers found little to ease the tedium. Meals followed the same dreary routine. Meat, either salt beef or pork, was served on Sundays, Mondays, Tuesdays, and Thursdays, and stockfish (dried cod or ling) with some cheese and biscuits, washed down with beer or water, on Wednesdays, Fridays, and Saturdays. Once a week, to break the monotony, they received some bacon and peas.

Over meals and in their quarters the settlers probably spent long hours telling stories. John White would have described his experiences in the West Indies and on Roanoke Island and may have talked about his first voyage across the Atlantic ten years earlier, when he sailed with Martin Frobisher to the frozen land of Meta Incognita. Manteo would have described his peoples and other Indians of Roanoke as well as what he knew of the peoples of the Chesapeake, their customs, and their way of life. He and White endeavored to convey what America was like, how utterly different from anything the settlers had known in England—the beauty of the rivers and forests, the staggering abundance of wildlife, and the local peoples—a land that seemed to English eyes like a vast garden, an Eden.

Yet these stories, no matter how vivid, would have alleviated only to a small degree the discomforts of the long voyage. The settlers had to cope with seasickness, which left them nauseated and debilitated. There was also the chronic worry of attack from Spanish warships or pirates and the ever-present fear of foundering in a storm or falling seriously ill from one of many potential shipboard maladies. As the journey continued, they had to put up with deteriorating sanitary conditions, sour beer and water, and rotting food. Once they reached tropical latitudes, the heat would have made their living quarters even more oppressive, which must have been particularly hard on Eleanor Dare and Margery Harvey, both seven or eight months pregnant by mid-June.[19]

After about three weeks, one of the boys or a vigilant lookout in the *Lion*'s crow's nest spotted a smudge on the horizon that turned out to be the island of Dominica. The sailors had been aware that they were approaching land for several days; there were small, telltale signs such as pieces of debris in the waves, increasing numbers of birds that followed in their wake, and a change in the wind that brought the faint but unmistakable sweet smell of land. A hum of anticipation likely coursed through the settlers and crew, who stood on deck straining to see the island as it grew closer, an emerald rising precipitously out of a dazzling blue sea. White knew it was Dominica—he had sketched the mountainous island two years before—and must have been relieved to see it again. Sailing between Dominica and Guadeloupe as the sun dropped below the horizon, White and the settlers could take heart from having safely reached the first of their destinations in American waters.

The two ships anchored off St. Croix (Virgin Islands) on June 22, and passengers and crew went ashore to spend a couple of days recovering from the voyage. For some settlers, their first encounter with a Caribbean island was not a happy one. Eager for fresh fruit, they ate some small fruits that looked like green apples, but turned out to be poisonous and burned their mouths and tongues so badly they could not speak. Many of the settlers also became sick from drinking contaminated water from a stagnant pond near the temporary shelters they constructed soon after landing. Even washing themselves in the water caused their faces to burn and swell, so that they were unable to see for nearly a week. That night the settlers had better luck and captured five large sea turtles, which provided a feast of fresh meat, a welcome relief after weeks of salt beef, dried fish, and moldy biscuits. On the second day White divided the men who were fit into three groups to search for water and any signs of human life. One of the groups found a spring in the mountains, from which they filled bottles of water. Another spotted some Indians and their settlement a few miles away, but did not make contact.

The following day they left St. Croix and moved on to a small island off the south coast of Puerto Rico before anchoring at "Muskitoes Baye," the Mosquetal (Guayanilla Bay), where Ralph Lane had built a fortified settlement in 1585. They remained in the area for three days, again searching for fresh water, with little success; the amount of beer they drank in the course of their search, White commented testily, exceeded the small amount of water they eventually collected.[20]

After leaving the island on July 1 White learned of a serious setback. Two of the men, Darby Glavin and Dennis Carroll, both Irish and possibly Catholics, had deserted. White must have had little doubt that the men would quickly find their way to local Spanish authorities and tell them about the plan to establish a colony on Chesapeake Bay. To make matters worse, Glavin had been with Lane's original expedition and would be able to describe the precise location of the English settlement on Roanoke Island. White realized that sooner or later the Spanish would send warships to the Chesapeake to search for them. The Irishmen's desertion had greatly increased the possibility of a Spanish attack.[21]

Further problems arose over the next two weeks, as the ships made their way from the West Indies to the North Carolina coast. Relations between White and Fernandes began to break down. Their bickering was a continuation of arguments and accusations that had started early in the voyage, on the other side of the Atlantic. White had blamed his master pilot for losing contact with the flyboat in the Bay of Portugal. He believed that Fernandes had intentionally abandoned Spicer, stealing away in the night in the hope that the Englishman would fail to find his way to Virginia or would be captured by Spanish frigates.

Tensions between the two men increased in the West Indies. At Rojo Bay, Puerto Rico, Fernandes promised to take in salt, as the English had done in 1585. Accordingly, White assigned fifty men to go ashore, but then Fernandes protested, claiming that if the pinnace went into the bay, she might not be able to get back out until the following day, by which time a storm might arise and the two ships separated. While they argued, White alleged in his journal, Fernandes recklessly brought the *Lion* into shallow waters and began to swear "and tear God in pieces," crying out that the pinnace was in great danger and they should bear up the helm hard. The mariners followed Fernandes's orders, and the pinnace bore away from the bay. White commented ruefully, "we were disappointed of our salt." Similarly, off both Puerto Rico and Hispaniola a few days later, when White looked for a place to land to purchase cattle and provisions and collect orange plants, pineapples, and plantains for cultivation in Virginia, Fernandes refused to cooperate, and the two ships sailed on.

Setting aside a deliberate attempt to sabotage the expedition for unknown reasons, there is only one explanation for Fernandes's behavior: He was reluctant to waste time on the islands gathering plants or salt when he could be patrolling offshore waters in search of booty. The *Lion* was well armed, carrying between a dozen and two dozen cannon, ranging from demiculverins and sakers (ship-smashing guns that could throw shot weighing five to ten pounds across a couple of thousand yards), to an array of smaller weapons such as fowlers and robinets. It is likely that Ralegh had planned a privateering expedition to take place after White's colonists were deposited safely in the Chesapeake Bay, which would cover the costs of the venture (approximately £6,000) and perhaps make a profit. But Fernandes and his men were eager to seize every opportunity for plundering Spanish shipping in the West Indies. Even a couple of modest prizes would be sufficient to give the pilot and mariners handsome dividends beyond their contract wages. From this standpoint, it is not surprising that Fernandes was much more interested in looting other ships than in transporting passengers and carrying cargo.[22]

White was enraged by Fernandes's behavior, but there was little he could do about it. He did not have authority over the mariners and was dependent on his pilot to guide the settlers to their destination. As relations between settlers and mariners deteriorated, mishaps continued. On reaching the American mainland, Fernandes mistook the latitude, and finding himself too far south, proceeded north along the coast, where in mid-July he almost wrecked the two ships on reefs near Cape Fear (Cape Lookout). Only Captain Stafford's vigilance in the pinnace saved them from calamity, "such was the carelessness, and ignorance of our Master," White complained.

Far worse was to follow. Off the Outer Banks in the third week of July, White's plans were thrown into complete disarray. According to the account that White later presented to Ralegh, Fernandes betrayed him and the settlers. Anchored off Hatarask, White had decided to make contact with the garrison left by Grenville on Roanoke Island as soon as possible. He set off for the island in the pinnace, accompanied by forty of his best men. As the pinnace pulled away, someone on the *Lion* called to the sailors, telling them not to bring any of the planters back, but to leave them there. Only White and two or three others were to be returned. The man who called to them, whom White mysteriously described as a gentleman who was to go back to England with Fernandes, explained that the mariners of the pinnace and the *Lion* had been persuaded by Fernandes to leave the settlers on Roanoke Island because "the Summer was far spent." In other words, the pilot and his men had decided not to take White and the settlers to the Chesapeake Bay.

Why would Fernandes and the sailors seemingly turn against White and the settlers when they were so close to their destination? There could be no doubt what Ralegh expected of the expedition's leaders on reaching Roanoke Island. Following his master's instructions, White was to learn about the state of affairs in the area from the men in the garrison and return to the ships. Fernandes would then pilot the fleet to the Chesapeake Bay, where the settlers would plant their "seate and forte."

The refusal of Fernandes and his men to take the settlers any farther was nothing less than an act of mutiny. Fernandes and the unnamed gentleman were flouting not only White's authority but also Ralegh's. And yet, surprisingly, White apparently did little to challenge them. Informed by sailors of the decision to leave the settlers on the island, he merely remarked (describing his own response in the third person), that "it booted [suited] not the Governor to contend with them, but [he] passed to Roanoke, and . . . went aland."

In White's telling, the incident makes little sense. If Fernandes and his men had decided to mutiny, it seems unlikely that they would have chosen to take White back with them to England, where he would surely have testified about their gross insubordination. It also seems unlikely that White would have accepted the dramatic change of plan without putting up an argument.[23]

But Fernandes may not actually have betrayed White. Perhaps the two men were in agreement about the change of plan. (In this scenario, White's later account to Ralegh was simply a means of placing blame for the failures of the voyage on Fernandes.) The phrase, "the Summer was far spent," used by the gentleman on the *Lion*, can be interpreted in two ways. Fernandes and his men had had no luck capturing prizes on the outward voyage, but if they helped the settlers establish themselves on

Roanoke Island, spent a few weeks provisioning their ship, and put to sea by mid-August, they might yet have an opportunity to plunder a straggler from the New Spain or Panama treasure fleets. Taking the settlers to the Chesapeake, on the other hand, would diminish their hopes of plunder. Fernandes had probably never sailed as far as the bay and might have been concerned that if the weather turned against him he would be delayed too long to allow him to reach the Azores in time to capture a prize.

Because a fort and houses already existed on Roanoke Island, Fernandes may have reasoned, why not make use of them for the time being before moving on to the Chesapeake at some later date, when White and the settlers were ready? He could leave the pinnace—which was ideal for sailing the sounds, inshore waters, and along major rivers—so that the settlers could transport themselves, their provisions, and equipment after the *Lion* departed.

White may have been thinking along similar lines. After ten weeks on board ship, the prospect of setting up temporary quarters on Roanoke Island, having fresh food and water, and exploring the country was probably appealing to settlers weary of the sea. And it is possible that White had already made up his mind to wait at Roanoke (another rendezvous point for the fleet) for Captain Edward Spicer and the rest of the settlers to arrive in the flyboat. Back on the Isle of Wight in May, White may have agreed with Carey that his privateers should call in at Roanoke Island to relieve Grenville's men before sailing on to the Chesapeake. If so, he might have calculated Carey's ships would reach the island within the next month and be able help with the transportation of the settlers to the bay. White had not given up the plan to plant a colony to the north, but had merely decided to delay implementing it.[24]

⌒⟋⟍⌒

That same evening, July 22, at sunset, White and his men landed on Roanoke Island at the place (possibly near Shallowbag Bay) where the small garrison of fifteen men had been left a year earlier by Grenville. There was no one there, only the bleached bones of one of the men, who White supposed had been killed by the Indians "long before." The following day he and some of the settlers marched to the north end of the island to Lane's fort. There they found the earthwork and palisade thrown down but the houses within and around still standing, uninhabited and "overgrown with Melons [gourds, squash] of many sorts, and Deer within them, feeding." This was good news—at least the houses would provide some shelter for the colonists—but there was still no sign of Grenville's men, and White concluded there was now probably little chance of finding any of them on the island. To discover what had happened they would have to wait until they visited Manteo's people on Croatoan.

Over the next few days the settlers and crew began unloading their gear and supplies from the ships—the pinnace sailing to and fro between the *Lion* and the island. They began repairing the houses left by Lane and prepared the ground for "newe Cottages," small single-unit dwellings, for the families. For John White, the sound of hammering and sawing, and the busy activity around the site, may have brought back fond memories of when Lane's fort was first built, a time when the potential of the region had only been glimpsed. Two years later, he (like Ralegh) was convinced of the untapped riches that Virginia offered and was now determined to succeed in establishing a permanent colony for the glory of God, his queen, and his master.

White's determination was reinforced when he received the best news in more than two months: on July 25 the flyboat arrived off Hatarask with the settlers safe and sound "to the great joye, and comfort of the whole company." Remarkably, of the 118 settlers who had left Plymouth, only two were lost: Glavin and Carroll, who had deserted in Puerto Rico.

By the end of July all the settlers were healthy and making good progress establishing their temporary quarters. To be sure, the settlement was not where it was meant to be. But White was confident they would be able to make their way to the Chesapeake Bay soon, perhaps later in the summer with the assistance of Carey's ships, should they call in at Hatarask. Even wintering on Roanoke Island would not be a major setback if they could find sufficient provisions to see them through to early spring. With Spicer's arrival, little short of a miracle considering he had never before sailed to Virginia, the settlers had survived the hazards of an Atlantic voyage and were together at last—poised to make the final leg of the journey to the Chesapeake Bay to found the City of Ralegh.[25]

5

The Broken Promise

My lost delights, now clean from sight of land,
Have left me all alone in unknown ways,
My mind to woe, my life in fortune's hand;
Of all which past, the sorrow only stays.

—Sir Walter Ralegh

THREE DAYS AFTER the flyboat arrived, George Howe stripped off his clothes by a small creek a couple of miles from the fort. He intended to catch some crabs, and taking a forked stick he gingerly waded into the water. The peace and quiet of the hot summer's day was a welcome respite from the noisy clatter at the settlement, where the colonists were rebuilding the houses and sorting out their gear. As he paused in his search for crabs and looked around at the beautiful countryside, he may have understood why John White had become captivated by Virginia. What a contrast the virgin expanse of land and water of Roanoke Island, populated only by wild creatures, offered to the stench and dirt of London's crowded streets, Howe's last memory of England.

Hidden in tall reeds nearby, a handful of Secotan warriors watched. They had learned of the settlers' return a few days before and had crossed over the sound from their town on the mainland to find out what the newcomers were doing. Coming upon the unarmed man in the creek, they decided the opportunity to avenge the killing of their people by the English the previous year was too good to miss. After making sure the man was alone, they struck.

Sixteen arrows riddled Howe's body, and he fell screaming into the water. In an instant the warriors were upon him, beating his head to a pulp with their war clubs, quickly silencing his cries. Then they were gone, heading back to the mainland, leaving the scene as undisturbed as they had found it save only for the bloody corpse floating gently in the water and a cloud of flies buzzing greedily around.[1]

News of Howe's killing was probably brought back to the settlement the same day by a search party sent to look for him. His death would have come as a profound shock to White and the colonists. They had endured a long voyage and the perils of the Atlantic together, and yet within a few days of arriving on Roanoke Island Howe had been brutally murdered by unknown Indians, apparently without provocation or cause. As the horror sank in, the settlers' view of the island must have shifted dramatically. No longer a place of innocent beauty, it had suddenly taken on an altogether different character, in which appalling violence lay hidden in the forest or by the water's edge. They could no longer assume they were safe outside the confines of the settlement and might not even be secure within if the Indians mounted an attack in force.

WHITE KNEW it was essential to find out who had killed Howe and the extent of the threat as soon as possible. The day after Howe's burial, Captain Edward Stafford set off in the pinnace with Manteo and twenty armed men to visit the Croatoans, about fifty miles to the south, who the English hoped were still friendly. When they reached Croatoan Island, a group of warriors who were gathered on the shore appeared ready to fight. When the Englishmen began to march toward them with their muskets primed, the warriors turned to flee, at which point Manteo called out to them in their own language. They had not recognized him, possibly because he was dressed as an Englishman, but to Stafford's relief, when the Indians realized who Manteo was they immediately threw down their weapons and went to embrace him. They asked him to plead with the Englishmen not to take their corn because they had little. Manteo answered that they had not come to take their corn or anything else, only to "renew the old love, that was between us, and them, at the first, and to live with them as brethren."

Pleased by this response, the warriors invited the men to their town, where they were welcomed by the people and invited to feast with them. The next day, in conference with the town's elders, Stafford learned that Howe had been killed by Secotan warriors, a "remnant" of Wingina's people, who lived at Dasemunkepeuc. The Croatoans told him that Wanchese was one of this group, but whether or not he had been involved in Howe's killing was not mentioned. Perhaps anticipating that the English would seek out the Secotans to take revenge for Howe's murder, the elders requested that their own people be given some badge or token by which the English would recognize them when the

Indians left their island. They told Stafford that the year before several Croatoans had been badly hurt by Ralph Lane's men in the fighting at Dasemunkepeuc. The elders understood that the English had mistaken them for Secotans and wanted to prevent similar confusion in the future.

Discussions between Stafford and the Croatoans solved another mystery: the fate of the fifteen men left by Grenville on Roanoke Island. The English learned that the men had been attacked by thirty warriors from Secotan, Aquascocock, and Dasemunkepeuc. Two Secotans had approached the English settlement and, feigning friendship, invited a couple of the Englishmen's leaders to meet with them unarmed. Foolishly the Englishmen agreed, whereupon the Indians struck one of the men over the head with a club, killing him outright. The other ran back to his company, pursued by the Secotans, shooting at him with their bows and arrows. The English took shelter in their storehouse, which the Indians set alight, forcing the men to run out to escape the flames. After more than an hour of vicious fighting a second Englishman was killed, shot in the mouth with an arrow. The rest of the Englishmen, together with four others who had been outside the settlement when the Indians attacked, escaped by boat and headed toward Hatarask. They had lived for a short time on a small island near the entrance to Port Ferdinando, but after a while had left. They had not been seen or heard of since.

The news was grave. Stafford was now aware that the killing of Howe was not an isolated incident perpetrated by a small group of warriors from Dasemunkepeuc. The attack on Grenville's men had been ruthlessly executed after careful planning by the leaders of three Secotan towns. Nevertheless Stafford, on behalf of White and the setters, told the Croatoans that they were willing to put past wrongs, even Howe's murder, behind them. He may have believed, as White possibly did, that the Secotans' aggression had been justifiably provoked by the violence of Lane's soldiers. Stafford informed the elders that if the Secotans would accept the settlers' friendship, they in turn would "willingly receive them again." To that end, the chiefs and elders of the mainland peoples should be notified by the Croatoans to visit John White on Roanoke Island or give their answer to the Croatoans within seven days. The elders agreed to send the message, and Stafford and his men departed.[2]

After a week passed with no word from chiefs on the mainland or from the Croatoans about a meeting, White concluded reluctantly that there was no other option than to launch a raid on Dasemunkepeuc. The decision was not made lightly. In 1585 White and Thomas Hariot had considered Pemisapan and his people firm friends. The Secotans had helped the English establish themselves on the island and provided them with food and vital information about the region. Hariot had told White about the many occasions on which the Indians had joined the English at their prayers and singing of psalms. White and Hariot had developed a genuine affection for Pemisapan's people, and when White returned in 1587 he hoped it would be possible to reestablish their friendship. Yet the safety of his own people was paramount, and he knew he could wait no longer for a conciliatory gesture from the Secotans.[3]

White, Captain Stafford, and Manteo, together with two dozen men, crossed over to the mainland in the early hours of August 9, while it was still dark. They quickly made their way to woods adjoining Dasemunkepeuc and launched their attack, falling upon a group of men sitting around a fire. The Indians fled into dense reeds, and the Englishmen followed, shooting one through the body, determined to "acquit [revenge] their evil doing towards us."

But White was mistaken. The people they had attacked were not Secotans but Croatoans, who had heard that the Secotans had abandoned the town shortly after killing Howe. The Croatoans had therefore gone to gather corn, tobacco, and pumpkins from the town's fields. In the darkness, the English could not tell friend from foe, "their men and women appareled all so like the others," White confessed. Had it not been for one of the Croatoans calling out to Stafford they might all have been slaughtered.

Manteo was greatly distressed by the injuries suffered by his people but ultimately sided with White, telling the Croatoans that if their chief men had sent messengers to the governor at the appointed time, the English could have informed them of their plans and thereby prevented the "mischance." Nevertheless, White's return to Roanoke after the raid with the unfortunate Croatoans in tow was not the victorious homecoming he had hoped for. The problem of the mainland peoples' hostility was unresolved, and even if White could count on the Croatoans' friendship, somewhat soured by the recent fiasco, the colony remained as isolated and exposed to attack as its predecessor had been under Lane.

BY MID AUGUST, much of the repair and building work at the colonists' settlement was completed. The men and boys probably moved into Lane's old houses, and the Archards, Dares, Harveys, Joneses, Paynes, Powells, Tappans, and Viccarses shifted their possessions into a cluster of new-built cottages more suitable for families; priority being given to the Dares and Harveys because both pregnant women had nearly reached the end of their terms.

The next two weeks were the happiest that White spent on Roanoke Island. On August 18 his daughter, Eleanor, gave birth to a girl, "the first Christian born in Virginia," who was given the name Virginia and christened the Sunday following (August 24). The happy event and accompanying celebrations brought a measure of cheer to the settlers after the difficult three weeks following George Howe's death. The healthy birth of baby Virginia restored the settlers' numbers and was perhaps a sign that the English would succeed after all in establishing themselves in America. Further good news came a few days later with the birth of a child to Margery, wife of assistant Dyonis Harvey.

Earlier, on August 13, White had officiated over another important ceremony at the settlement. In recognition of three years of invaluable service to the English, Manteo was christened and given the title of lord of Roanoke and Dasemunkepeuc, by right of Ralegh's claim to Virginia and Queen Elizabeth's authority. The granting of the title indicated that after White and the settlers left Roanoke to continue their journey to Chesapeake Bay, Manteo and his people would continue to hold the region for the English. Lord Manteo would be Ralegh's Indian governor, ruling over both Roanoke Island and the adjacent mainland, which the English deemed they had taken by their victory over the Secotans.

Manteo was the first Indian admitted into the Church of England on American soil. His baptism marked the beginning of the colonists' godly work to convert Indian peoples to Protestantism, a matter of great significance for White. In the spring of 1585 Okisko, chief of the Weapemeocs, had sworn allegiance to Elizabeth and Ralegh and sent his head men to Lane's fort to declare their fealty. But neither Okisko nor his people had converted to the Church of England. Manteo, on the other hand, was now a Christian lord who was intended to play an active role in winning over Indian peoples of the region to Protestantism and Englishness. The effort to convert the Secotans had failed amid the havoc caused by European diseases and the outbreak of hostilities that followed. Ralegh, who had ordered White to baptize Manteo, believed that the conversion of one of their own was another means of bringing Protestantism to the Indians. Manteo would first win over the Croatoans and perhaps in time the Indians of the mainland.

Ralegh and White's assumption that the Indians would convert to Christianity reflected the profound differences in how the English and Indians viewed one another. Whereas White envisioned settlers and Indians living in peace "as brethren," the Secotans had come to believe that the settlers' notion of living together assumed Indian peoples would submit to English ways. Wanchese (if he was still alive) and the chiefs of towns on the mainland were convinced that neither White nor any other English leader had in mind a union of equals, but rather expected Indians to willingly renounce their gods and traditions in favor of the strangers' beliefs. For Wanchese and those who fought with him, the matter could not be clearer: they were engaged in a life or death struggle, the outcome of which would determine their very existence.[4]

By the third week of August the sailors of the *Lion* and the flyboat had finished unloading the settlers' goods and equipment on Roanoke Island and began to prepare for the return journey across the Atlantic. On August 21, however, the ships' departure was delayed by a fierce nor'easter that pounded the Outer Banks and forced Fernandes, who was on board the *Lion*, to cut her anchor cables and put out to sea to avoid being driven ashore. Fearing the ship had been cast away or that Fernandes had abandoned the colony, as he had threatened to do when the settlers first arrived, White hastily gathered the assistants together to take stock.

The settlers had previously decided to send one of their number back to England on the flyboat to report to Ralegh and garner support for a relief expedition. Now none of them wished to go, perhaps because they did not wish to face the return journey without the escort of the heavily armed *Lion*, or possibly because they did not want to leave their families. Only Christopher Cooper, after much cajoling by White, showed any willingness, but he changed his mind after talking to friends.

The next day the entire company went to White and "with one voice" implored him to go to England himself. They believed his close association with Ralegh made him by far the best qualified to obtain supplies and additional settlers for the colony. White was aghast and refused point blank, arguing that as governor his abrupt departure would be tantamount to deserting his post. He would be greatly discredited by abandoning the expedition and those who depended on him. He pointed out that critics in England would slander him by accusing him of going to Virginia only to keep in Ralegh's good graces. They would say that he had led the settlers to "a Country, in which he never meant to stay himself, and there to leave them behind him." Rather less convincingly, he told them that because they "intended to remove 50 miles further up into the main presently," his possessions might be damaged or lost in his absence, so that when he eventually returned he would likely be ruined.

Not to be dissuaded, a group of settlers, including the assistants, continued to press him. They promised to bind themselves "under all their hands, and seals" to safeguard his goods and to justify his departure in writing. Accordingly, they had a testimonial drawn up and presented it to White on behalf of the entire company:

May it please you, her Majesty's Subjects of England, we your friends and Countrymen, the planters in Virginia, do by these presents let you, and everyone of you to understand that for the present and speedy supply of certain our known, and apparent lacks, and needs, most requisite and necessary for the good and happy planting of us, or any other in this land of Virginia, we all of one mind, and consent, have most earnestly entreated, and incessantly requested John White, Governor of the planters in Virginia, to pass into England, for the better and more assured help, and setting forward of the foresaid supplies: and knowing assuredly that he both can best, and will labor, and take pains in that behalf for us all, and he not once, but often refusing it, for our sakes, and for the honor, and maintenance of the action, hath at last, though much against his will, through our importunacy, yielded to leave his government, and all his goods among us, and himself in all our behalves to pass into England, of whose knowledge, and fidelity in handling this matter, as all others, we do assure ourselves by these presents, and will you to give all credit thereto. The five and twentieth of August.[5]

White agonized over the request for the better part of a day. Despite the setbacks since their arrival, the settlers' unanimous plea showed that they had not lost faith in him.

They were right about the importance of his connection to Ralegh. He was the only one among them likely to be able to persuade Sir Walter to raise the supplies and ships needed to relocate the colony to the Chesapeake Bay. Perhaps they were also right that no one else could be entrusted with such an important undertaking. Yet the decision was heartbreaking. On the one hand, White was convinced his duty was to remain with the settlers in Virginia, but on the other, the settlers believed he was needed more in London. He would have to leave behind his daughter, newborn granddaughter, kin, and friends to undertake a long and arduous journey with no certainty of ever seeing them again.

On August 26, White made the decision to return to England. He had little time to prepare for his departure and immediately threw himself into a flurry of activity. The first task was to make arrangements for the assistants to govern while he was away, possibly with Roger Bailey or Ananias Dare in charge. Then he and the assistants had to decide where the colonists would go when they left Roanoke Island. Mindful of the threat of attack by the Secotans, White and the settlers had decided to leave the island and move inland, where they hoped to find friendly Indian peoples to help them. The best prospect was somewhere near the head of Albemarle Sound, where the Chowanocs lived. White knew from discussions with Ralph Lane that both peoples had been loyal allies of the English the previous year. Possibly the aged Menatonon would be equally helpful to his settlers.

It was also likely that they would find plenty of food in the area. The English still had several months of provisions, but the failure to obtain cattle, salt, and supplies in the West Indies would necessitate short rations through much of winter and spring. Inland there were fish and game, invaluable supplements to the settlers' diet, as well as fresh water. They also might be able to acquire corn and other provisions from the Chowanocs.

The problem of how the settlers would transport themselves off Roanoke Island was settled in agreement with Stafford and Edward Spicer. They would leave behind the pinnace and a couple of ships' boats for the settlers' use, which would be sufficient to transport them around the sounds and along rivers. The pinnace could be used to skirt the coast to the Chesapeake Bay should the settlers choose to explore that route.

White also had to consider arrangements for his own eventual return to Roanoke and how to locate the settlers at that time. Neither he nor anyone else had decided on a specific location inland where the settlers would establish themselves, other than possibly near the mouth of the Chowan River. They had not yet scouted the region, although John Wright and James Lasie may have been with Ralph Lane's expedition to the town of Chowanoc in 1586 and possibly remembered something of the lands along the river.

The settlers therefore decided to leave a small contingent on Roanoke Island, who would keep in touch with the main group's movements inland. When White returned to Roanoke they would be able to tell him where the main group had gone. White would then have a couple of options, which would be largely determined by the number of new settlers he recruited while in England. If he returned with only a handful of recruits, he would order the settlers to abandon their temporary quarters inland. They would return to the island in preparation for boarding the ships he expected to bring with him to complete (belatedly) the last leg of the voyage to the Chesapeake. If he returned with a large number of new colonists, he might consider maintaining a small settlement at the head of Albemarle Sound. By this means he could keep an English presence in the area while the majority of settlers relocated to the Chesapeake.

Finally, White and his assistants made arrangements in case of an emergency. If the settlers had to leave the island or their inland settlement hurriedly, they would carve the name of where they planned to move on prominent trees so White would know where to find them. A cross over the letters would signify they had been attacked and forced to depart.

White had much to worry about. Besides Indian attacks, he was concerned about Spanish ships finding the colony. Darby Glavin and Dennis Carroll, who had deserted at Puerto Rico, would by now probably have informed Spanish authorities where White's colony was to be established, raising the strong possibility that the Spanish would soon investigate. In fact, unknown to White, Pedro Menéndez Marqués, governor of Florida, had scouted the Outer Banks and sailed as far as the entrance to Chesapeake Bay in June, only a month before White and the settlers arrived. Finding no sign of the English, Menéndez Marqués had nevertheless recommended that the king order a thorough exploration of the coast as far as St. John's (Nova Scotia) forthwith.[6]

By August 27 the flyboat was ready to sail. With little time to say good-bye to Eleanor, Ananias, and his close friends, White bundled his gear together and left the island to join the ship anchored off Hatarask, promising to return as soon as possible. Miraculously, that same morning Fernandes and the *Lion* reappeared at Port Ferdinando after six days riding out rough weather at sea. But for White the happy news of the ship's safe return was tinged with the realization that it came too late to alter plans for his departure. Deeply troubled, he sailed for England shortly after midnight, wondering when and in what circumstances he would be with his family and the rest of the settlers again.[7]

WHITE'S VOYAGE got off to a disastrous start. As the flyboat weighed anchor, one of the capstan's bars broke, causing it to spin out of control. Several men hauling in the cable were badly injured and others were flung to the deck. The ship had a crew of only fifteen men, and as a result of the accident most were barely able to perform their work. Nevertheless, Captain Spicer managed to keep the flyboat alongside the *Lion* until they arrived in the Azores in mid-September. Then the two ships went their separate ways: Fernandes patrolled off Tercera for prizes in the *Lion*, and Captain Spicer headed for England.

Again White's luck failed him. After three weeks of indifferent weather, the flyboat was hit by a strong storm off the coast of

Ireland, driving her back out into the Atlantic. By the time the ship eventually made landfall at Smerwick in Southwest Ireland on October 16, the men had exhausted their supplies and "expected nothing," White wrote, "but by famine to perish at Sea." Five sailors, a third of the crew, died on the voyage or soon after reaching Smerwick, and several others were in bad condition. Realizing the men would be unable to continue the journey to England, White rode to the nearby town of Dingle, where he arranged for the care of Spicer's sick and for fresh provisions to be delivered to the flyboat. Then he took passage on board the *Monkey* on November 1, bound for Southampton.[8]

When White arrived in England on November 8, he learned that the *Lion* had already docked at Portsmouth several weeks earlier. Fernandes had failed to take any prizes, and sickness had ravaged the *Lion*'s crew to such an extent that the ship had scarcely been able to make port. The return voyage of both ships had been terrible, but White was anxious to put his ordeal behind him and report to Ralegh as quickly as possible. He probably arrived in London a few days later but then had to wait more than a week to see Sir Walter.[9]

Unfortunately White's arrival and his efforts to organize a relief expedition could not have come at a worse time. England was preparing for invasion. In the late spring and summer of 1587, Sir Francis Drake had led a successful raid on Cadiz and ravaged Spanish shipping along the Iberian coast in an effort to disrupt preparations for the dispatch of the Armada, Philip II's great fleet, later that year. Yet as Elizabeth's councilors were aware, Drake's action had only delayed Philip's plans, not scuttled them. In early October, therefore, the Privy Council had ordered a general stay of English shipping, which prohibited ships from leaving port without permission because they might be needed to defend England's shores.

The following month Ralegh was appointed by the queen to her council of war. Along with Sir Richard Grenville, Ralph Lane, and eight others, he was to take charge of the country's land defenses. The English fleet would be the first line of defense, but should Spanish forces break through, it would be left to the county militias and levies to repulse the attack. The entire coast from Cornwall to East Anglia was vulnerable, and Ralegh and his fellow councilors were extremely busy throughout the winter overseeing the strengthening of coastal fortifications, organizing the militias and trained bands, and securing supplies of arms and equipment.[10]

On November 20, Ralegh managed to set aside his many responsibilities to meet White. White likely reported his differences with Fernandes and anxiety about the settlers' difficulties on Roanoke Island in the light of continuing Indian hostility. He may well have been anxious about how Ralegh would react. Would his master be so exasperated with the setbacks that he would decide to abandon the venture altogether? But Sir Walter remained optimistic. Edward Stafford, who had returned on the *Lion*, had already met with Ralegh and described the voyage as a success. He had delivered the good news of the colonists' safe arrival "in their wished [for] haven," an exaggeration given that the settlers had been left on Roanoke Island instead of the Chesapeake Bay. Yet Stafford had assured Ralegh that the colonists were determined "to prosecute this action more thoroughly than ever," which suggested they were committed to the venture and

ready to move on to the Chesapeake once provisions and reinforcements arrived from England.

Ralegh had also heard in October from Richard Hakluyt the
younger, who remained highly enthusiastic about the colony's
prospects. Hakluyt had returned to London in the spring of 1587
and had likely spoken to Thomas Hariot as well as Stafford about
Virginia. He had recently finished a translation of René de
Laudonnière's account of the French Huguenot settlements in
Florida, and in the dedication to Ralegh he urged him to take
possession of the "inward parts of the firme [mainland]." In the
interior, Hakluyt wrote, there were many thousands of Indians
who were more intelligent than the native peoples of Spanish
America. The Indians would be easily converted to the Anglican
Church and English ways. Inland, too, would be found "large
and ample regions" suitable for stock rearing and the cultivation
of all sorts of commodities. And most promising, the colonists
might perhaps find precious minerals and a route to the Pacific.
Although his argument largely repeated Hariot and Lane's findings of the previous year, Hakluyt encouraged Ralegh to perse-
vere with the venture now that it was so close to success.[11]

SIR WALTER immediately began organizing a relief expedition. He
promised White he would dispatch a pinnace with provisions and
equipment as soon as it could be fitted out, and he sent word to
Sir Richard Grenville at Bideford, in north Devon, to ready a
fleet for a full-scale expedition. He also wrote letters to the settlers telling them that he was preparing "a good supply of shipping and men with sufficiency of all things needful." God willing,
he assured them, the fleet would be with them by the summer.[12]

White must have been delighted by Ralegh's response. If he was concerned that the fleet would not sail for several months, nevertheless the scale of the planned expedition was a clear indication of Ralegh's commitment to the colony. Yet as December and the early new year passed, White became increasingly concerned. For reasons that are unclear, the promise to send out a pinnace was not fulfilled. Perhaps on second thought Ralegh and Grenville considered that dispatching a small ship unaccompanied across the Atlantic was too risky. Or possibly by the time preparations were made they decided there was little to be gained by sending the pinnace on ahead and arranged for her to sail with the fleet instead. Either way, White could only hope that Grenville's expedition would be ready to depart in the spring.

Grenville's fleet was as large as that of 1585 and may have carried several dozen colonists to reinforce White's settlers as well as plenty of supplies. The principal ships were the *Galleon Dudley* (250 tons), the *Virgin God Save Her* (200 tons), the *Tiger* (possibly part of the 1585 expedition), the *Golden Hind*, and the *St. Leger*. Grenville's plan was probably to head first to Roanoke Island, where he would pick up the settlers and transport them to Chesapeake Bay. After establishing the colony he would take the fleet to the West Indies, where he would harry Spanish shipping and cruise the Atlantic for valuable prizes.

White's hopes, however, were dashed at the end of March 1588. Just as the fleet was about to depart, Grenville was ordered by the Privy Council not to proceed with the voyage. Ralegh had been confident during the winter that he would be able to use his influence with the queen to bypass the general stay on shipping and arrange for the fleet to sail, but the escalating national crisis had overtaken his plans. By the spring, White explained in his account of the voyage, the talk throughout the whole country was of the king of Spain's "invincible fleets," which were about to sail against England. Grenville was told to send his ships to Sir Francis Drake at Plymouth, where they would join the queen's navy for service against the Armada.[13]

White was able to take some comfort from the fact that the voyage to Roanoke did not have to be abandoned entirely. Ralegh managed to salvage two small ships that were not required by Drake: the *Brave* (30 tons), captained by Arthur Facy, and the *Roe*, a 25-ton pinnace. Fifteen settlers were on board the two ships (seven women, four men, and four children), as well as supplies of biscuit, meal, and vegetables. White, who sailed on the *Brave*, was surely maddened by the turn of events, but at least the two small vessels would provide some relief to the settlers.[14]

The ships left Bideford on April 22, 1588, but unhappily for White and the other passengers, Facy showed no interest in getting them to Virginia. Shortly after leaving port he began plundering any vessel that came within reach. His rampage ended only when, on their way to Madeira, the *Brave* was attacked by two well-armed privateers out of La Rochelle. The larger of the two French ships carried 100 men and ten cannon and was faster than the English vessel. Facy had little choice but to surrender or fight. He chose to fight and signaled his intention by sending a volley of shot into the French ship at close range.

The attack set off a fierce battle that lasted for an hour and a half, during which twenty-three men on both sides were killed or badly wounded. White was in the thick of the fighting as the two ships came together and some thirty Frenchmen clambered over the sides of the *Brave*. The Frenchmen clustered on the forecastle and poop deck (fore and aft decks), where they rained a withering crossfire upon the English crowded below. Outnumbered and outgunned, Facy and his men fought desperately until the French captain called on them to surrender, promising to spare their lives. After the English had surrendered, the French pirates set about pillaging the ship and took away everything they could carry.

Facy was forced to abandon the voyage and limp back to England as best he could, "God justly punishing our former thievery of our evil disposed mariners," White commented angrily, referring to Facy's piracy. The English had been badly mauled in the hand-to-hand fighting. Three of the settlers were injured, the master and mate were so badly hurt they could not rise from their beds, and White had taken two wounds to the head from sword and pike and a graze from a bullet on his thigh. The ship arrived back at Bideford on May 22 and the *Roe*, which had been separated from the *Brave* before the battle, returned a few weeks later. Far more galling for White than the wounds he had suffered was the realization that there was now no chance of reaching the settlers by the summer or even later that year.[15]

WHITE WAS not the only one seeking the English colony in the spring of 1588. On the other side of the Atlantic the governor of Florida, Pedro Menéndez Marqués, was ordered by Spain's naval high command to prepare a ship to explore northward as far as San Juan (Bay of Fundy, Nova Scotia). Following Grenville and Drake's expeditions of 1585 and 1586, the Spanish had learned that the English had located themselves somewhere along the mid-Atlantic coast and believed the most likely place was the Bahia de Madre de Dios (Chesapeake Bay). Menéndez Marqués had sailed to the Chesapeake in the summer of 1587 but had found no trace of them. Now, on the eve of the invasion of England, the Spanish were determined to make another effort to locate the English colony and rid themselves of pirate interlopers in North America.

The governor turned to Captain Vicente Gonzáles, one of Florida's most experienced mariners, to lead the expedition. Gonzáles possessed expert knowledge of the region's coastal waters and had been to Chesapeake Bay several times before. He left San Augustine at the end of May 1588 in a small bark with thirty men, and after making rapid progress entered the Chesapeake Bay early the following month. The Spaniards explored the Western Shore and a number of the larger rivers. Along one of them they met many Indians who came down to the riverside, including a chief who wore a necklace of fine gold. Toward the end of June, having reached the head of the bay, they returned the way they had come. They then crossed to the Eastern Shore, where they landed on some small islands in sight of Cape Charles (Cabo de San Juan).

Leaving the bay and heading south, the Spanish encountered strengthening winds off the Outer Banks and sought shelter in one of the inlets. Quite by chance, Gonzáles then discovered what he had been looking for: evidence of an English settlement. The Spanish had entered Port Ferdinando. There, to the south they saw Pamlico Sound and to the north a large arm of land that was well wooded, probably the eastern side of Roanoke Island. On Hatarask they found a slipway, where small vessels could be drawn up for loading or repair, bits and pieces of discarded equipment, as well as some barrels placed in the ground to collect rainwater. The Spaniards did not see any sign of the English, however, and deciding not to stay any longer, Gonzáles returned to San Augustine to report his important discovery to the governor. By the summer, the Spanish knew precisely where the English had been seated, but where they had gone remained uncertain.[16]

AT THE END of May 1588 the decisive confrontation between England and Spain was at hand. Philip II's Armada of 130 ships left Lisbon, carrying more than 19,000 troops and 8,000 mariners, and began its stately journey north to link up with the Duke of Parma's army in Flanders. Such a fleet had never been seen in Atlantic waters: "the greatest and best furnished with men, munitions, and all warlike preparations that ever the Ocean did see," William Camden wrote. Many feared the English navy would be powerless to prevent its descent on England.

In its essentials Philip's plan of attack remained the same as that formulated several years earlier. The Armada, commanded by Alonso Pérez de Guzman, the Duke of Medina Sidonia (who had replaced Santa Cruz upon his death in February), was to proceed up the English Channel and take up a station near Margate on the extreme northeast coast of Kent. There he would protect Parma's army of 27,000 as they crossed the channel from Dunkirk. Philip knew that if Medina Sidonia was able to keep the English fleet at bay long enough to enable Parma to make a successful landing on the Kentish coast, there was little to prevent his army from reaching London. Parma's troops would follow the old Roman road to Canterbury, then on to Chatham and

Rochester before the final push to the capital. Though comparable or greater in number, Elizabeth's land forces were made up primarily of raw recruits mustered in trained bands and county militias. They would be no match for Parma's seasoned veterans, who would sweep through Kent and be in London within a week.

Philip's faith in his holy mission was unshakable. "As all victories are the gift of God Almighty," he assured Medina Sidonia, "and the cause we champion is so exclusively His, we may look for His favor, unless by our sins we render ourselves unworthy." Even serious setbacks failed to disturb the king's resolute belief. When bad weather forced the Armada to put into Corunna after a month at sea, Philip wrote, "If this were an unjust war, the storm might be taken as a sign of God's will that we should cease from our offence. As, however, it is so just, it is not to be believed that God will withhold His aid, but that He will rather favor that [our] cause even to the utmost of our desires."

Yet while Philip put his faith in God, Medina Sidonia and Parma were fully aware of the formidable logistical challenges they faced. The massive fleet was cumbersome and unwieldy, able to travel only as fast as the slowest of the ponderous urcas and hulks (transports and freight carriers), which sailed at a snail's pace. Nor was the vast Armada unified. Brought together from all over Europe, the fleet had never before operated as a single unit and had little cohesion in practice. And the Spanish were poorly prepared for the kind of fighting they would encounter against the English fleet. Many of the larger vessels were heavily armed with great guns, but Spanish naval tactics relied mainly on close-range combat, grappling with the enemy and overpowering them with boarding parties, a tactic ill-suited to fighting the English in their fast, maneuverable ships, who favored firing from a distance with their long-range cannon.

Timing was the key to victory. Medina Sidonia would have to battle his way up the channel, immobilize the English fleet, and arrive off Flanders at the same time Parma was ready to launch his transports carrying the army. The riskiest part of the operation by far was getting the flotilla of barges from the embarkation point at Dunkirk across the Straits of Dover to Margate, approximately fifty miles. If a heavy sea or gale should arise, the barges would be swamped, and if caught in open waters by English or Dutch warships, they would have little chance of escape. "Neither the valor of our men nor any other human effort could save us," Parma told the king in late June. Yet both Philip and Medina Sidonia remained confused about this most crucial aspect of the plan. Both men continued to believe that Parma had sufficient ships to be able to make his own way out of Dunkirk and rendezvous with the Armada at sea. This proved to be a fatal misunderstanding.[17]

John White's whereabouts on Friday, July 29, 1588, when the Armada was first sighted off the Lizard, the most southerly point of Cornwall, are unknown. He may have been with family and friends or was possibly at Durham House with Hariot. He would not have seen much of Ralegh, who was busy making last-minute arrangements for the defense of Cornwall and Devon and also attending the queen in his capacity as Captain of the Guard, responsible for her personal safety. News of the drama unfolding along the southern coast only gradually filtered through to the capital, and White, like most Londoners, had to make do with vague and sometimes confusing scraps of gossip.

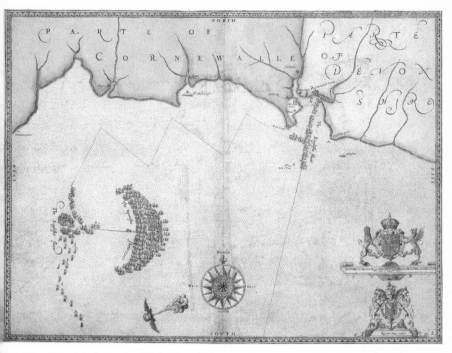

5.1 The Spanish Armada off the South Coast of England, 1588. The Armada is shown in a large crescent formation to the left of center. To the right, the English fleet is depicted leaving Plymouth and on the left taking up a station to the rear of the Spanish fleet. Lord Howard's flagship, the *Ark Ralegh* (or *Ark Royal*), leads the English fleet into action. The massive 800-ton ship was built by Sir Walter Ralegh at his own expense and given to Queen Elizabeth in early 1587.

Contrary to the expectations of Elizabeth's council of war, the Spanish made no attempt to capture deep water harbors such as Plymouth or Portsmouth, from which they could conduct their operations. Instead, they sailed slowly up the Channel toward France in a huge crescent formation, two miles across and several long.

Cannon fire thundered across the water over the next several days. Lord Admiral Charles Howard of Effingham and

Drake led the main body of the English fleet to harry the great Spanish galleons and prevent a landing on the English coast, all the while being careful to avoid being drawn into fighting at close quarters. As far as the latter was concerned, the English commanders need not have worried. Philip had expressly forbidden his commander to engage the enemy in a protracted action and emphasized that he should bring his ships safely to the rendezvous point with Parma. Following orders, Medina Sidonia avoided any serious contact, and after a week of inconclusive skirmishes, neither side had inflicted any major damage. On August 6 the Spanish fleet came to anchor at Calais to wait for word that Parma's transports were ready to begin the crossing.

The English now had an ideal opportunity to attack. As Howard's fleet maneuvered into position outside Calais, Elizabeth sent an urgent message to the Lord Admiral. Ralegh was possibly the messenger and would have surely relished a central role in the drama unfolding off the French coast. Stepping onto the deck of the flagship *Ark Royal*, which he had built at his own expense and given to the queen the previous year, Ralegh informed Howard that the queen expected him to drive the Spanish out of the harbor or engage them. Drake and Howard needed no prompting, however, and had already prepared eight fireships, covered in pitch, resin, and wildfire. On the night of August 7 the fireships were sent blazing into the heart of the enemy with devastating effect, the "whole Sea glittering and shining with the Flame thereof," Camden wrote. In confusion and panic, the Spanish were forced to cut their cables and scramble to avoid the fireships and get out of the congested harbor.

The Spanish fleet headed north to take up a station off Flanders, where they would be able to protect Parma's troops during the crossing. Howard and Drake led the pursuit and were joined by Lord Henry Seymour's squadron of forty ships, which had been guarding the Kentish coast where Parma was expected to land. Then, off Gravelines, near Dunkirk, on August 8 the entire English naval force of 150 ships caught up with the Spanish. At close range the English poured volley after volley of shot from their great guns into the Spanish galleons. Medina Sidonia could only fight a desperate rearguard action to hold position off Gravelines while waiting for Parma to appear.

But Parma did not appear. His army was still not ready to make the crossing and in any case could not get away from Dunkirk without being caught by Dutch flyboats patrolling the shallow coastal waters. Even if Parma could have left port, Medina Sidonia's ships were in no condition to protect him. Many of the largest ships had by now been badly damaged and could not hold their positions. Several sank or had to be beached on the Flanders coast. The battle was over, and as a strong wind pushed the Armada in a northeasterly direction up the Channel, the English fleet was content to shepherd the Spanish away from the English coast. When Elizabeth left London in her royal barge on August 18 to visit the Earl of Leicester's camp downriver at Tilbury, what was left of the battered Spanish fleet was rounding the northern coast of Scotland in what would prove a long and dreadful voyage back to Spain. The seemingly invincible Armada had been decisively defeated, and there would be no invasion of England, at least for the time being.

The country had survived a great ordeal. The threat of invasion and foreign occupation that had loomed over England for the best part of two decades had at last been lifted. Public prayers and thanksgiving services were held throughout England during the late summer and fall, culminating in a triumphant ceremony at St. Paul's Cathedral on November 24, 1588, attended by the queen.

Sumptuously dressed in gold, silver, and pearls, Elizabeth celebrated not only her victory over the Spanish foe but also the thirtieth anniversary of her reign. A procession of noblemen, courtiers, her ladies of honor, the Lord Mayor and aldermen, magistrates, and great merchants moved along streets decked out in blue cloth, lined by the liveried companies and cheering crowds. At the cathedral, flanked by the banners of the vanquished hung for all to see, Elizabeth heard a sermon in which "the Glory was given to God alone." She thanked Lord Howard and his gallant captains, "as men born for the Preservation of their Country," and commended those who had fought valiantly and served faithfully. For the remainder of her reign, a national day of thanksgiving was set aside at the end of November to commemorate England's greatest victory and salvation from Spanish tyranny.[18]

CHRISTMAS 1588 came and went, and John White remained in London, fretting. It had been nearly eighteen months since he had left Roanoke Island, and he had made little progress in organizing supplies and settlers for Virginia. If anything, the outlook seemed less bright than it had twelve months earlier, when Ralegh had appeared eager to send ships as soon as possible. In the aftermath of the defeat of the Armada, Ralegh and Grenville had been dispatched by the queen to guard the Irish Sea in case Medina Sidonia endeavored to regroup the Spanish fleet and launch a surprise attack from Ireland. The threat had quickly fizzled out, and the two men had then attended to their own interests, touring their vast estates in Munster.

Instead of turning once again to the plight of the Roanoke settlers, Ralegh busied himself with the development of his Irish lands. He had been granted a princely fiefdom of more than 42,000 acres in late February 1587, centered on the beautiful, fertile valley of the River Blackwater and the town of Youghal, and had subsequently acquired valuable ecclesiastical estates, including Molana Abbey, together with the magnificent castle at Lismore, which he was rebuilding as his palace. At the time of his visit he would have found several hundred settlers on his lands, most from Devon, Somerset, and Dorset, and entire villages rapidly growing into thriving farming communities. The prospects were strong for continued growth and prosperity because of the expansion of trade between southern Ireland and the north coast of Devon and Cornwall. Perhaps Ralegh thought that he had already achieved in Munster what he had so far failed to accomplish in Virginia.

Sir Walter also may have been distracted by developments at court. A new star was competing for Elizabeth's affections, the dashing, twenty-three-year-old Robert Devereaux, 2nd Earl of Essex. He had arrived at court a few years before and by 1588 was already a firm favorite of the queen, who was dazzled by his youth and charm. Bitter rivals, Ralegh and Essex detested each other, and in December 1588 Essex challenged Ralegh to a duel. What caused the quarrel between the two is unknown, but the

Privy Council was barely able to prevent them from coming to blows.[19]

Whether he was preoccupied with his Irish estates or his spat with Essex, Ralegh showed little of his usual energy in organizing another expedition to Roanoke. He may have introduced White to his kinsman and financier, William Sanderson, and to Thomas "Customer" Smythe, the wealthy London merchant, both of whom became backers of a fresh venture. But it was probably White who in early March 1589 pulled together the rest of the group who pledged to support a voyage to relieve the settlers. Sir Walter continued to guard jealously his overall rights to North America as stipulated in his patent, but owing to White's tireless efforts in the winter of 1588–1589 he would no longer have to shoulder the entire financial burden for the colony.

The outcome was a formal agreement in which Ralegh granted exclusive trading privileges with the "city of Ralegh" to a syndicate of nineteen London merchants and supporters who had joined with John White, two assistants in England (John Nichols and Humphrey Dimmocke), and the seven surviving assistants in Virginia. As a token of his good faith, Ralegh contributed £100 for "planting the Christian religion, in, and amongst the said barbarous and heathen countries," and for use by the group for their own purposes. In return, the merchants were to provide capital, supplies, trade goods, and arms for the colony, the intention being to reinforce the settlers' position, not to bring them home.[20]

Despite his progress, White must have been in an increasingly desperate mood. It was too late to fit out an expedition for April or May, and he could not find ships and men to undertake the voyage. In the spring of 1588, Ralegh's plans to send a fleet to Roanoke had been wrecked by preparations to repulse the Spanish Armada. Now, a year later, White's efforts to organize a relief expedition were frustrated by English plans for a large-scale attack by sea and land on Spanish ports and shipping.

When the full extent of the defeat inflicted upon the Armada had dawned on Elizabeth's commanders, merchants, and privateers, they had realized that there was a golden opportunity to mount a major assault on the undefended Iberian coast to further weaken Philip's naval power. The plan of attack that evolved over the winter of 1588–1589 was to destroy Spanish ships as they underwent repairs in various ports—Santander, Corunna, and Lisbon; to restore the royal claimant, Dom Antonio, to the Portuguese throne; and to deploy a fleet off the Azores to intercept the Indies treasure fleet. The English fleet was commanded by Drake and the land forces by General John Norris. In the face of this massive expedition that promised handsome returns to its investors, White had little hope of finding mariners for a voyage to the unprofitable shores of Virginia.

In mid-April 1589 the huge merchant fleet of 143 vessels and half a dozen royal ships, carrying 18,000 soldiers, set out from Plymouth. The expedition was a complete failure. Poorly coordinated and executed, the combined land and naval forces were repulsed from Corunna and Lisbon, with heavy losses. To Elizabeth's fury, Drake and Norris made no attempt to attack Santander. The English failed to inflict any serious damage on the Spanish fleet and returned to England a few months later with little plunder. Ralegh was one of the few investors who gained anything from the voyage—his ships took prizes off Portugal; most, including Elizabeth, lost heavily. Yet London and West

Country merchants continued to invest eagerly in privateering ventures. Even small-scale voyages could bring good profits, and there was always the chance of striking it rich by taking a great merchantman. Desperately worried about his family and the rest of the settlers, all White could do was hope that his luck would soon change.[21]

Not until early 1590 did White at last manage to persuade a group of privateers bound for the West Indies to take him on to Roanoke. Three well-armed ships were made available by John Watts, one of London's leading privateering entrepreneurs, and his partners, among whom was Ralegh. The fleet included the *Hopewell* (140–160 tons), captained by Abraham Cocke, which carried about sixty men and twenty guns; the *Little John* (100–120 tons), captained by Christopher Newport, able to carry approximately a hundred men and nineteen guns; and the pinnace the *John Evangelist*, captained by William Lane. In addition, William Sanderson fitted out the *Moonlight* (80 tons), captained by Edward Spicer, carrying forty men and seven guns, to sail with them.

Besides White, the privateers were supposed to carry "a convenient number of passengers, with their furnitures and necessaries [gear and provisions] to be landed in Virginia." Nothing is known about them, but they may have included settlers from the previous year's abortive expedition or men and women recently recruited by White and financed by the City of Ralegh syndicate.

Unfortunately, apart from Spicer, the privateers had little interest in going to Roanoke. They had only consented because on February 1, 1590, the Privy Council had issued a general restraint and stay on shipping in response to government fears of another Spanish attack on England. The voyage to Roanoke allowed the privateers to circumvent the ban, because Ralegh had received permission from the queen to allow the ships to proceed with their planned voyage to the West Indies as long as they stopped in at the colony.

At the end of February White suffered yet another misfortune. When his group was about to board the ships riding at anchor in the Thames, Watts and his captains refused to carry any passengers other than White himself. White later complained bitterly about his treatment by Watts's men, saying they regarded "very little the good of their countrymen in Virginia" and were only willing to seek plunder and spoils. His arguments did not persuade the privateers to reconsider, and fearing that if he left the ships to protest to Ralegh they would sail without him, he boarded the *Hopewell*. From the large-scale expedition of two years earlier, White was now reduced to returning to the settlers alone.[22]

Cocke left port on March 20 and led his ships to the coast of Africa, then on to the Canaries and across the Atlantic to Dominica, which they sighted at the end of April. Over the next several months the privateers hunted down prizes, with considerable success, capturing a large merchantman out of Seville that carried hides, sugar, and ginger valued at over £5,000. At the end of July the *Hopewell* and *Moonlight* left the West Indies and set a course for Virginia, parting company with the other two ships, which made their way back across the Atlantic to the Azores.

The two captains, Cocke and Spicer, made good progress along the Florida coast until August 1, when they ran into a hurricane, "with much rain, thundering, and great [water] spouts," White wrote. Bad weather followed them all the way to the Outer Banks and obliged them to stand out to sea for nearly a week before the storm cleared. The ships eventually reached Hatarask in mid-August and anchored a couple of miles from Port Ferdinando, where White reported seeing "a great smoke rise in the Ile Roanoke near the place where I left our Colony in 1587." The smoke, he continued, "put us in good hope that some of the Colony were there expecting my return out of England."

On August 16 two boats were readied to go ashore on Hatarask Island. The *Hopewell*'s master gunner was instructed to fire three cannon in succession to alert the colonists that the English had at last come back. As the boats pulled away from the ships, another "great smoke" was spotted to the southwest of Kenricks Mounts, the high dunes near a prominent cape (Cape Kenrick) that jutted out into the ocean midway along Hatarask Island. White must have wondered whether another group of settlers to the south had signaled to them.

The English landed first at Port Ferdinando and walked some fifteen miles along Hatarask Island, but found no sign of the settlers or any indication they had been there recently. Tired and disappointed, the men marched back to the harbor where they had left their boats and decided not to attempt going over to Roanoke Island until the next day. They then returned to their ships for the night.

At mid-morning the two boats set off again, once more with Cocke's boat in the lead and Spicer following. A nor'easter was blowing a gale, churning up the surf and creating a fierce current through the inlet at Port Ferdinando. Passing through, Cocke's boat was hit by a large wave and half filled with water, but by the skilful navigation of the captain the boat was brought to shore on the other side of Hatarask with no harm done, apart from the men's weapons and supplies being soaked.

Shortly after, Spicer's boat entered the inlet and was also pounded by the heavy sea. The master's mate, Ralph Skinner, was unable to keep the prow heading into the waves, and the boat was struck sideways on, swamped, and flipped over. As White and Cocke's men looked on in horror, Spicer and his men struggled to stay afloat, clinging to the upturned boat, but were repeatedly beaten down by the waves. Seven of the men, including Spicer and Skinner, were drowned. Only four were saved despite the valiant efforts of Captain Cocke, who stripped off his clothes and with a few men rowed out to rescue them.

The loss of the seven men was a terrible blow to the mariners, who demanded to return immediately to their ships. After some coaxing, White and Cocke managed to persuade them to go on—perhaps by arguing that this was no time to try passing back through the inlet. Having rescued the upended boat, they left Hatarask and sailed up Roanoke Sound as the sun set behind the island, casting deep shadows across the water. By the time they reached Shallowbag Bay it was pitch dark, and they overshot their intended landing place near Baum's Point. White may have considered this a stroke of good fortune, because soon after the men picked out a flickering light in the darkness at the north end of the island and began rowing toward it as hard as they could. Nearing the place, they moored against the shore, sounded a trumpet, and played "many familiar English Tunes and Songs, and called to them friendly." But there was no answer.

White passed what surely must have seemed the longest night of his life aboard the boat with the other men, waiting for the dawn to come. What went through his mind as he stepped on shore in the early morning light of August 18 can only be imagined. When he had departed three years earlier he had promised his family and friends to return with more settlers and supplies as soon as possible. Neither he nor they could have known it would take him so long to get back or that when he returned he would come empty handed. How would he explain his long absence and failure to secure provisions and reinforcements to those who had depended on him, or convey all he had been through in his attempts to reach them?

Leaving several men to guard the boats, White, Captain Cocke, and the rest of the company made their way through the woods to where they had seen the fire. There they found only smoldering grass and some rotten trees burning, presumably from a lightning strike. They heard nothing but a gentle wind soughing through tall pines and cedars and the busy sounds of birds and small creatures among the undergrowth.

White must have become increasingly worried as he led the men to the western side of the island directly across from Dasemunkepeuc. There was no sign of human life apart from the footprints of a couple of Indians, which judging by the freshness of the tracks in the sand had been made the night before. The men continued on their way, following the water's edge around the northern point of the island and down the eastern side until they approached the settlement. Climbing over a sandy bluff from the beach, White saw "CRO" carved on a tree in "fair Roman letters." Then, fearing the worst, he entered the clearing.[23]

The settlement was deserted, the houses had been dismantled, and the colonists were gone. His first response was dismay. He had dreaded finding the settlement abandoned. What had forced the settlers to leave? But as he looked around he felt a gradual sense of relief. There was no sign that the settlement had been attacked. The palisade built by the settlers was intact, and he discovered the word "CROATOAN" carved on one of the main gateposts, without any cross or signs of distress that would have indicated the settlers had been in grave danger. As they continued to look around the site, Cocke's men found iron bars, a couple of pigs of lead, four fowlers (cannon), saker shot, and other heavy gear scattered about, almost overgrown with grass and weeds.

Anxious to find further clues to what had happened to the colonists, White and Cocke searched the surrounding area. Picking their way down to the waterside and following the shore to the point of a creek nearby, they found the settlers' boats and pinnace were gone, along with the cannon left with them. The absence of boats confirmed that the settlers had departed from the island in a planned move and had not been captured or killed by the Secotans or Spanish.

Returning to the fort, they found the sailors eager to show them the remains of five chests carefully hidden in a trench. Three of the chests belonged to White, who described the scene ruefully: "About the place many of my things [were] spoiled and broken, and my books torn from the covers, the frames of some of my pictures and Maps rotten and spoiled with rain, and my armor almost eaten through with rust." The Secotans, he surmised, had waited for the settlers to leave and then ransacked the site.

Saddened by the loss of his possessions, White nevertheless returned to the *Hopewell* that evening in good heart, "greatly pleased" at finding "a certain [sure] token of their [the colonists] safe being at Croatoan, where Manteo was born, and the Savages of the Island our friends." If he had initially been disappointed that he had not been reunited with the settlers that day, at least he knew where to find them. And above all, he knew they were safe.[24]

White was now eager to move on to Croatoan as soon as possible, especially as the weather was worsening. During the night conditions turned stormy, the wind and seas "so greatly risen," White recounted, "that wee doubted our Cables and Anchors would scarcely hold until Morning." Fortunately, he had made a friend in Captain Abraham Cocke. By transporting him to Roanoke, the captain had done all that was required according to the terms of his contract and could have insisted on returning to the Caribbean or sailing for the Azores, but instead he agreed the next morning to take White to Croatoan Island to find the colonists.

Disaster struck again as the *Hopewell*'s crew was hauling in the anchor. The cable broke and the ship quickly gathered way toward Hatarask Island. Cocke ordered the men to drop another anchor, but it came home so fast that they had to let it go to avoid running aground on Cape Kenrick. The chance discovery of a deep water channel along the shore saved them at the last moment from foundering.

The storm had caused them to lose three of their four anchors as well as valuable time, during which the weather had worsened. Concerned about dwindling food supplies and his lack of fresh water, Cocke decided to postpone efforts to reach the colonists and head either for St. John's (Puerto Rico), Hispaniola, or some other island. In consultation with his men and White, they agreed to winter in the West Indies. After reprovisioning and repairing their ship during the winter months, they would return to plundering Spanish shipping in the spring and then sail to Croatoan Island in early summer. Cocke put the same suggestion to the men of the *Moonlight*, who had been waiting offshore. Claiming their ship was in no fit state to continue, they elected to go back to England.

Cocke set the *Hopewell* on a course for Trinidad, the most southerly of the Caribbean islands, off the Orinoco Delta. Uninhabited by the Spanish, it was a favorite haunt of privateers. Once again, bad weather intervened. After making good progress for a couple of days, strong northwesterly winds drove the ship far out to sea and persuaded Cocke to head for the Azores, where he joined a great squadron of English ships led by Sir John Hawkins that was lying in wait for the Spanish treasure fleet. Toward the end of September, realizing that the Spaniards had eluded them, Hawkins's ships dispersed, and Cocke returned to England. For White, there was no joy in the homeward voyage, only a bitter sense of loss.[25]

☙

By the time he arrived at Plymouth in late October, White knew it was unlikely he would ever see his family and the settlers again. Ralegh had seemingly lost interest in the colony, and there was little prospect of involving merchants and privateers, who had shown themselves to be far more interested in plundering Spanish ships than transporting White to America. So concluded, he wrote sorrowfully a few years later, "my fifth and last voyage to Virginia, which was no less unfortunately ended then forwardly begun, and as luckless to many, as sinister [unfortunate] to myself."[26]

6

"INTO THE MAIN"

It is a spacious, and ample Tract of Land, from North to South, upon a right line, it may be 700 miles; from East to west in the narrowest place, supposed some 300 miles, and in other places 1000 a sufficient space, and ground enough.

—WILLIAM STRACHEY

IN THE SUMMER OF 1590, while John White was struggling to reach Roanoke Island, Ralegh's life took an unexpected turn. He had met a pretty young woman, Elizabeth (Bess) Throckmorton, one of the queen's maids-of-honor, and fallen in love. She was the daughter of Sir Nicholas Throckmorton, a distinguished diplomat and former ambassador to France and Scotland. Following the death of Sir Nicholas, Bess was looked after by her elder brother, Sir Arthur Throckmorton, who arranged her introduction to the court in 1584, when she was twenty. A later portrait shows her as an attractive woman with an open countenance, hazel eyes, and a quizzical smile. Intelligent and experienced in the ways of the court, she must have known the likely consequences of entering into an affair with Ralegh. At Elizabeth's court disloyalty was not tolerated, and in the queen's view there could be no greater personal affront than clandestine affairs between her maids and male favorites.

Ralegh also knew the queen would be displeased, but believed she would soon reconcile herself to the relationship. He decided not to tell her about it and continued the affair in secret over the next year. By the summer of 1591 Bess was pregnant, and in November she and Ralegh were married. Again, he opted not to tell Elizabeth. But when Ralegh's son was born the following spring, it was no longer possible to keep the relationship secret. The queen was outraged. Angered more by his dishonesty and callous attitude about breaking her trust than by his weakness in falling for a pretty maid, the queen first placed Ralegh under arrest at Durham House and then, as the city sweated in a sickly summer heat, consigned him and Bess to the Tower of London.[1]

There was no longer any hope that Ralegh would organize a fleet to locate the settlers in Virginia. Although Ralegh and his wife were released toward the end of 1592, they were banished from the queen's presence. The two retired to his newly acquired estate at Sherborne, Dorset.

Yet even if he had not been in disgrace, it is unlikely that Ralegh would have taken up the colonists' plight. He had shown little interest in White's last voyage and was now focused instead on his privateering ventures and regaining the queen's favor. One part of his strategy was to give her presents of rich prizes taken by his ships, and the other was to achieve a spectacular discovery in America that would bring wealth to the crown (and him) and cripple Spanish power in the Indies. In the 1580s his ambitions had centered on Roanoke and the Chesapeake Bay, but now, ten years later, he had set his sights instead on Guiana, in South America, and the lost city of El Dorado.

The legend of El Dorado had its origins in Peru in the early1540s. Spanish chroniclers and conquistadors reported stories by local Indians of a kingdom rich in gold mines across the mountains to the east, ruled, in the words of the historian Fernández de Oviedo, by a "Golden Chief or King." This chief wore no clothing but each morning was covered from head to toe in fine gold dust, looking "as resplendent as a gold object worked by the hand of a great artist." During the next half century, the rumor was further embellished with incredible accounts by explorers who had braved the interior and heard news of the rich and populous realm of the golden Indian.[2]

Ralegh had become fascinated by the story of El Dorado in 1586. That spring he had dispatched two small pinnaces, the *Mary Spark* and the *Serpent*, on a voyage to the Azores, which turned out to be a remarkably profitable venture. In August the two ships brought home valuable merchandise including sugar, brasilwood, and ivory, and also a high-ranking Spaniard, Don Pedro Sarmiento de Gamboa, governor of Patagonia.

Sarmiento was an expert on Peru, and in the course of his many years in South America he had picked up a great deal of information about lands in the interior. During conversations at Durham House the Spaniard told Sir Walter about the flight of Incas led by their emperor, Manco Capac, into the surrounding mountain fastnesses in the 1530s to escape Spanish invaders. Sarmiento also passed on what he had heard about El Dorado. In particular, he told Ralegh about an elderly Spanish gentleman and soldier, Antonio de Berrio, who had led a recent exploration along the Orinoco River.

Berrio's ideas about the location of El Dorado were highly influential in shaping Ralegh's thinking. In 1579 Berrio had inherited valuable estates in New Granada (Colombia) and the governorship of a huge province that stretched hundreds of miles east of the Andes into the Orinoco River basin. Two years later Berrio moved with his family to New Granada to manage his estates and search for El Dorado, which he believed was somewhere in the jungle highlands of Guiana between the Orinoco and Amazon Rivers. He had heard rumors of a fabulous city called Manoa beside a great lake of the same name and had made an expedition along the Orinoco River in 1583–1584 to find it. Although he failed to find Manoa, Berrio did discover the highlands south of the Orinoco; he was convinced the city was located there.

Years later, as Ralegh pondered his reduced circumstances in exile at Sherborne, he turned to the idea of mounting an expedition to the Orinoco himself. Connecting what he had learned from Sarmiento about the flight of the Incas and Berrio's ideas about the whereabouts of Manoa, he concluded that the golden city had probably been founded by Inca refugees. Manco Capac had established a new empire in the interior of South America that was even greater than that destroyed by the Spanish in Peru. Sir Walter was enough of a realist to appreciate that the likelihood of finding El Dorado was remote. But there was nonetheless a possibility of discovering information that might eventually lead him to the fabled city or to rich mines and other treasures.[3]

Roanoke, on the other hand, offered little prospect of profit. White had reluctantly admitted as much to his friend Richard

Hakluyt in a letter in February 1593. The mariners who had sailed with White on his last voyage had ignored orders from Ralegh to take a small group of settlers recruited by White to Roanoke Island. Apart from Abraham Cocke and Edward Spicer, they had been interested only in privateering. In the years since his return to England, White had been unable to raise financial support for another voyage and did not have enough money of his own to fit out a ship. "I would to God my wealth was answerable to my will," he wrote disconsolately. With no hope of returning to the Outer Banks to search for his family, he had moved to Ireland to live on Ralegh's estate at Newtown in Kylmore, County Cork. He was to play no further part in efforts to establish a colony in North America and probably died in Ireland in the early years of the seventeenth century.

Over the next eighteen months Ralegh threw himself into preparations for a voyage to Guiana with all his old enthusiasm. He was convinced that staking a claim to Guiana would afford Elizabeth a glorious opportunity to acquire an empire that, as he wrote later in his account of the voyage, "has more quantity of Gold by manifold [many times], than the best parts of the Indies, or Peru." Philip II's Indian gold endangered all the nations of Europe, he argued, not his trade in wines and Seville oranges. If the English could possess an empire of riches greater than Spain's, they would eventually surpass Spanish wealth in the New World and weaken Philip's influence in Europe. It was a familiar argument, only in this version England's empire would be founded in South, not North, America.

Sir Walter spent about a month in the summer of 1595 exploring the lower Orinoco and the mouth of the Caroni (Caroli) River, but despite his high hopes the adventure brought little tangible return. The ore and "precious" stones he brought back to London proved worthless, and he had failed to acquire definite knowledge of the whereabouts of El Dorado. Even so, he continued to believe that enormous riches would be discovered in Guiana and that the region would offer the queen a fortune that would surpass the wealth of Spanish America. Elizabeth and the investors remained skeptical, however, and any plans Ralegh might have had for a further voyage languished.[4]

Fortunately for Ralegh, the failure of the venture hardly mattered. Within eighteen months he was back in the queen's favor following one of her notoriously capricious changes of heart, and he gradually regained much of his former influence at court. Reconciliation with Elizabeth did not incline Ralegh to take up large-scale colonizing projects, but his interest in Virginia did resurface briefly in the opening years of the new century. In 1602 and 1603 he dispatched two small-scale exploratory expeditions to the Outer Banks and Chesapeake Bay.

The reason for his renewed interest in Virginia and the lost colonists is unclear. Possibly he wished to underline his continuing claim to North America by virtue of his charter of 1583, or perhaps his decision to sell his estates in Munster in 1602 led him to consider once again profits to be had from exploiting the Roanoke region. He was probably thinking more of returns from natural commodities than from spectacular discoveries, but he may have wondered whether finding the colonists would lead him to the greater riches he had hoped to find in the interior.

Sir Walter sent Samuel Mace (who had sailed with Ralegh to Guiana) to the Outer Banks in March 1602. Mace spent about a month near Cape Fear (modern Cape Lookout), about sixty miles south of Croatoan Island, collecting sassafras and other medicinal plants. He was supposed to sail farther north to look for the settlers, but "extremity of weather" apparently made the journey up the coast impossible.

An attempt the following year met with even less success. In April 1603 Bartholomew Gilbert, a London goldsmith and explorer, sailed for the Chesapeake Bay "to seek out the people for Sir Walter Raleigh left near those parts in the year 1587." The voyage ended in disaster. Running low on water and provisions, Gilbert put ashore somewhere along the Eastern Shore, where he and four of his companions were killed by Indians.[5]

Apart from these ill-fated attempts, however, Ralegh did little to promote Virginia after White's return from Roanoke. The fate of the lost colonists remained a mystery; they had not been seen or heard of for more than a decade. Rumors circulated in London and Madrid about their survival and possible location, but no one could say for sure if they were still alive. Yet there could be little doubt that the longer it took to organize an expedition to search for them, the less likely it was that they would ever be found.[6]

RALEGH'S WORLD was turned upside down with the death of Queen Elizabeth on March 24, 1603. The queen was succeeded by her cousin and heir, James I, who had been king of Scotland since 1567, when his mother Mary, Queen of Scots, had been deposed. Before succeeding to the English throne James had been careful to win over many of the queen's principal ministers and influential courtiers, but he detested Ralegh, whose position and influence he believed were wholly a consequence of Elizabeth's unseemly infatuation with him. Ralegh was quickly shorn of his privileges, including his right to establish colonies in North America, and ejected from his beloved Durham House. By the summer he was once again in the Tower, this time charged with high treason on trumped-up charges of being involved in a Catholic plot to topple the king.[7]

James's succession also marked a dramatic change in foreign policy. He had little desire to continue the long sea war against Spain, which he believed was destructive to trade and ruinous for the royal treasury. He negotiated a treaty in 1604 that secured peace and prohibited the plunder of Spanish shipping and possessions. For a generation that had lived through the long war with Spain, the abrupt cessation of hostilities must have seemed a welcome beginning to James's reign that at once brought not only relief from the threat of invasion but also fresh commercial opportunities.

Peace and the end of Ralegh's American monopoly encouraged those who had long been on the fringes of colonizing ventures to play a more active role. West Country merchants were anxious to exploit fish, oil, furs, and timber in New England, while in London a group of leading merchants and statesmen who supported the settlement of the Chesapeake Bay formed the Virginia Company of London.[8]

After eighteen months of negotiations among various mercantile groups and their political supporters, North America was formally divided into two separate areas of interest by the royal charter of April 10, 1606. The Plymouth Company, dominated by merchants and financiers from the West Country, was permitted to settle an area between latitudes 38 degrees and 45 degrees north, stretching from the Chesapeake Bay to just above present-day Maine. The Virginia Company of London was allowed to establish a colony to the south between Cape Fear, North Carolina, and New York (latitudes 34 degrees and 41 degrees north). Neither group was granted exclusive rights to all the territory within the regions specified, but they were permitted to establish a settlement within those bounds and given jurisdiction over lands 50 miles north and south of the colony and 100 miles inland and out to sea.[9]

The Virginia Company adopted much the same rationale for colonization that Ralegh's circle had put forward twenty years earlier. The conclusion of hostilities with Spain meant that a North American colony would not be developed as a privateering base, but the potential for profits from natural resources and precious minerals remained strong.

Richard Hakluyt the younger continued to champion Virginia, by which he meant the Chesapeake and North Carolina. He had written enthusiastically in 1599 that the interior was "so rich and abundant in silver mines, so apt and capable of [supplying] all commodities which Italy, Spain, and France" produced that even the Spaniards acknowledged it was a more promising region than Mexico or New Spain. It is likely that seven years later he assisted the Virginia Company in drawing up instructions for the expedition to be dispatched to the Chesapeake Bay in the winter of 1606.

The instructions laid out the company's hopes and priorities. Once the colonists arrived in Virginia, they were to explore the major rivers and establish their settlement on a river that had its source in the mountains or from lakes connected to "the Other Sea." Company officials believed that a passage to the Pacific

Ocean was to be found inland and shared Ralegh's belief that mines might be discovered in the mountains. They differed from Ralegh, however, in thinking that the passage and mines were located not hundreds of miles to the south in the highlands of Florida, but rather in the Chesapeake Bay region.

The colonists were warned to be wary and vigilant. They should be cautious in their dealings with local peoples in case the Indians proved hostile, and they were told to locate their settlement 100 miles inland to avoid being taken by surprise by the Spanish. The advice was a reminder that although England was at peace with Spain, the Spanish did not recognize English claims to North America and would not tolerate interlopers. Forty years after the destruction of the French Huguenot settlers at Fort Caroline in 1565, the company still referred to the massacre as a reminder that the greatest threat to the colonists was an attack by the Spanish.[10]

Shortly before Christmas 1606 three ships, the *Susan Constant* (120 tons), *Godspeed* (40 tons), and *Discovery* (20 tons), set sail for Virginia carrying 105 settlers and 39 crew members. Under the command of Christopher Newport, the fleet followed the usual Atlantic crossing via the Canaries and West Indies. After spending two weeks in the West Indies resting and exploring the islands, during which time one of the settlers died, Newport led the three ships along the Florida coast and sighted the Chesapeake Bay on April 26, 1607.

The colonists spent the next week exploring the lower reaches of the bay and then entered the James River to search for a suitable site to establish their settlement. Eventually they chose a marshy peninsula about fifty miles from the coast, which they named

6.1 John Smith, Map of Virginia, engraved by William Hole, 1612. Smith's map was the result of his explorations of major rivers and the Chesapeake Bay between 1607 and 1608. Jamestown lies on the James River ("Powhatan flu") center left. Far left are the lands of the Mangoaks and Chowanocs.

Jamestown Island. The colonists disembarked on May 14 and all the men, including the mariners, were put to work unloading the settlers' gear, putting up tents and temporary shelters, and erecting a light defensive fortification from brushwood around the camp. The defensive work proved completely inadequate, however. Following a large-scale Indian attack later in the month, during which two of the colonists were fatally wounded, the Englishmen built a sturdy, three-sided palisade with bulwarks for cannon.

A week after landing, Captain Newport and two dozen men left the settlement on a voyage of discovery. Eager to assess the wealth of the region, they sailed along the James River into the interior in search of mountains and a passage to the South Sea. After about fifty miles, however, when they were a little way above the town of Powhatan (near present-day Richmond), they found only rocks and shoals, which made progress impossible.

Despite his disappointment that the river did not flow farther inland, Newport considered the voyage a success. He now had a good idea of the extent of the river and had encountered many friendly peoples living along its banks who were willing to trade. From them the English had learned of a great chief, Wahunsonacock, who ruled the powerful Powhatan people as well as another thirty peoples. Newport had learned also that the Indians obtained their copper from mountains inland and, as he passed through the fertile lands of the Pamunkey people on his way back downriver to the settlement, he had seen Indians wearing plates of copper and pearls in their hair and as ornaments.[11]

By the time Newport was ready to return to England with the *Susan Constant* and *Godspeed* on June 21, the settlers were confident about the natural wealth of the country. There was an abundance of trees suitable for many different uses. Virginia could supply all the timber, clapboard, wainscot, dyestuffs, and medicinal drugs that England needed. One of the colony's leaders, Gabriel Archer, believed not only that Virginia could provide many of the crops grown in northern latitudes, but also that the settlers would be able to produce oils, wines, iron, and copper. The great sturgeon found in the rivers would be worth at least £1,000 annually, and enormous quantities of cod and herring taken off the coast would provide a steady income. Most intriguing of all, in the mountains to the west, perhaps gold and other precious minerals awaited discovery.[12]

Newport arrived back in London in early August and gave a glowing report of the expedition to Virginia Company members. Rumors that the settlers had found gold-bearing ore in Virginia spread rapidly around the city. And even when it was discovered that the barrels of earth brought back by Newport did not contain gold, company investors still remained excited about the colony's potential. Sir Walter Cope, a leading member, wrote, "Our new discovery is more Like to prove the Land of Canaan than the land of Ophir," a land of milk and honey rather than a land of gold. But most company supporters had not given up hopes of finding riches and believed there was sufficient good news to justify sending more settlers and supplies. Preparations were soon underway for another voyage.[13]

While Newport was in London, however, the colony all but collapsed. Throughout August and September many settlers died from a virulent camp fever and diseases that swept through the settlement, as well as from wounds inflicted by Indians in sporadic attacks. By the fall, barely 40 ragged and dispirited men were left of the 104 who had first arrived on the island. As a bitterly cold winter set in, they huddled together in the fort by the frozen banks of the James River, waiting for Newport to return to rescue them.

Along with the threat of Indian attack, the colonists' most pressing problem was their rapidly dwindling food supply. Knowing their stores would not last much longer, the colonists sent a brash young soldier, Captain John Smith, to get provisions by trade or force from Indians along the James River. Smith was a veteran of wars against the Turks in Eastern Europe and was an ambitious and resourceful man. Invariably convinced that he knew best, he had made enemies of the expedition's leaders on the voyage to Virginia and had spent much of the passage in the *Susan Constant*'s brig on charges of mutiny. At the settlement he continued to be a constant source of irritation, rarely missing an opportunity to point out the leaders' shortcomings in blunt language. By the winter, they sought to rid themselves of him by sending him on missions to get provisions, possibly hoping that he might eventually be killed by Indians. For his part, Smith was willing to go. He was keen to be in charge of a group of men and have the chance to explore the rivers and make contact with local peoples. Besides corn, the Indians possessed much information about the region that could turn out to be valuable.[14]

If the colonists' leaders hoped Smith might not return from one of his missions, their wish nearly came true. Initially his expeditions went well. He conducted two successful trading voyages along the Chickahominy River in November, bringing provisions back to the settlement. But then, hoping to discover specific information about a passage to the mountains or riches farther inland, he returned to the Chickahominy early the following month to explore the river to its source.

There, far upriver, in a "vast and wild wilderness," Smith was suddenly confronted by 200 Pamunkey warriors. Using the Indian guide who had accompanied him on his exploration as a human shield, he tried to hold off the warriors long enough to reach his boat, tied up nearby, but as he backed away he lost his footing and slipped into an icy quagmire. He could fight no longer and threw down his pistol and surrendered, at which point the Pamunkeys pulled him out of the swamp and took him to their war chief, an old, imperious-looking man, named Opechancanough.

Face to face with the chief and fearing for his life, Smith considered his best option was to try to persuade Opechancanough that he was a man of power who might be useful. He took from his pocket a compass, which he presented to the chief. Describing how it worked, he talked about the roundness of the earth, and of the sun, moon, and planets in the heavens. He described the extent of the oceans, the different countries of the world, and the variety of their peoples. The ploy seemed to work. The chief restrained his men from killing Smith and he was led away, the warriors keeping a close guard and shouting in triumph as they made their way through the woods to a hunting camp nearby.

Smith was treated well. He was given plenty of food, and the items taken from him during his capture were returned. Opechancanough took delight in quizzing him about the Englishmen's ships; how they sailed the seas; and their beliefs about the earth, skies, and God. In return, the war chief was pleased to tell him about the Indians' own country. He told the Englishman that within four or five days' journey of the falls of the James River "was a great turning of salt water." He mentioned also that there were "certain men clothed at a place called Ocanahonan, clothed like me," Smith reported in a detailed account he sent to England in the summer of the following year. What the information meant may not have immediately been apparent to him, but would become clear in the next few weeks.[15]

Smith was then taken to be questioned by Wahunsonacock. The Indians led him on a long march across the wintry country from the Chickahominy to the Rappahannock River and back to the York River to the great chief's principal residence at Werowocomoco. The Englishman's arrival was anticipated. Smith entered the smoky interior of the chief's longhouse and stood before Wahunsonacock, who lay in pomp on a bed near a large fire. Flanking him, in rows of ten seated on the ground, were his councilors, priests, and wives, all of whom wore white beads and had their heads and shoulders painted red. Smith was impressed by the spectacle and especially by the chief, who displayed "such a grave and Majestic countenance," he recalled, "as drove me into admiration to see such state in a naked Savage."

Smith may have been concerned about whether he would leave the longhouse alive, but his mind was soon put at rest. The chief assured him of his friendship and told him he would be released within a few days. After courtesies were exchanged, he asked Smith why the English had come to Virginia. Smith decided to avoid revealing the colonists' intention of establishing a settlement in the region, because he believed the Indians would be hostile to it. So he concocted a story about having been in a sea battle with the Spanish and subsequently forced into the Chesapeake Bay by bad weather. They had been directed up the James River by friendly Indians, he continued, and their pinnace had sprung a leak, compelling them to camp temporarily on Jamestown Island to make repairs and wait for the return of their leader, Captain Newport, with ships to take them away.

Whether Wahunsonacock believed the story is unclear, but perhaps prompted by Smith, he entered into a lengthy description of his lands and those of neighboring peoples. To the west, far up the James River where storms caused the water to become briny, lived a fierce people called the Pocoughtronack, who "did eat men." Northward, at the top of the Chesapeake Bay, was a powerful nation whose warriors shaved their heads and carried swords like pole axes, and farther north was a region where "people with Short Coates, and Sleeves to the Elbows . . . passed that way in Ships." The latter probably referred to French, Basque, and English mariners who sailed every year to the Gulf of St. Lawrence to exploit the rich fishing grounds.

Then the chief told Smith startling news. Two to six days south of Tsenacommacah (the Powhatan name for Virginia) were the lands of the "Mangoge," "Chawwonock," and "Roanoke," and a "people clothed at Ocanahonan." Beyond, the chief said, "to the south part of the back sea" was a land called "Anone, where they have abundance of Brass, and houses walled as ours." The Englishman paid careful attention to Wahunsonacock's description, noting that the information confirmed his earlier discussions with Opechancanough.[16]

Smith had stumbled upon information that might yet save the colony from failure. Both chiefs had told him about salt water beyond the falls of the James River, which suggested that perhaps within 120 miles of Jamestown there was a great salt lake or an arm of the South Sea. The chiefs may have also revealed the whereabouts of the lost colonists. The "Mangoge," "Chawwonock," and "Roanoke" were the Mangoaks, Chowanocs, and people of Roanoke Island and the adjoining mainland (Secotans). Smith had read Ralph Lane's account of the first Roanoke colony published by Richard Hakluyt, and was familiar with the story of the disappearance of John White's settlers twenty years before. He would have immediately recognized the names of the lands to the south of Wahunsonacock's own territory. Finally, references to "people clothed at Ocanahonan" and a land called "Anone," where there were houses built like those of the English, could only be news of the lost colonists, living somewhere 50 to 150 miles south of the James River.

From Opechancanough and Wahunsonacock Smith had picked up the first credible reports of the Roanoke colonists' whereabouts since John White's voyage of 1590. Armed with this knowledge, he was keen to find survivors of the lost colony. He had little doubt that the lost colonists and their children, having lived in the country for twenty years, would have extensive connections with local peoples of the region, who had sheltered them and traded with them. The English and Indian peoples of "South Virginia" (North Carolina) might well know of mines in the interior or of a river passage to the great sea in the west. Smith had uncovered vital information that could lead him to gold and silver mines and possibly a route to the Pacific Ocean; he was determined to make the most of it.[17]

SHORTLY AFTER Smith's return to Jamestown on New Year's Day 1608, Newport arrived from England with fresh supplies and an additional hundred settlers. Newport was delighted to hear Smith's news and readily agreed to dispatch an expedition south to look for the Roanoke colonists. The English persuaded Wow-inchopunck, chief of the Paspaheghs, who knew the lands south of the James River well, to lead the expedition.

The party set off at the end of January. The Paspaheghs and two Englishmen headed southeast toward a place called Pana-wicke, beyond Roanoke, where Wowinchopunck believed many of the settlers were still to be found. They proposed to make their way along the Pagan River to the Blackwater and then head due south to the lands of the Chowanocs. It was the same route, in reverse, that Lane had mapped out following discussions with Menatonan in 1586, by which the English commander connected the Chowan River region to the James.

How far the men traveled south and whether they reached Panawicke are uncertain; no details of the expedition exist. Yet Smith was highly displeased when the men returned only three or four days after setting out. He accused Wowinchopunck of trying to shortchange the English by claiming payment for guiding the search party and then cutting short the expedition. But if Wowinchopunck's party got no farther than the Chowan River, they must have learned much more about the lost colonists from Indian peoples of the area than they were able to discover for themselves. The information the expedition gathered about where some of the lost colonists still lived was extremely important. Smith had already discovered the general whereabouts of the lost colonists from the two Powhatan chiefs, and now he had specific information about their locations.

Smith incorporated the news in a rough sketch map of Virginia and North Carolina that he drafted over the next few months. The map was sent back to England in June 1608 and surely caused a sensation among Virginia Company members when it came into their hands later that summer. Drawing upon everything Smith had learned about Virginia from his own explorations and conversations with local peoples during the past year, the map illustrated the huge extent of the country from south of Roanoke Island to the Eastern Shore of the Chesapeake Bay. Yet the map was meant to be more than an illustration of the geography of the country; it was intended to reveal the secrets of the region's wealth.[18]

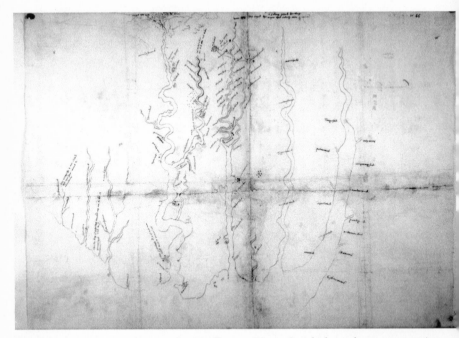

6.2 John Smith's sketch map of 1608 (Zuñiga Map). Smith drew the map sometime during the spring of 1608. His knowledge of regions to the north of Jamestown is vague at this point and the rendering of the Rappahannock River and Chesapeake Bay (right) is therefore crude. His depiction of the region to the south of the James River is similarly vague (left), but the map provides vital information about the whereabouts of survivors of John White's colony that Smith had picked up earlier in the year.

Smith claimed to have found a river passage to the Pacific Ocean. At the head of the James he drew the shore of a sea with the note, "Hear the salt water beats into the river amongst these rocks being the south sea." Company leaders could not have failed to recognize the significance of his findings. For the first time since John White had worked with Jacques Le Moyne on their map of Virginia and Florida more than twenty years earlier, an Englishman had detailed a route through the American land-

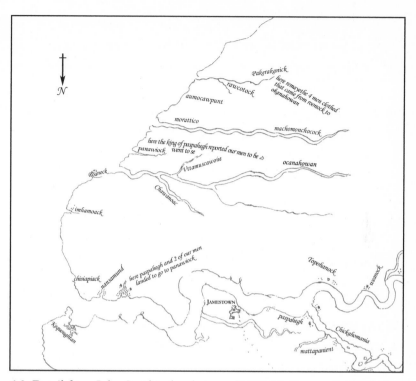

6.3 Detail from John Smith's sketch map of 1608 (Zuñiga map). Drawn by Rebecca L. Wrenn.

mass to the South Sea. His map provided specific evidence that the passage was not to the south along a strait, inland from Port Royal (the short-lived French settlement near the border of modern-day Georgia and South Carolina) where White and Le Moyne had located it. Rather, it was accessible by way of the Chesapeake Bay and the James River, within easy reach of where the English were seated.

But that was not all. Smith's map also showed the locations of survivors of the lost colony. The information was provided on the lower left-hand side of the map in three groupings: (1) on the southern bank of the James River at Warraskoyack, near the Pagan River, "here paspahegh and 2 of our men landed to go to panawiock"; (2) near the Roanoke River, "here the king of paspahegh reported our men to be and went to see"; and (3) at "Pakerakanick," "here remain the 4 men clothed that came from roonock to okanahowan." Smith's notations suggested that some of the lost colonists were at Ocanahonan and that four of the settlers who had moved from Roanoke Island to Ocanahonan later ended up at Pakerakanick. In addition, it is possible that some of White's settlers remained at Panawicke ("Panawiock"), but they were not found by the expedition that Smith had sent to make contact with them.

Although Smith's map provided the Virginia Company with extremely valuable information about the lost colonists it was difficult to interpret. The southern (Roanoke) portion is in fact best viewed from the perspective of Wowinchopunck's search party as it traveled down the Blackwater River to the lands of the Chowanocs. Of most interest to the Englishmen were the areas between the Chowan and "morattico" (Roanoke) Rivers and the region to the south adjoining the next major river, the Tar. "Ocanahowan," which Smith placed on a tributary of the Chowan River, was without doubt the Ocanahonan described by Opechancanough and Wahunsonacock and was situated beyond the Chowan on the Roanoke River. Panawicke was south and west of Cashie Creek, the historic border between the Chowanocs and Tuscaroras. And finally Pakerakanick, a Tuscarora town, may have been located on the south bank of the Tar River.[19]

Smith's sketch map illustrated a possible route to the South Sea and located the lost colonists at Ocanahonan, Panawicke, and Pakerakanick. Smith made no attempt to explain how the lost colonists came to be living in those particular Indian towns, and it is unlikely that he knew. But in any case, how the settlers got there was of far less interest to the English than the possibility of making contact with them. If they could find them, the Virginia Company might be able to bring the two groups of colonists together, creating settlements well to the south of the James River as well as along it. At the very least, company leaders may have reasoned, the Jamestown colonists might be able to exploit the Roanoke settlers' knowledge of the country to their own advantage.

THE COMPANY'S first priority was to find out more about the interior beyond the falls of the James River. When Captain Newport returned to Jamestown in mid-October 1608, he led a large expedition about forty or fifty miles into the Virginia piedmont to look for mines and a passage to the Pacific. He and his men discovered a fertile and well-watered country. They were the first Englishmen to glimpse the Blue Ridge Mountains, but they did not discover gold or a river passage, only a small quantity of silver.

John Smith, however, remained eager to continue the search for the lost colonists. A few weeks after Newport left for England in early December, Smith entered into discussions with Tackonekintaco, chief of the Warraskoyacks. He arranged for one of his men, Michael Sicklemore, accompanied by two guides, to journey to "Chowanoke," either the lands of the Chowanocs or the Indians' capital. There are few details of the expedition, only Sicklemore's pessimistic assessment, reported by Smith in the new year, that the small search party returned with "little hope and less certainty of them [that] were left by Sir Walter Rawley." Smith may have wondered whether Sicklemore's information was more reliable than that of the earlier search party and whether White's settlers were beyond the reach of the English.[20]

Critical new information about the lost colonists did come to light in early 1609—not in Virginia but in London. The source, once again, was an Indian. Along with a cargo of clapboard, wainscot, pitch, tar, and soap ashes produced by the colonists, Newport had taken back to London two Powhatans, Namontack and Machumps. They had been ordered to accompany the English by Wahunsonacock, who wanted to learn more about the colonists' own country. Namontack was one of the chief's advisors and had already been to England once before, in 1608. Little is known about Machumps other than that his sister, Winganuske, was one of the great chief's favorite wives.

What Namontack and Machumps did during their four months in London is unclear. One of them, probably Namontack, visited Thomas Hariot at his residence at Syon House near London, where the Englishman and Powhatan quite likely conversed in Algonquian. Machumps's movements are unknown, but whatever else he did while in the city, it is certain he told the English an astonishing story about what had happened to the lost colonists.[21]

Machumps's account was recorded by William Strachey, a young, footloose gentleman who had arrived in London a few years earlier. He had enrolled at Gray's Inn and became a member of fashionable literary circles as well as a supporter of the Blackfriars Theater, where he rubbed shoulders with leading playwrights of the day such as Ben Jonson, John Marston, and Will Shakespeare. Following a year abroad, he had returned to

London in the summer of 1608. In need of money, he decided to try his luck in Virginia, having no better prospects at home. He planned to travel with the large-scale expedition the Virginia Company was preparing for departure in the spring of 1609. Possibly thinking already of writing an official account of the colony, and hearing about the arrival of the Indians in London, he may have wondered whether they could provide him with a description of the Powhatans and their country. Evidently Machumps agreed and provided a great deal of information about his people and, tangentially, about neighboring lands.

During one of his many long conversations with Strachey, Machumps recounted the extraordinary tale of the lost colonists. Strachey, who began working on his history of the colony in 1609, recorded the Indian's story. In the fruitful region south of the James River, Machumps told him, at Ocanahonan and Pakerakanick "the People have houses built with stone walls, and one story above another, so taught them by those English who escaped the slaughter at *Roanoak*." He explained that in the same region where the English survivors now lived there was a place called "Ritanoe." The chief, Eyanoco, held seven of the English there—four men, two boys, and a young maid—who had fled up the Chowan River. There were mines at Ritanoe, Machumps told Strachey, and the English were "preserved" by the chief to beat his copper, perhaps meaning that they worked the copper into ornaments.

Machumps likely told Strachey who was responsible for the killing of the English. It was probably he who informed the Englishman that the lost colonists had lived peaceably for "20 and odd" years with the Indians, until they were suddenly attacked without provocation by Wahunsonacock's warriors. The attack occurred about the same time that Newport's fleet arrived in the Chesapeake Bay in the spring of 1607.

"Slaughter at *Roanoak*" is how Machumps described what had happened, or possibly how Strachey interpreted it. By "Roanoke" Strachey referred to "South Virginia," the region from Roanoke Island inland into the piedmont, inhabited by the Chowanocs and Tuscaroras. Some colonists had escaped the slaughter and were to be found in the Tuscarora towns of Panawicke, Ocanahonan, and Pakerakanick. Others had fled up the Chowan River, where they were protected by a powerful chief, Eyanoco, at Ritanoe. The majority of White's settlers had been killed in the attack, but some survived.

Why Machumps told Strachey about the attack is unknown. Possibly he was boasting about Wahunsonacock's influence over peoples of the Roanoke region, or perhaps the information came out indirectly in questioning about rumors, commonplace among peoples south of the James River, telling of strangers who lived in the interior. Yet whatever persuaded the Indian to tell the story, Strachey and those Virginia Company leaders informed of Machumps's testimony found it convincing. The Indian's account accorded remarkably with the information sent to the company the previous summer by John Smith. Like Smith, Machumps located the lost colonists south of the James, and he mentioned specifically their locations at Panawicke, Ocanahonan, and Pakerakanick. The slaughter explained why the two expeditions dispatched by Smith from Jamestown had been unable to make contact with the settlers.[22]

Machumps had provided the vital missing information that explained what had happened to the colonists. Captain Smith had discovered the whereabouts of English people in the interior of North Carolina but had been unable to explain how they had come to be there. Now Machumps had related the devastating news of their fate.

DESPITE THE SHOCKING revelations, company leaders were still eager to locate one or more of the lost colonists, because their local knowledge, they believed, might yet be of significant benefit. Machumps's report, together with that of Smith, were of a significant influence on company leaders' thinking as they shaped a new vision of the colony.

The company had already begun plans the previous summer for a thorough overhaul of Virginia. Company leaders such as Sir Thomas Smythe acknowledged that initial explorations of the Chesapeake Bay and the James River had indicated the promise of the region, but the colonists had so far failed to produce any return on the small fortune already invested in the venture. By January 1609, following discussions with Newport and others who had recently returned from Virginia, it was obvious to Sir Thomas that the colony had to be put on a completely different footing.

A series of wide-ranging reforms were put forward by Smythe and other leaders to restructure the company as well as the colony. They strengthened the power of the principal authority in the colony, the governor, to ensure that discipline and order were enforced among the colonists. Sir Thomas West, 12th Baron De La Warr, a high-ranking nobleman and soldier, was appointed the colony's first lord governor and captain general, supported by Sir Thomas Gates, a veteran of the wars in the Netherlands, as lieutenant governor. Company leaders also broadened financial support for the colony and reformed the company's organization to place more power in the hands of the governing council.

A new charter, granted to the company by King James in May, incorporated the reforms and greatly expanded the colony's territory. From north to south, the colony now stretched from the Roanoke region to the head of the Chesapeake Bay, and from east to west, from the Atlantic to the Pacific Ocean. The latter provision expressed the company's confidence in eventually discovering a river passage through the mountains to the South Sea.[23]

Virginia was first and foremost a commercial venture, and the colony had to be made profitable. Richard Hakluyt and Thomas Hariot were fully involved in discussions about the colony. Both most likely had a hand in drafting the confidential instructions delivered to Gates in May, shortly before he left Plymouth for Jamestown with a fleet of eight ships and 500 settlers. The instructions laid out four principal ways of making the colony profitable: The first was the discovery of a passage to the South Sea and gold or silver mines; the second was trade with Indians, within the region and beyond; the third was extracting tribute (tithes) from local peoples in return for liberating them from the tyranny of Wahunsonacock and his priests; and the fourth was producing all sorts of commodities in demand in England, as well as harvesting the natural wealth of the land and rivers.

The company leaders' most radical proposal, however, derived from the information that they had acquired from Smith and Machumps. Only a few of the lost colonists survived in the interior of North Carolina, but they might nevertheless provide a means of making alliances with Indians of the region, who were hostile to the Powhatans. With the encouragement of Hakluyt and Hariot, the company adopted an expansive view of the Virginia colony that brought together Roanoke ("South Virginia") with the James River Valley. Earlier, the company's efforts had been concentrated on the settlement at Jamestown. Now, in the spring of 1609, the company envisioned a colony that extended much farther to the south and would include local peoples and surviving lost colonists as well as new settlers brought with Gates's expedition.

The new Virginia would have two principal settlements. The colony's chief seat was to be above the falls of the James River, away from major rivers and accessible only by small boats or from overland. Jamestown would be reduced to a small garrison because company leaders considered the site unhealthy and vulnerable to attack by Spanish warships. The company feared the Spanish were about to seek out the colony and attempt to destroy it. The second principal settlement was to be located farther south, at or near Ocanahonan. Gates was told that the area was near the rich copper mines of Ritanoe and within easy reach of Pakerakanick. There he would find four of the English alive, "left by Sir Walter Rawely," who had escaped the slaughter by the Powhatans.[24]

WHILE VIRGINIA COMPANY leaders were developing their plans for the colony, at Jamestown Captain John Smith had decided to send another search party to look for the lost colonists. The year before, Michael Sicklemore had explored the Chowan River and found little. Local peoples were few, and the country was overgrown with pines. Nevertheless, Smith believed that one last attempt to find the colonists was justified.

In February or March 1609 Smith sent two of his most reliable men, Nathaniel Powell and Anas Todkill, beyond the Chowan River into the lands of the Mangoaks. The outcome was discouraging. "Nothing could we learn," Smith wrote, "but [that] they were all dead." How Powell and Todkill had picked up the news, where the two men had searched, and which Indian peoples they had met, Smith did not say.

A very different version of Powell and Todkill's expedition was presented in a pamphlet published hurriedly by the Virginia Company at the end of the year, in response to devastating news. On July 24, 1609, en route to Virginia, Sir Thomas Gates's fleet had encountered a powerful hurricane that scattered the fleet in all directions. The colony's new leadership, including Gates, as well as 150 settlers on board the flagship *Sea Venture*, was shipwrecked on Bermuda. Gates and the settlers spent the next ten months there before making the 600-mile crossing to Jamestown in two small boats constructed on the island. But that winter, when a report of the disappearance of the *Sea Venture* reached London, the company could only assume the ship and all on board had been cast away.

In view of this major setback, company leaders reaffirmed their intention to pursue their plans for Virginia. In an effort to persuade investors to continue backing the venture, they set out in *A True and Sincere Declaration* a lengthy explanation that underlined their conviction that the colony would in time become profitable. Amid a range of reasons to support the venture, the company reported some recent good news. Two men (presumably Powell and Todkill) had discovered survivors of the lost colony living within fifty miles of Jamestown. They had been denied contact with the colonists by local Indians but had discovered "crosses and letters, the characters and assured testimonies of Christians," freshly cut in trees.

The assertion is puzzling. If company leaders were referring to the expedition of Powell and Todkill, why did their account differ so markedly from Smith's? Perhaps the company had acquired further information that had been unavailable to Smith. Or perhaps the company had fabricated the story for their own purposes: to show they remained hopeful about potential financial benefits that might accrue from locating survivors in South Virginia. Yet the mention of crosses and letters cut in trees is specific and closely related to John White's description from his 1587 voyage. Had survivors of the lost colony carved crosses as a distress signal and written words to direct Powell and Todkill to where they had gone (or been taken), as they had been instructed to do twenty years earlier? And if so, where were they?[25]

IN THE TWO DECADES since John White had returned to Roanoke Island in 1590 to find the colonists' settlement deserted, no direct evidence of the settlers' whereabouts had come to light. Ralegh's expeditions of 1602 and 1603 had failed to make contact, and none of the search parties dispatched by John Smith had found survivors. But information gathered by the English from local Indian peoples on both sides of the James River between 1607 and 1609 clearly indicated that survivors still lived in the interior of North Carolina. Although we cannot know with any certainty what became of the lost colonists, it is possible, based on the evidence provided by numerous sources, to reconstruct what most likely happened to them.

When White sailed for England in August 1587, the settlers had already decided that they should leave Roanoke Island and journey inland to the lands of the Chowanocs. White had left the pinnace and ships' boats to enable the settlers to move off the island, and the settlers saw little reason for delay. They may well have preferred to move to the mouth of the Chowan River in the fall so as to be settled in their new quarters before winter. They could not be certain whether the Secotans were planning another attack or whether the Spanish might soon find them. The two Irishmen, Glavin and Carroll, had deserted at Puerto Rico during the voyage to Roanoke, who had probably told local Spanish authorities about English plans to call in at Roanoke Island on their way to the Chesapeake Bay. The fact that the Spanish knew where the settlers had gone had greatly increased the likelihood of attack.

For the same reasons, the settlers probably decided that leaving a small group on Roanoke Island to wait for White's return was too risky. They therefore likely opted to send them to Croatoan Island instead, where they would be safe with Manteo's people. Knowing it would take a couple of months to make the move to their new locations, the colonists chose to strengthen the palisade at the settlement on Roanoke Island in case the Secotans attacked. White had remarked on the high palisade of great trees when he returned to the island in 1590.

Possibly soon after White left, several of the colonists' leaders set out with Manteo and a couple of dozen men in the pinnace to make arrangements with the Chowanocs for establishing a temporary settlement at a site near the entrance to the Chowan

6.4 John White, detail from *A map of that part of America, now called Virginia*, 1585–86 (engraving by Theodor de Bry, 1590) showing Albemarle Sound and the towns of Tandaquomuc and Metackwem. White's settlers may have located themselves somewhere in this area after they left Roanoke Island in the fall of 1587.

River. The Chowanocs had been allies of the English in the summer of 1586, and the settlers' leaders hoped the Indians would see advantages in trading with the English or would view them as potential allies against hostile Iroquoian peoples to the south and west. Whether or not the English and Chowanocs negotiated a formal agreement to allow the settlers to build their settlement is unknown. But if the English did gain permission, they may have chosen a site close to the town of Metackwem, on modern-day Salmon Creek. This location would have offered a superb vantage point for keeping watch down the length of Albemarle Sound and allowed easy access to both the Chowan and Roanoke Rivers.[26]

Before the main group left Roanoke Island, approximately two dozen settlers were transported to Croatoan Island. The exact number is uncertain, but it is unlikely that the Croatoans could have supported many more, especially during a time of drought and with winter coming on. The settlers left messages carved on prominent trees and posts at the settlement to tell White where they had gone. They assumed that White would return to Roanoke Island, go on to Croatoan to pick up the settlers there, and then make contact with the main group inland. The pinnace could probably carry up to forty passengers on short journeys without gear, but given that the settlers had to take all their possessions, they probably made two trips from Roanoke Island.

Who went to Croatoan is also unknown. The group may have included families with young children, possibly Ananias and Eleanor Dare and their daughter, Virginia; Dyonis and Margery Harvey with their baby; and two other families with young children, the Viccars and Archards. Eleanor and Margery had given birth only a couple of months before and may not have welcomed taking part in the arduous work of building a new settlement on the Chowan River. Some single men probably also went to the island. They were probably well armed in case of attack by the Spanish or mainland Indians.

The main group that went inland was likely made up of between 90 and 100 settlers. The group may have included several couples—Edward and Winifred Powell, Griffin and Jane Jones, Henry and Rose Payne, and Thomas and Audrey Tappan—along with most of the single men and women.

Moving to the new location inland would have required all the boats as well as the pinnace. Again, several journeys would have been necessary to transport the settlers together with their weapons, equipment, and dismantled houses. Once they had prepared the ground at their settlement at the head of Albemarle Sound, the settlers could begin the job of constructing their new living quarters using the timbers and materials brought from Roanoke Island. With the help of the Chowanocs, they could have had the settlement substantially completed by late December and been able to enjoy their first Christmas in their inland quarters, hopeful that John White would be back in the spring with fresh supplies and settlers.[27]

The settlers must have been worried and perplexed by White's failure to return by the early summer of 1588. He had been gone for nearly a year, and they likely wondered what could have delayed him for so long. It is possible that around this time some of the settlers from the inland group went to Croatoan Island to confer with the settlers there. Some of those living with Manteo's people may have decided that they would continue to wait and watch in case White returned. Others possibly opted to join the settlers inland.

As the months turned into years, hope of White returning faded. Most of the settlers had probably resigned themselves to living with the Indians for the rest of their lives. When news reached the Croatoans of two ships (the *Hopewell* and *Moonlight*) passing by on their way to Roanoke Island in 1590, the settlers lit fires in a desperate effort to attract White's attention—this was the "great smoke" seen by the *Hopewell*'s crew to the south-west of Kenricks Mounts—but White continued on to Roanoke. The settlers must have hoped the ships would return, but bad weather intervened, and White did not come back. Joy at the news of White's long-awaited return quickly turned to bitter disappointment.

After a few years the main group of colonists inland probably began to break up. Most of the settlers were single men, or if married to wives in England realized they had little chance of seeing them again. Some may have decided to marry into the Chowanoc people who had befriended them and stay at the head of Albemarle Sound, possibly joining local peoples of Tandaquo-muc and Metackwem. Others may have gone upriver closer to the Chowanoc capital. Others still, perhaps dreaming of finding riches in the province of Chaunis Temoatan, may have begun exploring the Roanoke River and eventually settled down at Panawicke near Cashie Creek or moved farther inland to Ocana-honan, a Tuscarora town near the falls of the Roanoke River. Panawicke was known locally for its salt production ("salt stones"), and Ocanahonan was close to an important trading route that led northward and inland to the mountains beyond.

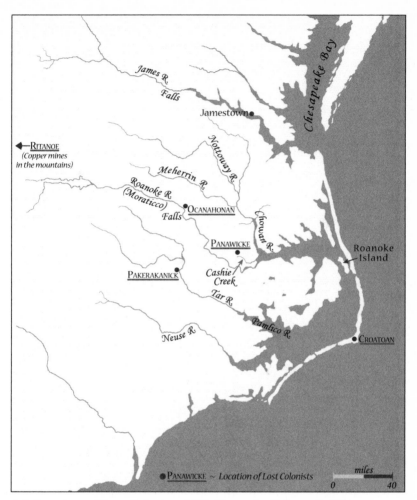

6.5 Locations of Lost Colonists, 1608. Drawn by Rebecca L. Wrenn.

The settlers probably dispersed into four main groups: those who went to live on Croatoan Island, those on the west bank of the Chowan River, those near Cashie Creek, and a final group at Ocanahonan. The English heard about all of these locations, initially from John White (Croatoan), and later from Smith and Machumps (the Chowan River, Panawicke, and Ocanahonan). Other than the Croatoan group, the timing of the settlers' movements is impossible to determine, but it is likely that most of them had joined local Indian communities by the early to mid-1590s.

The settlers lived peacefully with the Tuscaroras and Chowanocs for nearly two decades. By the early seventeenth century, the majority of settlers had spent the greater part of their adult lives with Indians along the Chowan and Roanoke Rivers. They had not forgotten their English background, but those who survived and lived in Indian communities would have by now thoroughly adapted to Indian ways. They spoke the Indians' language and dressed like local peoples. The men would have hunted and fought, perhaps using their steel swords and axes, and the women looked after the fields and homes. Using their sharp metal tools they perhaps created copper ornaments, and they showed the Indians how to build houses with walls and an upper floor, like those they had built on Roanoke Island.

Then a catastrophe overwhelmed them. Machumps had told Strachey early in 1609 that the lost colonists were killed by the Powhatans at the same time that Captain Newport was exploring the lower reaches of the Chesapeake Bay and the James River in April and May 1607. The Indian gave no details of the attack, other than that it occurred in South Virginia. Forty years later, however, a story picked up by a small group of English explorers led by Edward Bland may have stumbled upon what happened.

In August 1650, Bland and five companions, with two Indian guides, made their way into the interior of North Carolina. South of the Meherrin River, one of the major tributaries of the Chowan, the group halted on a path between two remarkable trees. One of the guides told the English that many years before the great chief Opechancanough had come to the region with hundreds of warriors and several chiefs to make war on the Tuscaroras and Chowanocs. Where Bland and his men had halted marked the place where the chief of the Chowanocs had been murdered by Parahunt, one of Opechancanough's chiefs. Bland's guide made no comment on whether the Powhatans launched other attacks against the Chowanocs following the chief's murder, but it is possible that the killing initiated attacks on their settlements.

Bland and his party then moved on to the falls of the Roanoke River, near Ocanahonan. A local Tuscarora guide who had joined them showed them a field three miles from the river where heaps of bones were piled up. He told Bland that one morning Opechancanough and 400 warriors had treacherously slaughtered 240 Tuscaroras. The site of the killing, which Bland called "Golgotha," was sacred to the Indians.

The date of the raid is not given by Bland, and there are no references in his account to white settlers being killed. The attack on the Tuscaroras and Chowanocs could have been later, possibly in the period between 1616 and 1622, when Opechancanough became de facto chief of the Powhatans. Yet the similarity between the information Bland picked up in 1650 and Machumps's report of the Powhatan attack is striking. Were the stories recounted by Bland's Indian guides a distant echo of the tragedy that befell the lost colonists in 1607?[28]

The settlers and their Indian kin were victims of fighting along an unstable border zone. In the broad scheme of regional rivalries, Opechancanough's raid reflected deep-seated antagonisms among three major peoples vying for dominance, the Powhatans, Tuscaroras, and Chowanocs. Over the previous twenty-five years, Wahunsonacock and Opechancanough had aggressively expanded their territories to embrace much of Tidewater Virginia, but they were faced by powerful Iroquoian and Siouan peoples in the west and north beyond the fall line, and to the south their expansion was blocked by the Chowanocs and Tuscaroras.

In addition, Wahunsonacock was concerned about the arrival of the Jamestown colonists. He may have wondered whether the Roanoke settlers would serve as go-betweens in forging alliances between the new English arrivals and Indian peoples that they (the lost colonists) lived with, potentially threatening his influence in the region and raising the possibility of peoples to the south and west of his territories allying themselves with the English.

The chief's power was based primarily on fear and control of prestige goods such as copper and highly prized European commodities. He could not allow the English to establish themselves in (or adjacent to) his dominions, where they might act as protector and benefactor of his own and neighboring peoples. Unwilling to take any chances of the Jamestown colonists joining forces with the Roanoke English, he ordered his warriors to track down as many of White's colonists as they could find and kill them.[29]

THE VIRGINIA COMPANY's vision of a new colony stretching from the Roanoke to the James River was also a victim of war. Conflict with the Powhatans erupted in the fall of 1609 and occupied the English fully for the next five years, destroying any possibility of establishing settlements in South Virginia as well as the James

River Valley. After the war ended in 1614, the discovery of a type of tobacco suited to English tastes that could profitably be cultivated in Virginia led settlers to turn away from stories of gold mines deep in the interior or the elusive passage through the mountains to the South Sea and focus instead on raising a crop that fetched handsome prices on the London market. No further effort was made to expand English settlement to the Chowan or Roanoke Rivers for forty years, and no more search parties were dispatched to look for the lost colonists. In the scramble for profits that characterized Virginia society for a decade and a half after the beginning of large-scale tobacco cultivation in 1616, Roanoke and England's first colonists were forgotten.[30]

THE MEN AND WOMEN of London and other parts of England recruited by John White to establish a colony in Virginia never reached the Chesapeake Bay; they never established a great city in Ralegh's name or discovered gold mines in the distant province of Chaunis Temoatan. El Dorado did not lie in the mountains to the west any more than it lay in Ralegh's Guiana, and there was no convenient route that would take the English to the South Sea and Cathay.

The lost colonists could not have guessed the adversities faced by White that prevented him from returning. When he failed to come back with supplies and reinforcements, they turned to local peoples for help and lived peacefully with them for nearly twenty years. How many survived the calamity of Opechancanough's attack is unknown. According to Machumps, seven (four Englishmen and three Anglo-Indian children) were protected by a powerful chief, Eyanoco, an "enemy to Powhaton." They were highly valued workers who beat his copper at Ritanoe, which lay in the mountains deep in the interior. But others, mentioned by Captain John Smith, also escaped and lived with Tuscarora peoples at Panawicke, Ocanahonan, and Pakerakanick, where they had built their "walled" houses like those of the English. They blended into Indian communities, making their homes and raising families with peoples they had found when the English thought them lost.[31]

EPILOGUE

⌒ᙢᙢᓕ

RALEGH'S SHIP

In 1700 a footloose Londoner, John Lawson, bent on traveling overseas, met by chance a gentleman who had lived many years abroad. The man persuaded him that "Carolina" was the best country in the world to visit, and so, finding a ship in the Thames ready to depart for America, Lawson made arrangements to take passage.

Following a long voyage that lasted three months, Lawson arrived in New York in August and after a two-week layover boarded his ship to complete the voyage to Charleston. On arrival, he was pleasantly surprised by the city. It was well laid out between two rivers and had fair streets with many sturdy buildings of brick and wood. Trade with Europe and the West Indies was flourishing, and the people were prosperous. The colony, he considered, was probably more valuable to Britain than any of the other mainland provinces, with the exception of Maryland and Virginia.

How Lawson occupied himself during his first few months in Charleston is unknown, but in December he was appointed by the colony to make a survey of the interior of Carolina. Shortly after Christmas, he embarked on a journey of more than 500 miles with five Englishmen and four Indians to explore the country and gather botanical specimens, which he intended to send back to England. He hoped his exploration and collection of specimens would make him eligible to become a member of the prestigious Royal Society, which was dedicated to the pursuit of scientific knowledge.

Lawson's party left Charleston on December 28 and traveled up the Santee River by canoe and on foot, pushing through swamps of cane and cypress until they reached the higher ground of the piedmont. They continued to head north and west, passing through beautiful rolling country where they encountered many different Indian peoples, each with their own distinctive culture: the Santees, Waxhaws, and Catawbas. In the final week of January 1701, they entered North Carolina and headed north and then east, traveling through the fertile lands of the Saponis, Occaneechees, and Tuscaroras. Eventually, toward the end of February, Lawson crossed the Neuse River and completed his journey at the plantation of Richard Smith on the Pamlico River.

Lawson chose to stay in North Carolina and built a house on the Neuse River, near an Indian town called Chattoka (the future site of New Bern). He continued to undertake surveying work and over the next eight years traveled widely throughout the province. Sometime after 1705 he became deputy to the colony's Surveyor General, Edward Moseley, and in the spring of 1708 was appointed to succeed Moseley in that position.

Lawson prospered in North Carolina. He laid out land holdings for the new town of Bath on the Pamlico River, established a grist mill in the town, and became clerk of the Court of Bath County. In 1709 he returned to London to arrange the publication of his description and natural history of the province. Besides his epic journey of 1700–1701, he recounted his recollections of places he had visited and stories he had heard during the previous few years.

One story in particular stood out in Lawson's mind. On a visit to Roanoke Island, he had seen the ruins of an old fort as well as "some old *English* Coins, which have been lately found; and a Brass-Gun, a Powder-Horn, and one small Quarter deck-Gun, made of Iron Staves, and hooped with the same Metal." More than a hundred years after the English had departed, the site was still littered with debris left behind by Lane and White's settlers.

But Lawson had an even more astonishing story to tell. A group of Hatteras Indians (Croatoans), who either lived on Roanoke Island or often visited it, told him "that several of their Ancestors were white People, and could talk in a Book, as we [the English] do. . . . The truth of which," he added, "is confirmed by gray Eyes being found frequently amongst these *Indians*, and no others." The Indians thought highly of themselves because of their kinship with the English.

Then the Indians recounted a story that had been passed down the generations. They told Lawson "that the Ship which brought the first Colonies [colonists], does often appear amongst them, under Sail, in a gallant Posture, which they call Sir *Walter Raleigh*'s Ship; And the truth of this has been affirm'd to me, by Men of the best Credit in the Country."

Lawson had discovered the great- and great-great-grandchildren of the settlers who had gone to live on Croatoan Island in the fall of 1587. They had waited patiently for John White to come back, keeping watch for English ships on the distant horizon. But no ship came—only Ralegh's ghost ship, which from time to time could still be seen plying the treacherous waters off the North Carolina coast.[1]

Chronology

1545   Discovery of silver mines in Mexico and Peru.

1547–1553   English Protestantism advances during reign of the boy king, Edward VI.

1553   Mary I (Tudor) succeeds Edward VI and reinstates the Catholic Church.

1554   Sir Thomas Wyatt's rebellion against Mary is quashed. Princess Elizabeth is sent to the Tower on suspicion of sympathizing with the rebels. Mary marries Philip of Spain in July. Walter Ralegh is born at Hayes Barton, East Budleigh, Devon.

1558   Elizabeth I ascends the throne and restores the Church of England

1562   Outbreak of civil war in France between Catholics and Protestants (Huguenots). Jean Ribault establishes a Huguenot settlement at Charlesfort in Spanish Florida.

1564–1565   The French move their settlement to Fort Caroline (near present-day Jacksonville, Florida). It is destroyed the following year by the Spanish governor of Florida, Don Pedro Menéndez de Avilés, who establishes a string of garrisons along the coast.

1566   Humphrey Gilbert authors a treatise on the Northwest Passage to Cathay. The Spanish are the first Europeans to explore the Outer Banks of North Carolina. John White marries Thomasine Cooper at St. Martin Ludgate in London.

1567   Philip II of Spain orders the Duke of Alba to crush opposition to Spanish rule in the Netherlands. Mary, Queen of Scots is forced to abdicate the Scottish throne in favor of her infant son, James VI.

1568   A fleet of English privateers led by John Hawkins is destroyed at St. Juan de Ulúa, Vera Cruz, Mexico. Mary, Queen of Scots flees to England. Ralegh goes to France to fight for the Huguenots. Eleanor, daughter of John and Thomasine White, is born.

1570   Pope Pius V issues an injunction encouraging Catholics to depose Elizabeth I. A small group of Jesuits establishes a mission on the Pamunkey (York) River in the Chesapeake Bay with the support of Governor Menéndez; they are killed by Indians the next year

1572   St. Bartholomew's Day Massacre in Paris incites the killing of thousands of Huguenots throughout France.

1572–73 Francis Drake raids the Spanish Caribbean and Main.

1575 Elizabeth I is invited to become sovereign of the rebellious Dutch provinces; she refuses.

1576–1578 Martin Frobisher leads three expeditions to Baffin Island (Meta Incognita) in search of the Northwest Passage and gold. John White accompanies the second voyage.

1577–1580 Francis Drake circumnavigates the globe and is knighted by the queen.

1578 Elizabeth I grants Sir Humphrey Gilbert a patent to plant a colony in North America. Gilbert fails to reach America.

1580 Annexation of Portugal by Philip II. Ralegh takes part in the massacre of Italian and Spanish troops at Smerwick on the west coast of Ireland.

1581 Dutch rebels in the Spanish Netherlands declare Philip II deposed.

1582 Francis, Duke of Anjou, Elizabeth's last suitor, leaves England. Ralegh becomes the queen's favorite and moves into Durham House on the Strand, London, early the following year.

1583 Death of Sir Humphrey Gilbert at sea in September returning from Newfoundland. In November Francis Throckmorton confesses to a Catholic plot to kill Elizabeth and put Mary, Queen of Scots on the throne.

1584 Ralegh dispatches a reconnaissance mission to North America. Philip Amadas and Arthur Barlow discover Roanoke Island and the Outer Banks of North Carolina. Richard Hakluyt the younger writes "Discourse on Western Planting" advocating an English America. William of Orange, leader of the Dutch rebels, is assassinated in July. Amadas and Barlow arrive back in London in September, bringing two Indians, Manteo and Wanchese. The Bond of Association is distributed throughout England.

1585 Ralegh is knighted. Sir Richard Grenville leaves Plymouth for Roanoke in April with seven ships and 600 men. A garrison of 108 men under the command of Ralph Lane is established in August on Roanoke Island. Grenville and most of the men, including John White, return to England. Elizabeth signs a treaty with the Dutch in August pledging military support. Drake sails with a fleet of twenty-five ships to raid the West Indies and Spanish Main.

1586   Lane sends an exploratory party north from Roanoke Island to Chesapeake Bay. In March the English learn of a possible attack being planned by local Indians and send an expedition against the Chowanocs. Lane hears of the distant province of "Chaunis Temoatan" and of a powerful Indian chief to the north, possibly Wahunsonacock (Powhatan). The English attack the town of Dasemunkepeuc in June and kill the Secotan chief Wingina (Pemisapan). After plundering the West Indies and destroying the Spanish garrison at San Augustine, Florida, Drake arrives off Hatarask and removes Lane's men back to England. Grenville arrives with six ships and 200 colonists in July, but finding Roanoke Island deserted, departs after establishing a small garrison of fifteen to eighteen men. A Catholic plot to assassinate Elizabeth is foiled. Mary, Queen of Scots is implicated in the conspiracy. During the fall and winter Ralegh develops plans for a civilian colony to be led by John White. The queen grants Ralegh lands in England and 12,000 acres in Munster, southern Ireland.

1587   White and Grenville recruit settlers for a new colony to be founded on the Chesapeake Bay. Mary, Queen of Scots is executed on February 19, setting off an international crisis with Spain. White leaves Plymouth in April with three ships and 118 men, women, and children. They arrive at Roanoke Island in July and are deposited there by the master pilot, Simon Fernandes, who refuses to go on to the Chesapeake. In August White returns to England with Fernandes to seek aid for the colonists. The queen grants Ralegh 42,000 acres in County Cork, centered on Youghal and Lismore.

1588   A general stay of shipping in March prevents a large expedition commanded by Grenville from returning to Roanoke to reinforce the colonists. The following month White leaves with two privateers but fails to reach the colony. In July Captain Vicente Gonzales discovers the English had settled on Roanoke Island but finds no trace of the settlers. The Spanish Armada descends on England and is defeated off the Flanders coast in early August. Elizabeth celebrates victory and the thirtieth year of her reign.

1589   White is unable to mount an expedition to relieve the colonists. Ralegh grants trading privileges with the colony to a syndicate of merchants and others, including White, in return for their involvement in financing another voyage to reinforce the settlers.

1590   White leaves Plymouth in March with three privateers bound for the West Indies and Roanoke. He arrives at Roanoke Island in August and finds the settlement abandoned. A message carved on a post by the colonists suggests they might be at Croatoan Island, but persistent bad weather prevents White from reaching them. He returns to England.

1591   Ralegh secretly marries Elizabeth (Bess) Throckmorton. His son is born the following year.

1592   Ralegh is sent by the queen to the Tower in disgrace and then exiled to his country estate at Sherborne, Dorset. He begins planning an expedition to the Orinoco River to discover El Dorado.

1593   John White resides on Ralegh's estates at Newtown, County Cork. He writes to Richard Hakluyt in February.

1595   Ralegh explores the Orinoco River but does not find El Dorado. His *Discoverie of the Large, Rich, and Bewtiful Empyre of Guiana* fails to stimulate support for further expeditions.

1597   Ralegh is restored to the court and Elizabeth I's favor.

1602   Samuel Mace is sent by Ralegh to the Outer Banks but does not make contact with the lost colonists.

1603   Ralegh dispatches Bartholomew Gilbert to the Chesapeake Bay. Gilbert is killed by Indians on the Eastern Shore. Death of the queen in March and the accession of James I lead to Ralegh's fall from power. He is convicted of treason and sent to the Tower.

1604   James I negotiates a peace treaty with Spain that ends the privateering war.

1606   The Virginia Company of London is established in the spring. Three ships carrying 105 settlers are dispatched in December to found a colony on the Chesapeake Bay.

1607   The English arrive at the Chesapeake Bay and establish Jamestown on the James River. The Powhatans possibly launch a large-scale attack on the Tuscaroras, Chowanocs, and Chesapeakes. Captain John Smith hears of the existence of survivors of the lost colony south of Jamestown. By winter, Jamestown is on the brink of collapse.

1608   Smith sends an expedition to look for the lost colonists. The English search for mines in the interior beyond the fall of the James River and for news of a passage to the South Sea.

1609   The Virginia Company is thoroughly reformed, and 500 settlers are sent to the colony. The company urges establishing settlements in North Carolina as well as Virginia. Captain Francisco Fernández de Écija coasts the Outer Banks. Another expedition to find the lost colonists is dispatched early in the year. War with the Powhatans erupts in the fall. John Smith returns to England.

1616   Large-scale tobacco production develops along the James River Valley. Ralegh is released from the Tower in the spring to lead another expedition to the Orinoco River.

1618   Ralegh is executed following the disastrous outcome of the expedition.

1622   John Pory sets off from Jamestown to explore the Chowan River.

1650   Edward Bland leads a small group of explorers from Fort Henry on the Appomattox River through the interior of North Carolina to the Chowan and Roanoke Rivers.

1650s   The English begin to settle the Roanoke and Chowan River areas.

1653   A small English expedition visits Roanoke Island and discovers the ruins of Lane's fort.

1701   John Lawson encounters a group of Hattaras Indians from Roanoke Island and nearby who tell him stories about their English ancestors.

The Settlers of 1587

The Governor, the Assistants, and Their Families/Kin

John White (Governor)
Roger Bailey (Assistant)
Ananias Dare (Assistant)
Eleanor (White) Dare
Christopher Cooper (Assistant)
Dyonis Harvey (Assistant)
Margery Harvey (Wife)
George Howe (Assistant)
George Howe (Boy)
Roger Pratt (Assistant)
John Pratt (Boy)
John Sampson (Assistant)
John Sampson (Boy)
Thomas Stevens (Assistant)

The Settlers

Morris Allen
Arnold Archard
Joyce Archard (Wife)
Thomas Archard (Infant)
Richard Arthur
Mark Bennet
William Berde
Henry Berrye

Richard Berrye
Michael Bishop
John Borden
John Bridger
John Bright
John Brooke
Henry Browne
William Browne
John Burden
Thomas Butler
Anthony Cage
Dennis Carroll
John Chapman
Alice Chapman (Wife?)
John Cheven
Thomas Chevan (or Pheven)
William Clement
Thomas Colman
—— Colman (Female)
John Cotsmur
Richard Darige
Henry Dorrell
William Dutton
John Earnest
Robert Ellis (Boy)
Thomas Ellis
Edmond English
John Farre
Charles Flurrie (Flory)
Thomas Gramme (Graham)
John Gibbes
Darby Glande (Glavin)
Elizabeth Glande (Glavin) (Wife?)
Thomas Harris
Thomas Harris (Different person from above)
John Hemmington
Thomas Hewet
Thomas Humphrey (Boy)
James Hynde

Henry Johnson
Nicholas Johnson
Jane Jones (Wife?)
John Jones
Griffen Jones
Richard Kemme
James Lasie (Lacey)
Margaret Lawrence
Robert Little
Peter Little
William Lucas
Jane Mannering (Mainwaring)
George Martyn
Emme Merrimoth
Michael Myllet (Millett)
Henry Milton
Humphrey Newton
William Nichols
Hugh Patterson
Henry Payne
Rose Payne (Wife)
Joan Peers (Pierce/Pearce)
Edward Powell
Winifred Powell (Wife)
Henry Rufoote
Thomas Scot
Richard Shaberdge
Thomas Smart (Boy)
Thomas Smith
William Sole
John Spendlove
John Starte
John Stilman
Martyn Sutton
Thomas Tappan
Audry Tappan (Wife)
Richard Taverner
Clement Taylor
Hugh Taylor

Richard Tomkins
John Tydway
Ambrose Viccars
Elizabeth Viccars (Wife)
Ambrose Viccars (Infant)
Thomas Warner
Joan Warren (Warner?) (Wife?)
William Waters
Cuthbert White
Robert Wilkinson
Brian Willes (Wyles)
John Willes (Wyles)
William Willes (Wyles)
Agnes Wood
Lewis Wotton
John Wright
Richard Wylde
William Wythers (Boy)

Notes

Prologue: John White's Last Letter

1. White wrote the letter to Richard Hakluyt from his house in Newtown (called Ballynoe today) in February 1593, but the scene portrayed is imaginary. The entire letter is reproduced in David Beers Quinn, ed., *The Roanoke Voyages, 1584–1590*, 2 vols. (London, 1955), vol. 2, 712–716. Kim Sloan, *A New World: England's First View of America* (Chapel Hill, NC, 2007), 46–48.

1. To "Annoy the King of Spain"

1. David Beers Quinn, ed., *The Voyages and Colonizing Enterprises of Sir Humphrey Gilbert*, 2 vols. (London, 1940), 1: 53–90; 2: 419–420.

2. Ralegh's father first married Joan Drake, a relative of Francis Drake and daughter of an important trader in Exmouth. Their two sons, George and John (who had left home by the time young Walter was born), took up privateering, sometimes in partnership with the Drakes. More distant relatives included the Grenvilles, Carews, and Sandersons, all of whom would later play important roles in Ralegh's overseas ventures. Raleigh Trevelyan, *Sir Walter Raleigh* (New York, 2002), 1–8; Robert Lacey, *Sir Walter Ralegh* (New York, 1974), 3–12; and Joyce Youings, "Raleigh's Devon," in *Raleigh and Quinn: The Explorer and His Boswell*, ed. H. G. Jones, 69–72 (Chapel Hill, NC, 1987).

3. Quinn, *Voyages and Colonizing Enterprises*, 1: 102–117, 129–165 (the map follows page 164). Gilbert may have first become interested in western voyaging when serving in France in 1562–1563 with an army of occupation. Seeing little action in plague-ridden Le Havre, a Huguenot (French Protestant) stronghold, he had plenty of time to talk to local merchants and mariners about French raids on Spanish shipping in the West Indies. Perhaps he met Jean

Ribault, recently returned from North America. See John T. McGrath, *The French in Early Florida: In the Eye of the Hurricane* (Gainesville, FL, 2000), 50–95; and David B. Quinn, *North America from Earliest Discovery to First Settlements: The Norse Voyages to 1612* (New York, 1975), 240–243.

4. A group of London merchants and financiers led by Michael Lok took up the search for a Northwest Passage in 1576. Gilbert was aware of their plan and gave it his blessing but did not participate. He displayed unusual judgment, because after three voyages to Baffin Island (off the northeast coast of Canada) between 1576 and 1578, led by Martin Frobisher, the venture collapsed in acrimony and debt. See James McDermott, *Martin Frobisher: Elizabethan Privateer* (New Haven, 2001), 103–256. Privateers were commissioned by government authorities to plunder enemy ships. Pirates were uncommissioned and might attack any ship, friend or foe.

5. Ralegh registered first at Lyons Inn in 1575 before moving to the Middle Temple. John Stow, *The Survey of London* (New York, 1956), 70–71; and David Beers Quinn, *Set Fair for Roanoke: Voyages and Colonies, 1584–1606* (Chapel Hill, NC, 1985), 4–5.

6. For advocates of American ventures, see David B. Quinn, ed., *New American World: A Documentary History of North America to 1612*, vol. 3, *English Plans for North America. The Roanoke Voyages. New England Ventures* (New York, 1979), 27–34 (Christopher Carleill), 49–53 (Sir George Peckham), and 61–123 (the two Richard Hakluyts). Others of Gilbert's London circle included his brother, Adrian, Sir George Peckham (a prominent Catholic), the influential and wealthy merchant "Customer" Sir Thomas Smythe, and John Dee. Benjamin Woolley, *The Queen's Conjuror: The Science and Magic of Dr. John Dee, Adviser to Queen Elizabeth I* (New York, 2001), 117–122.

7. E. G. R. Taylor, ed., *The Original Writings and Correspondence of the Two Richard Hakluyts*, 2 vols. (London, 1935), 1: 5–7, 12–13; and Peter C. Mancall, *Hakluyt's Promise: An Elizabethan's Obsession for an English America* (New Haven, 2007), 19–23.

8. J. H. Elliott, *Imperial Spain, 1469–1716*, (Harmondsworth, UK, 1970. Pelican edition), 230–233; J. H. Elliott, *Spain and Its World, 1500–1700: Selected Essays* (New Haven and London, 1989), 7–24; Geoffrey Parker, *The Grand Strategy of Philip II* (New Haven and London, 1998), 3–6; Penryn Williams, *The Later Tudors, England 1547–1603* (Oxford, 1995), 258; and Susan Brigden, *New Worlds, Lost Worlds: The Rule of the Tudors, 1485–1603* (New York, 2000), 159–162, 210–211.

9. Often referred to as the "papal donation," Alexander VI's 1493 bull *Inter caetera* became the basis of Spain's legal claim to the Americas. Some conces-

sions were made—Portuguese rights to discoveries in the Atlantic were recognized by the treaty of Tordesillas in 1494, which confirmed to them all those lands they had discovered or would discover up to 370 leagues (approximately 1,100 miles) west of the Cape Verde Islands. Anthony Pagden, *Lords of All the World: Ideologies of Empire in Spain, Britain and France, c.1500–c.1800* (New Haven and London, 1995), 29–52; and James Muldoon, "Papal Responsibility for the Infidel: Another Look at Alexander VI's *Inter Caetera*," *Catholic Historical Review* 64 (1978): 168–184.

10. Woodbury Lowry, *The Spanish Settlements within the Present Limits of the United States: Florida, 1562–1574* (New York, 1959), 155–207; Eugene Lyon, *The Enterprise of Florida: Pedro Menéndez de Avilés and the Spanish Conquest of 1565–1568* (Gainesville, FL, 1976), 100–130; and McGrath, *French in Early Florida*, 25–26, 133–155.

11. Kenneth R. Andrews, *Trade, Plunder and Settlement: Maritime Enterprise and the Genesis of the British Empire, 1480–1630* (Cambridge, 1984), 129–134, 141–145; and generally, I. A. Wright, ed., *Documents Concerning English Voyages to the Spanish Main, 1569–1580* (London, 1932); Harry Kelsey, *Sir Francis Drake: The Queen's Pirate* (New Haven and London, 1998), 36–39, 45–66, 93–220; and Samuel Bawlf, *The Secret Voyage of Sir Francis Drake, 1577–1580* (New York, 2003), 67–181.

12. Quinn, *Voyages and Colonizing Enterprises*, 1: 170–180; Andrews, *Trade, Plunder and Settlement*, 116–134; Peter E. Pope, *Fish into Wine: The Newfoundland Plantation in the Seventeenth Century* (Chapel Hill, NC, 2004), 13–14; and Kelsey, *Sir Francis Drake*, 11–67.

13. Quinn, *Voyages and Colonizing Enterprises*,1: 35, 188–194. The wording was conventional, resembling earlier grants for this purpose issued by Elizabeth's father and grandfather.

14. Quinn, *Voyages and Colonizing Enterprises*, 1: 39–48.

15. Trevelyan, *Sir Walter Raleigh*, 27–51; Lacey, *Sir Walter Ralegh*, 20–36; and Stephen Coote, *A Play of Passion: The Life of Sir Walter Ralegh* (London, 1993), 37–56.

16. Trevelyan, *Sir Walter Raleigh*, 17, 46; Lacey, *Sir Walter Ralegh*, 34–35; and John W. Shirley, *Sir Walter Ralegh and the New World* (Raleigh, NC, 1985), 6–25.

17. Trevelyan, *Sir Walter Raleigh*, 46–49; Coote, *Play of Passion*, 60–65, 70; and J. Hannah, ed., *The Poems of Sir Walter Raleigh . . .* (London, 1892), 15–16, 29, 77–78.

18. Brigden, *New Worlds, Lost Worlds*, 270; Alison Plowden, *Elizabeth I* (Sparkford, 2004), 511–526; Christopher Hibbert, *The Virgin Queen: Elizabeth*

I, Genius of the Golden Age (Cambridge, MA, 1991), 123–129, 191–202; Carolly Erickson, *The First Elizabeth* (New York, 1983), 293–303, 323–330; and Susan Doran, *The Tudor Chronicles, 1485–1603* (New York, 2008), 335.

19. Plowden, *Elizabeth*, 139–152; Erickson, *First Elizabeth*, 29–30, 206–210, 241–242, 244–258, 272–273; and Brigden, *New Worlds, Lost Worlds*, 262–272.

20. Lacey, *Sir Walter Ralegh*, 43–44; and Coote, *Play of Passion*, 59, 68–70.

21. Trevelyan, *Sir Walter Raleigh*, 55–59; and Stow, *Survey of London*, 296, 400–401.

22. Stow, *Survey of London*, 296, 402–403. London's population in the mid-1570s, when Ralegh arrived, was approximately 100,000. By the end of the century it had risen to 150,000. Williams, *Later Tudors*, 162–163.

23. Quinn, *Set Fair for Roanoke*, 7.

24. Quinn, *Voyages and Colonizing Enterprises*, 1: 49–62; 2: 278–279, 391; and Andrews, *Trade, Plunder and Settlement*, 190–191.

25. Quinn, *Voyages and Colonizing Enterprises*, 1: 71–82; 2: 272.

26. Andrews, *Trade, Plunder and Settlement*, 194–197; and Quinn, *Voyages and Colonizing Enterprises*, 1: 50–52, 62–67, 82–89; 2, 378–379, 390–420. The precise location where the *Delight* was lost is unknown.

27. Quinn, *Set Fair for Roanoke*, 7–9, 45–46; and John W. Shirley, "American Colonization through Raleigh's Eyes," in *Raleigh and Quinn: The Explorer and His Boswell*, ed. H. G. Jones, 105–107 (Chapel Hill, NC, 1987).

28. Mancall, *Hakluyt's Promise*, 92–102, 138–154; Taylor, *Original Writings*, 1: 175; 2: 242; Andrews, *Trade, Plunder and Settlement*, 64–69, 139–141, 167–179, 183–199; David B. Quinn, *Explorers and Colonies, America, 1500–1625* (London, 1990), 207–223, 239–241; Quinn, *England and the Discovery of America*, 246–254; Quinn, *Set Fair for Roanoke*, 20–21; Peter J. French, *John Dee: The World of an Elizabethan Magus* (London, 1972), 178–199; David Armitage, *The Ideological Origins of the British Empire* (Cambridge, 2000), 105–108; and Benjamin Woolley, *The Queen's Conjuror: The Science and Magic of Dr. John Dee, Adviser to Queen Elizabeth I* (New York, 2001), 84–85, 97–122, 176, 201.

29. Quinn, *Explorers and Colonies*, 239–241; and Quinn, *Set Fair for Roanoke*, 20–21. In 1582 Richard Hakluyt the younger argued for the creation of a lectureship to instruct captains and sailing masters in the new navigational techniques, which both Sir Francis Drake and "Customer" Smythe supported.

30. John White was listed as a member of the Painters Stainers' Company in 1580. William S. Powell, "Who Were the Roanoke Colonists?" in *Raleigh and Quinn: The Explorer and His Boswell*, ed. H. G. Jones, 56, 65–66. (Chapel Hill,

NC, 1987). See also Kim Sloan, *A New World: England's First View of America* (Chapel Hill, NC, 2007), 23–27; and Paul Hulton, *America 1585: The Complete Drawings of John White* (Chapel Hill, NC, 1984), 7–8. For St. Martin, Ludgate, see Stow, *Survey of London*, 303.

31. Paul Hulton, *The Work of Jacques Le Moyne de Morgues, a Huguenot Artist in France, Florida, and England*, 2 vols. (London, 1977), 1: 10–12. Le Moyne was born about 1533 in Dieppe and lived in the parish of St. Anne's, Blackfriars, by 1581, which is the date of his letters of denization (making him a legal resident of a foreign country). Hulton believes he arrived only a year or two earlier, but given that he immigrated to England "for religion" it is more likely he left France shortly after the St. Bartholomew's Day Massacre of 1572.

32. McGrath, *French in Early Florida*, 20–22, 25–26; Eugene Lyon, *The Enterprise of Florida: Pedro Menéndez de Avilés and the Spanish Conquest of 1565–1568* (Gainesville, FL, 1976), 10–18; and Paul E. Hoffman, *A New Andulucia and a Way to the Orient: The American Southeast During the Sixteenth Century* (Baton Rouge, 1990), 128–129.

33. Olivia A. Isil, "Simon Fernandez, Master Mariner and Roanoke Assistant: A New Look at an Old Villain," in *Searching for the Roanoke Colonies: An Interdisciplinary Collection*, ed. E. Thomson Shields and Charles R. Ewen, 66–81 (Raleigh, NC, 2003); and Louis-André Vigneras, "A Spanish Discovery of North Carolina in 1566," *North Carolina Historical Review* 46 (1969): 398–415.

34. Sarah Lawson, *A Foothold in Florida: The Eye-Witness Account of Four Voyages made by the French to that Region and the Attempt at Colonization, 1562–1568* (East Grinstead, UK, 1992), 5, 94–95, 127; David B. Quinn, ed., *New American World: A Documentary History of North America to 1612*, vol. 2, *Major Spanish Searches in Eastern North America. Franco-Spanish Clash in Florida. The Beginnings of Spanish Florida* (New York, 1979), 363; W. P. Cumming, R. A. Skelton, and D. B. Quinn, *The Discovery of North America* (New York, 1972), map 198; McGrath, *French in Early Florida*, 80; and Paul Hulton, "Images of the New World: Jacques Le Moyne de Morgues and John White," in *The Westward Enterprise: English Activities in Ireland, the Atlantic, and America, 1480–1650*, ed. K. R. Andrews, N. P. Canny, and P. E. H. Hair, 195–214 (Liverpool, UK: 1978).

35. Quinn, *Set Fair for Roanoke*, 3; and David Beers Quinn, ed., *The Roanoke Voyages, 1584–1590* 2 vols. (London, 1955), 1: 82–89. The wording followed closely the grant issued by Elizabeth to Sir Humphrey Gilbert in 1578. Ralegh was expressly prohibited from interfering with Newfoundland fishing fleets.

2. Roanoke

1. David Beers Quinn, ed., *The Roanoke Voyages, 1584–1590*, 2 vols. (London, 1955), 1: 92. The two unnamed ships were described as barks, generally small vessels with three masts. The fore and main masts were square rigged and the mizzen fore-and-aft rigged. A deposition by Richard Butler, who claimed to have been a member of the expedition, taken by Spanish authorities in 1596 suggests that about 100 soldiers and sailors were involved in the voyage. David B. Quinn, ed., *New American World: A Documentary History of North America to 1612*, 5 vols. (New York, 1979), 3: *English Plans for North America: The Roanoke Voyages: New England Ventures*, 330. It is difficult to imagine how two small ships could have accommodated 100 men together with provisions, and therefore I have estimated a lower figure of around 75.

2. For Amadas and Barlowe, see Joyce Youings, "Raleigh's Devon," in *Raleigh and Quinn: The Explorer and His Boswell*, ed. H. G. Jones, 75–76 (Chapel Hill, NC, 1987); and David Beers Quinn, *Set Fair for Roanoke: Voyages and Colonies, 1584–1606* (Chapel Hill, NC, 1985), 21–22. Olivia A. Isil, "Simon Fernandez, Master Mariner and Roanoke Assistant: A New Look at an Old Villain," in *Searching for the Roanoke Colonies: An Interdisciplinary Collection*, ed. E. Thomson Shields and Charles R. Ewen, 66–81 (Raleigh, NC, 2003).

3. In 1524 the Florentine explorer Giovanni da Verrazzano, one of the first European explorers to see the Outer Banks, described them as an isthmus a mile wide and 200 miles long and mistook the sounds for "the eastern sea [Pacific]," an error that influenced European thinking for the next century and a half. Paul Hoffman, *Spain and the Roanoke Voyages* (Raleigh, NC, 1987), 2; and Timothy Silver, *A New Face on the Countryside: Indians, Colonists, and Slaves in South Atlantic Forests, 1500–1800* (Cambridge, 1990), 8–17.

4. Quinn, *Roanoke Voyages*, 1: 84, 93–97.

5. Reference to the shipwreck in 1558 can be found in Arthur Barlowe's account; see Quinn, *Roanoke Voyages*, 1: 111. For the arrival of the Spanish in 1566, see Quinn, *New American World*, vol. 2, *Major Spanish Searches in Eastern North America: Franco-Spanish Clash in Florida: The Beginnings of Spanish Florida*, 550–554; and Paul E. Hoffman, *A New Andulucia and a Way to the Orient: The American Southeast During the Sixteenth Century* (Baton Rouge, 1990), 244–245. French and Spanish activities in the southeast down to the early 1580s are outlined in David B. Quinn, *North America from Earliest Discovery to First Settlements: The Norse Voyages to 1612* (New York, 1975), 140–168, 206–288; David J. Weber, *The Spanish Frontier in North America* (New Haven and London, 1992),

30–75; and John T. McGrath, *The French in Early Florida: In the Eye of the Hurricane* (Gainesville, FL, 2000). On the Spanish Jesuit mission in the Chesapeake Bay, see Clifford M. Lewis and Albert J. Loomie, eds., *The Spanish Jesuit Mission in Virginia, 1570–1572* (Chapel Hill, NC, 1953).

6. Michael Leroy Oberg, *The Head in Edward Nugent's Hand: Roanoke's Forgotten Indians* (Philadelphia, 2007), 17.

7. General descriptions of the Carolina Algonquians can be found in Seth Malios, *The Deadly Politics of Giving: Exchange and Violence at Ajacan, Roanoke, and Jamestown* (Tuscaloosa, AL, 2006), 15–17; Oberg, *Head in Edward Nugent's Hand*, 1–30; and Karen Ordahl Kupperman, *Roanoke: The Abandoned Colony*, 2nd ed. (Lanham, MD, 2007), 41–64. See also Lee Miller, *Roanoke: Solving the Mystery of the Lost Colony* (New York, 2000), 265–272. For John White's paintings, see Kim Sloan, *A New World: England's First View of America* (Chapel Hill, NC, 2007), 108–131, 138–145. The linguistic and cultural affiliation of the Pamlicos, Neuse, and Coree cannot be determined with certainty; see Quinn, *The Roanoke Voyages*, 2: 871–872. Population estimates are derived from Christian F. Feest, "North Carolina Algonquians," in *Hand book of North American Indians*, vol. 15, *Northeast*, ed. Bruce G. Trigger, 271–279 (Washington, D.C., 1978); Douglas L. Rights, *The American Indian in North Carolina* (Winston-Salem, NC, 1957), 259; Quinn, *Roanoke Voyages*, 1: 113, 369; and Thomas C. Parramore, "The 'Lost Colony' Found: A Documentary Perspective," *North Carolina Historical Review* 78 (2001): 77.

8. See note 7 above. Quinn, *Roanoke Voyages* 1: 105–106, 337–362; and Philip L. Barbour, ed., *The Complete Works of Captain John Smith*, 3 vols. (Chapel Hill, NC, 1986), 1: 162–163.

9. Quinn, *Roanoke Voyages*, 1: 368–369, 417–420, 423–424, 430–431.

10. Quinn, *Roanoke Voyages*, 1: 372–373, 424–425; and Oberg, *Head in Edward Nugent's Hand*, 24–30. Temples generally took the form of longhouses, with a small room at one end that contained a raised platform on which the remains of former chiefs were placed. A statue of Kiwasa was placed on the platform to keep watch over the dead bodies and prevent them from coming to harm.

11. The identification of peoples inhabiting the interior is problematic. Little evidence of the names of peoples or towns beyond the coastal plain in the second half of the sixteenth century has survived. Some ethnohistorians have associated the Mangoaks with the Tuscaroras, Meherrin, or Nottoway. Lee Miller argues they were the Eno; see *Roanoke*, 252–256. Douglas W. Boyce, "Iroquoian Tribes of the Virginia-North Carolina Coastal Plain," in *Hand book of North American Indians*, vol. 15, *Northeast*, ed. Bruce G. Trigger, (Washington,

D.C., 1978), 282–286, 288; Thomas C. Parramore, "The Tuscarora Ascendancy," *North Carolina Historical Review* 54 (1982): 308–309; Daniel K. Richter, *The Ordeal of the Longhouse: The Peoples of the Iroquois League in the Era of European Colonization* (Chapel Hill, NC, 1992), 1–48; Quinn, *Roanoke Voyages*, 1: 260; David Stahle et al., "The Lost Colony and Jamestown Droughts," *Science* 280 (1998): 564–567; and Dennis B. Blanton, "If It's Not One Thing It's Another: The Added Challenges of Weather and Climate for the Roanoke Colony," in *Searching for the Roanoke Colonies*, ed. Shields and Ewen, 169–176.

12. Quinn, *Roanoke Voyages*, 1: 98–103.

13. Quinn, *Roanoke Voyages*, 1: 101–104. For John White's illustrations of the wives of chiefs, see Kim Sloan, *A New World: England's First View of America* (Chapel Hill, NC, 2007), 108–131, 138–145.

14. Quinn, *Roanoke Voyages*, 1: 106, 115, 414.

15. The sequence of events is difficult to unravel, and much of this paragraph must necessarily remain speculative. Based on Butler's deposition in 1596 (see note 1, above), Quinn suggests that Amadas and Fernandes might have sailed as far north as the entrance to the Chesapeake Bay, where they were attacked by hostile Powhatans. *Set Fair for Roanoke*, 39–43. This, however, seems unlikely. Butler's account states that Fernandes sailed twelve leagues, or about thirty miles, north of their original port of entrance, which if it was Port Ferdinando (Hatarask) would have brought them to the entrance of Albemarle Sound. This implies Fernandes and Amadas landed on the northern shore of the sound, where they were attacked by Weapemeocs. News of the attack and other details are derived from a confused account by an unnamed Englishman captured by the Spanish in Jamaica in 1586, who claimed the Indians "ate" thirty-eight men. See Irene A. Wright, ed., *Further English Voyages to Spanish America, 1583–1594* (London, 1951), 174–176. For Butler's deposition, see Quinn, *New American World*, 3: 329–330.

16. Quinn, *Roanoke Voyages*, 1: 110, 114–116. The unnamed Englishman captured by the Spanish in 1586 said that friendly Indians (probably Secotans) gave Fernandes "four pounds of gold and a hundred of silver and hides and many other valuable things." Wright, *Further English Voyages*, 175.

17. J. H. Elliott, *Spain and Its World,1500–1700: Selected Essays* (New Haven and London, 1989), 8–10; J. H. Elliott, *Empires of the Atlantic World: Britain and Spain in America, 1492–1830* (New Haven, 2006), 25; John Lynch, *Spain, 1516–1598: From Nation State to World Empire* (Oxford, 1991), 429–439; Susan Brigden, *New Worlds, Lost Worlds: The Rule of the Tudors, 1485–1603* (New York, 2000), 262–271; and Penryn Williams, *The Later Tudors, England 1547–1603* (Oxford, 1995), 283–288.

18. John Lynch, *Spain, 1516–1598: From Nation State to World Empire* (Oxford, 1991), 398–400; Jonathan I. Israel, *The Dutch Republic: Its Rise, Greatness, and Fall, 1477–1806* (Oxford, 1998), 140–168; Geoffrey Parker, *The Grand Strategy of Philip II* (New Haven, 1998), 121–122; Williams, *Later Tudors*, 258; and Brigden, *New Worlds, Lost Worlds*, 219–220, 245–246.

19. Israel, *Dutch Republic*, 179–220; Parker, *Grand Strategy*, 170–171; Lynch, *Spain*, 441; and Alison Plowden, *Elizabeth I* (Sparkford, UK, 2004), 338. Mary had been kept in close confinement in England ever since she had fled Scotland in 1568. By a strange coincidence, Throckmorton was executed on the same day William of Orange was assassinated, July 10, 1584.

20. Lynch, *Spain*, 439–445; and Parker, *Grand Strategy*, 169.

21. Williams, *Later Tudors*, 301; Plowden, *Elizabeth I*, 338–339; and Brigden, *New Worlds, Lost Worlds*, 282.

22. Even the title of Walsingham's plan, "A plott for the annoying of the king of Spayne," recalled Gilbert's proposal of November 1577. Harry Kelsey, *Sir Francis Drake: The Queen's Pirate* (New Haven and London, 1998), 242–243; Mary Frear Keeler, ed., *Sir Francis Drake's West Indian Voyage, 1585–86* (London, 1981), 14–15; and Quinn, *Roanoke Voyages*, 2: 728–729.

23. Raleigh Trevelyan, *Sir Walter Raleigh* (New York, 2002), 75.

24. Cited in Kenneth R. Andrews, *Trade, Plunder and Settlement: Maritime Enterprise and the Genesis of the British Empire, 1480–1630* (Cambridge, 1984), 9.

25. E. G. R. Taylor, ed., *The Original Writings and Correspondence of the Two Richard Hakluyts*, 2 vols. (London, 1935), 2: 222–230, 234–239, 243–250; and David Harris Sacks, "Discourses of Western Planting: Richard Hakluyt and the Making of the Atlantic World," in *The Atlantic World and Virginia, 1550–1624*, ed. Peter C. Mancall, 446–452 (Chapel Hill, NC, 2007). For an appraisal of the "Discourse," see Peter C. Mancall, *Hakluyt's Promise: An Elizabethan's Obsession for an English America* (New Haven, 2007), 139–154.

26. Taylor, *Original Writings*, 2: 254, 283–289.

27. Taylor, *Original Writings*, 2: 327–343; Quinn, *Roanoke Voyages*, 1: 126–129; and Quinn, *Set Fair for Roanoke*, 45–46.

28. Trevelyan, *Raleigh*, 76–77; Quinn, *Roanoke Voyages*, vol. 1, 144–145, 147–150.

29. Quinn, *Roanoke Voyages*, 1: 155–156; 2: 728–731.

30. John L. Humber, *Backgrounds and Preparations for the Roanoke Voyages, 1584–1590* (Raleigh, NC, 1986), 18–37.

31. Quinn, *Set Fair for Roanoke*, 55–56, 87–98; William S. Powell, "Who Came to Roanoke?" in *Searching for the Roanoke Colonies*, ed. Shields and Ewen,

50–61; Quinn, *Roanoke Voyages*, 1: 118–157, 174–175, 179–180, 194–197; 2: 741; and Gary Carl Grassl, *The Search for the First English Settlement in America: America's First Science Center* (Bloomington, IN, 2006), 113–115, 209–234.

32. Samuel Eliot Morison, *The European Discovery of America: The Northern Voyages, A.D. 500–1600* (Oxford, 1993), 631–638; Quinn, *Roanoke Voyages*, 1, 178–187; and Quinn, *Set Fair for Roanoke*, 57–63.

33. Quinn, *Roanoke Voyages*, 1: 187–189; and Quinn, *Set Fair for Roanoke*, 63.

34. Quinn, *The Roanoke Voyages*, 1: 416–417, 422–23, 428; and Sloan, *New World*, 112–113.

35. Quinn, *Roanoke Voyages*, 1: 189–191, 416; and Quinn, *New American World*, 3: 330.

36. For the fortifications and earthworks on Puerto Rico, see Sloan, *New World*, 100–103; and Morison, *European Discovery*, 633–636, 655. The design of the fort and layout of the settlement on Roanoke Island are conjectural. See Ivor Noel Hume, *The Virginia Adventure: Roanoke to James Towne: An Archaeological Odyssey* (New York, 1994), 30–33, 37–43; Quinn, *Set Fair for Roanoke*, 57–61, 75–82, 379–412; and Quinn, *Roanoke Voyages*, 1: 210; 2: 790–791, 903–910. Pedro Diaz, a Spanish pilot captured by Grenville on the *Santa Maria de San Vicente* in September 1586 and taken back to England, provides the only description of the fort: "a wooden fort of little strength." Its exact location is unknown. Traditionally, it has been associated with the National Park Service site at Fort Raleigh, near the northeastern tip of the Island. The First Colony Foundation, a private not-for-profit organization, is currently conducting archaeological investigations on Roanoke Island to locate the original fort and the settlement of the lost colonists.

37. Quinn, *Roanoke Voyages*, 1: 263–264; Quinn, *New American World*, 3: 330; and Wright, *Further English Voyages*, 175.

38. Quinn, *Roanoke Voyages*, 1: 197–210.

39. My assumptions about what Manteo and Wanchese might have seen during their stay in London in 1584–1585 are based on Alden T. Vaughan, "Sir Walter Ralegh's Indian Interpreters, 1584–1618," *William and Mary Quarterly* 3rd ser., 59 (2002): 346–348; and Oberg, *Head in Edward Nugent's Hand*, 51–55. The attitudes and opinions attributed to Manteo, Wanchese, and Wingina are speculative.

3. *"Chaunis Temoatan"*

1. David Beers Quinn, ed., *The Roanoke Voyages, 1584–1590*, 2 vols. (London, 1955), 1: 169–170; and Irene A. Wright, ed., *Further English Voyages to Spanish*

America, 1583–1594 (London, 1951), 12–14. A ducat is here valued at roughly 6s. 4d. See John J. McCusker, *Money and Exchange in Europe and America, 1600–1775* (Chapel Hill, NC, 1978), 99. Susan Ronald estimates that £1 in 1599 would be worth approximately £130 today (which suggests 40,000 ducats represented more than £1.6 million or $3 million). *The Pirate Queen: Queen Elizabeth I, Her Pirate Adventurers, and the Dawn of Empire* (New York, 2007), xviii.

2. Quinn, *Roanoke Voyages*, 1: 217–222; and David B. Quinn, ed., *New American World: A Documentary History of North America to 1612*, 5 vols. (New York, 1979), vol. 3, *English Plans for North America, The Roanoke Voyages, New England Ventures*, 294. Much of the gold, silver, and pearls probably ended up in the hands of Ralegh, Grenville, the queen, and high-ranking ministers and investors.

3. Whether or not John White returned to England in August 1585 is a matter of debate. Most historians have assumed he remained in the colony, but there is no evidence that he did. His name is not included in the list of colonists who stayed after Grenville's fleet left, and he does not appear in any of the existing documents for the period down to June 1586, when Lane abandoned the colony. The theory that he had to be in the colony to draw the map of the region, including the entrance to Chesapeake Bay, on the expedition of 1585–1586 is mistaken. Any competent surveyor or his assistant could have made the necessary measurements and sketches, and White, it should be remembered, was a painter, not a surveyor. The absence of any paintings of Indian peoples or towns by White after the initial exploration of July and August 1585 implies that he was not present for the entire year. Kim Sloan, *A New World: England's First View of America* (Chapel Hill, NC, 2007), 44; and Quinn, *Roanoke Voyages*, 2: 515. For White's paintings, see Paul Hulton, *America 1585: The Complete Drawings of John White* (Chapel Hill, NC, 1984); and Sloan, *New World, passim*.

4. Quinn, *Roanoke Voyages*, vol. 1, 108. Eleanor White was married to Ananias Dare at St. Clement Danes on June 24, 1583.

5. David Beers Quinn, *Set Fair for Roanoke: Voyages and Colonies, 1584–1606* (Chapel Hill, NC, 1985), 106–108; and Quinn, *Roanoke Voyages*, 1: 257–258, 286–287. The leader of the expedition is identified subsequently only as "the Colonel of the Chesepians." It is assumed the expedition sailed on the pinnace and probably included a couple of dozen men. Given Amadas's experience of sailing the pinnace during the earlier exploration of the Albemarle, he would have been Lane's likeliest choice for command. While staying near Skicóak the Englishmen were visited by several chiefs of adjoining territories, the Mangoaks, "Tripanicks, and Opossians" (the latter possibly the Nansemonds and

Warrascoyacks), which suggests a good deal of interest in the strangers. Thomas Hariot may have acted as an interpreter, taken measurements along the way, and recorded information about their discoveries. Much of this material was lost when the colonists abandoned Roanoke Island in June 1586.

6. Quinn, *Roanoke Voyages*, 1: 278, 378–381; Michael Leroy Oberg, *The Head in Edward Nugent's Hand: Roanoke's Forgotten Indians* (Philadelphia, 2007), 79–80. A comet passed over the Outer Banks sometime between mid-October and mid-November 1585.

7. Oberg, *Head in Edward Nugent's Hand*, 78–83.

8. Quinn, *Roanoke Voyages*, 1: 265–266. The linguistic and cultural affiliation of the Moratucs, a lesser people inhabiting the lower reaches of the Roanoke River, cannot be determined with certainty; they may have been Algonquian or Iroquoian. See Quinn, *The Roanoke Voyages*, 2: 871–872.

9. Quinn, *Roanoke Voyages*, 1: 259–261.

10. Quinn, *Roanoke Voyages*, 1: 263–264, 268–270.

11. Quinn, *Roanoke Voyages*, 1: 264–272. The approximate extent of the Tuscaroras' territory is described in Douglas W. Boyce, "Iroquoian Tribes of the Virginia-North Carolina Coastal Plain," in *Handbook of North American Indians*, vol. 15, *Northeast*, ed. Bruce G. Trigger, 282 (Washington, D.C., 1978).

12. Pemisapan/Wingina's "conspiracy" is described at length by Lane, perhaps in an attempt to justify his actions. Quinn, *Roanoke Voyages*, 1: 275–288. Michael Oberg suggests that the plot was probably more imagined than real, arguing that Skiko was the source of much of the intelligence about Pemisapan's plans, and he may have been settling an old score with the Secotan chief for trying to turn the English against his father and the Chowanocs. See *Head in Edward Nugent's Hand*, 81–100.

13. Whether or not the Mangoaks were involved in the conspiracy is open to question. See Quinn, *Set Fair for Roanoke*, 125.

14. Quinn, *Roanoke Voyages*, 1: 288. Lane says Stafford was on Croatoan Island, but almost certainly he was stationed at the southern end of Hatarask, or possibly on the high dune at Kenricks Mounts about midway along the Island. See Quinn, *Set Fair for Roanoke*, 133–134.

15. The classic English account of the West Indies voyage is Walter Bigges, *A summarie and true discourse of Sir Francis Drake's West Indian voyage* (London, 1589), in *Sir Francis Drake's West Indian Voyage*, ed. Mary Frear Keeler, 210–277 (London, 1981). For Spanish accounts, see Irene A. Wright, ed., *Further English Voyages to Spanish America, 1583–1594* (London, 1951), xxxiii, 16–202. An excellent recent history is Harry Kelsey, *Sir Francis Drake: The Queen's Pirate*

(New Haven and London, 1998), 240–249. Quinn, *Roanoke Voyages*, 1: 294–306; and Paul E. Hoffman, *A New Andalucia and a Way to the Orient: The American Southeast During the Sixteenth Century* (Baton Rouge, LA, 2004), 256 (orig. pub. 1990).

16. Quinn, *Set Fair for Roanoke*, 136.

17. Keeler, *Drake's West Indian Voyage*, 272–273; William Camden, *The History of the Most Renowned and Victorious Princess Elizabeth Late Queen of England*, ed. Wallace T. MacCaffrey (Chicago, 1970), 210; and Quinn, *Roanoke Voyages*, 1: 291–292, 308.

18. Three men who were inland were left behind. Quinn, *Roanoke Voyages*, 1: 289–294, 307; and Quinn, *Set Fair for Roanoke*, 138.

19. Quinn, *Roanoke Voyages*, 1: 312–313; Keeler, *Drake's West Indian Voyage*, 41–44; and Kelsey, *Drake*, 278–279.

20. Quinn, *Roanoke Voyages*, 1: 465–480, 494; 2: 787–792; and Quinn, *Set Fair for Roanoke*, 140–147. Pedro Diaz, a Spanish pilot captured by Grenville, later testified before Spanish authorities that he had been forced to accompany Grenville on the abortive voyage of 1586. He said the reason the English had settled on Roanoke Island was "because on the mainland there is much gold and so that they may pass from the North to the South Sea, which they say and understand is nearby; thus making themselves strong through the discovery of great wealth."

21. Quinn, *Roanoke Voyages*, 1: 273–275.

22. Quinn, *Roanoke Voyages*, 2: 761–765. Jean Ribault established Charlesfort on Parris Island, South Carolina, in 1562, but the site was abandoned by the French two years later in favor of a new location farther south on the St. Johns River, which was named Fort Caroline. Santa Elena was established by Pedro Menéndez de Avilés in 1566.

23. Zacatecas, Mexico, was in fact some 1,800 miles overland from Santa Elena. David J. Weber, *The Spanish Frontier in North American History* (New Haven and London, 1992), 70–71. Charles Hudson, *The Juan Pardo Expeditions: Exploration of the Carolinas and Tennessee, 1566–1568* (Washington, D.C., 1990); David B. Quinn, *North America from Earliest Discovery to First Settlements: The Norse Voyages to 1612* (New York, 1975), 271–275; David B. Quinn, ed., *New American World: A Documentary History of North America to 1612*, 5 vols. (New York, 1979), vol. 2, *Major Spanish Searches in Eastern North America. Franco-Spanish Clash in Florida. The Beginnings of Spanish Florida*, 543–544, 546, 548; and Georgia Archives, Mary L. Ross Papers, folder 44, item 16, ff. 12–15. Tales from previous Spanish expeditions, notably those of Alvar Núñez Cabeza de

Vaca and Hernando de Soto, also contributed to the rumors about gold and precious gems in Florida's interior that circulated in Europe, but Pardo's expedition was the last significant Spanish effort to penetrate inland and offered specific details about the location of mines.

24. William P. Cumming, *The Southeast in Early Maps*, 3rd ed. (Chapel Hill, NC, 1998), 121 and map 8.

25. Cumming, *Southeast in Early Maps*, 118–120 and map 7; Paul Hulton, "Images of the New World: Jacques Le Moyne de Morgues and John White," in *The Westward Enterprise: English Activities in Ireland, the Atlantic, and America, 1480–1650*, ed. K. R. Andrews, N. P. Canny, and P. E. H. Hair, 209, 213–214 (Liverpool, 1978); and R. A. Skelton, "The Le Moyne-De Bry Map," in *The Work of Jacques Le Moyne de Morgues, a Huguenot Artist in France, Florida, and England*, ed. Paul Hulton, 1: 45–54 (London, 1977). English maps from the early 1670s are more explicit and show the southwestern course of the Roanoke River that Lane and Hariot described; see, for example, the maps of John Locke (1671), John Lederer (1672), John Ogilby and James Moxon (ca. 1672), and John Speed (1676) in Cumming, *Southeast in Early Maps* 159, 161–163, 166–167; maps 65, 68, 70, and 77.

26. Quinn, *Roanoke Voyages*, 1: 317–337, 382–383. Hariot mentioned that Indians had told him about grains of silver found in rivers in the mountains but was careful to avoid sensationalism. He made no reference to gold or gems.

27. Quinn, *Roanoke Voyages*, 1: 273; and Hoffman, *New Andalucia*, 299.

4. A City on the Bay

1. David Beers Quinn, ed., *The Roanoke Voyages, 1584–1590*, 2 vols. (London, 1955), 1: 204, 322–323, 381, 493–494; and David Beers Quinn, *Set Fair for Roanoke: Voyages and Colonies, 1584–1606* (Chapel Hill, NC, 1985), 243–245, 250. The Spanish did not acknowledge English claims to Chesapeake Bay or any other part of North America. Espejo's expedition explored New Mexico and Arizona and returned with exaggerated claims about the region's potential. See David J. Weber, *The Spanish Frontier in North America* (New Haven, 1992), 79.

2. Raleigh Trevelyan, *Sir Walter Raleigh* (New York, 2002), 100–102; and Robert Lacey, *Sir Walter Ralegh* (New York, 1973), 104–107. Nicholas Canny, "Raleigh's Ireland," in *Raleigh and Quinn: The Explorer and His Boswell*, ed. H. G. Jones, 91–97 (Chapel Hill, NC, 1987).

3. Quinn, *Roanoke Voyages*, vol. 1, 387; vol. 2, 835. Hariot also planned to prepare a "Chronicle," a chronological sequence of events, but it was never published and subsequently disappeared.

4. Liza Picard, *Elizabeth's London: Everyday Life in Elizabethan London* (New York, 2003), 148–155, 230–243; Jeremy Boulton, "London 1540–1700," in *The Cambridge Urban History of Britain, 1540–1840*, ed. Peter Clark, 315–346 (Cambridge, 2000); A. L. Beier, "Engine of Manufacture: The Trades of London," in *The Making of the Metropolis: London, 1500–1700*, ed. A. L. Beier and Roger Finlay), 153–159 (London, 1986); Susan Ronald, *The Pirate Queen: Queen Elizabeth, Her Pirate Adventurers, and the Dawn of Empire* (New York, 2007), 38–45; Adrian Prockter and Robert Taylor, *The A to Z of Elizabethan London* (London, 1979), viii–ix; Roy Porter, *London: A Social History* (Cambridge, MA, 1995), 46–51; Rosemary Weinstein, *Tudor London* (London, 1994), 36–49; Penryn Williams, *The Later Tudors, England 1547–1603* (Oxford, 1995), 162–175; Paul Slack, *Poverty and Policy in Tudor and Stuart England* (London, 1988), 69; A. L Beier, *Masterless Men: The Vagrancy Problem in England, 1560–1640* (London, 1985), 40–47; and John Stowe, *The Survey of London* (New York, 1956), 374–381, for the spread of suburbs.

5. Quinn, *Roanoke Voyages*, 1: 494; vol. 2, 506–512, 539–540, 571; William S. Powell, "The Search for Ananias Dare," in *Searching for the Roanoke Colonies: An Interdisciplinary Collection*, ed. E. Thomson Shields and Charles R. Ewen, 62–65 (Raleigh, NC, 2003); and Quinn, *Set Fair for Roanoke*, 262–264.

6. Anyone researching the English backgrounds of the lost colonies owes an enormous debt to the pioneering work of William S. Powell, and more recently to lebame houston and Olivia A. Isil. I am grateful to Ms. houston for generously sharing her unpublished research with me and to Dr. Susan Shames of the John D. Rockefeller Jr. Library at the Colonial Williamsburg Foundation for her invaluable research and advice. Colonists' places of origin were derived from the online International Genealogical Index of the Church of Jesus Christ of Latter Day Saints. They were cross-checked against parish records and printed sources such as the *Harleian Society*, volumes 1–81, and Joseph Lemuel Chester, ed., *Allegations for Marriage Licenses Issued by the Bishop of London, 1520 to 1610* (London, 1887). Manuscript parish records were checked at the London Metropolitan Archives, the Guildhall Library, and the City of Westminster Archives in London. At the Outer Banks History Center (OBHC), Manteo, North Carolina, are several dozen boxes of materials relating to research undertaken in London archives by houston and Isil as well as unpublished materials by Powell. See also William S. Powell, "Who

Were the Roanoke Colonists?" in *Raleigh and Quinn*, ed. Jones, 51–67; Powell, "Who Came to Roanoke?" in *Searching for the Roanoke Colonies*, ed. Thomson Shields and Ewen, 50–61; and Quinn, *Roanoke Voyages*, 2, 533, 539–543, 793. The findings put forward here, however, are tentative and should be treated with caution.

7. William S. Powell, "The Search for Ananias Dare," in *Searching for the Roanoke Colonies*, ed. Shields and Ewen, 62–65. John Dare was born to Ananias and Eleanor sometime between 1584 and mid-1586. Thomasine Dare, "the daughter of Ananias," was buried at St. Clement Danes on March 13, 1588/1589. See St. Clement Danes Parish Register, burials, 1558-1638/39, OBHC, microfilm. She is assumed to have been their child. In the same register were the baptisms of John and Elizabeth Whyte in 1584 and 1585, son and daughter of John. It is uncertain whether they were children of John White, the artist.

8. Powell, "Who Were the Roanoke Colonists?" in *Raleigh and Quinn*, ed. Jones, 55, 57–58, 61, 63–64; and Quinn, *Roanoke Voyages*, vol. 2, 539, 541. An Anthony Cage, of Grays Inn, gentleman, married Dorothy Rudstone, spinster, on April 17, 1572. See Chester, *Allegations*.

9. Mary Frear Keeler, ed., *Sir Francis Drake's West Indian Voyage* (London, 1981), 16–17, 69, 269; and Powell, "Who Were the Roanoke Colonists?" in *Raleigh and Quinn*, ed. Jones, 55.

10. David Quinn first raised the possibility that some of White's colonists may have been Puritans more than twenty years ago, but historians have generally ignored the suggestion. See *Set Fair for Roanoke*, 260–261. For the Puritan movement in London from the 1550s through the early 1580s, see Patrick Collinson, "The Puritan Classical Movement in the Reign of Elizabeth I" (PhD diss., University of London, 1957), 34–169; and his subsequent *The Elizabethan Puritan Movement* (London, 1967), 84–85, 113–121, 152; H. Gareth Owen, "The London Parish Clergy in the Reign of Elizabeth I" (PhD diss., University of London, 1957), 471–549; and Susan Brigden, *London and the Reformation* (Oxford, 1989), 407, 462, 635, 637, and *passim*. J. G. Nichols, ed., *The Chronicles of the Grey Friars of London*, Camden Society, o.s., 53 (1852), 54–57; John V. Kitto, ed., *St. Martins in the Fields: The Accounts of the Churchwardens, 1525–1603* (London, 1901), 177–178, 298; and William Henry Overall, ed., *The Accounts of the Churchwardens of the Parish St. Michael Cornhill in the City of London from 1456–1608* (London, 1871), 150–152, 170. "St. Clement Danes, Churchwarden Accounts, 1557–1575," 3 vols., City of Westminster Archives, London, microfilm 370.

11. Collinson, *Elizabethan Puritan Movement*, 159–316; Diarmaid MacCulloch, *The Reformation: A History* (London, 2003), 382–389; and Penryn Williams, *The Later Tudors, England 1547–1603* (Oxford, 1995), 476–481.

12. Quinn, *Roanoke Voyages*, 1: 490–491; 2: 513–515; E. G. R. Taylor, ed., *The Original Writings and Correspondence of the Two Richard Hakluyts*, 2 vols. (London, 1935), 2: 214, 216; David Harris Sacks, "Discourses of Western Planting: Richard Hakluyt and the Making of the Atlantic World," in *The Atlantic World and Virginia, 1550–1624*, ed. Peter C. Mancall), 446–452 (Chapel Hill, NC, 2007; and Trevelyan, *Raleigh*, 5, 9–15,166–167.

13. Quinn, *Roanoke Voyages*, 2: 516; John L. Humber, *Backgrounds and Preparations for the Roanoke Voyages, 1584–1590* (Raleigh, NC, 1986), 38–39; and Quinn, *Set Fair for Roanoke*, 264–268. The *Lion* may have been the same ship that accompanied Grenville on the 1585 expedition. It was the same size as the *Susan Constant*, which carried seventy-one passengers and crew on the 1607 Jamestown voyage. The numbers of settlers on the three ships is speculative, but given the size and purpose of the vessels, it is unlikely to be far off the mark.

14. Williams, *The Later Tudors*, 252–258; and Alison Plowden, *Elizabeth I* (Sparkford, UK, 2004), 363. The Babbington plot is described by William Camden in *The History of the Most Renowned and Victorious Princess Elizabeth Late Queen of England*, ed. Wallace T. MacCaffrey (Chicago, 1970), 226–237. In recognition of his services in uncovering the plot, Ralegh was rewarded with Babbington's extensive estates throughout the Midlands and Lincolnshire.

15. Camden, *History*, 235–300; Plowden, *Elizabeth*, 363–365; Carolly Erickson, *The First Elizabeth* (New York, 1983), 360–363; Williams, *Later Tudors*, 92–98, 313–315; Susan Brigden, *New Worlds, Lost Worlds: The Rule of the Tudors, 1485–1603* (New York, 2000), 286–290; and Keith Thomas, *Religion and the Decline of Magic: Studies in Popular Belief in Sixteenth- and Seventeenth-Century England* (London, 1971), 482–483.

16. Garrett Mattingly, *The Armada* (New York, 1959), 39, 80–81; and Neil Hanson, *The Confident Hope of a Miracle: The True Story of the Spanish Armada* (New York, 2003), 37–45.

17. Quinn, *Roanoke Voyages*, 2: 512–517; and Quinn, *Set Fair for Roanoke*, 268–271. The dedication is from Hakluyt's Latin translation of Peter Martyr in *De Orbe Novo . . .* (Paris, 1587). See Peter C. Mancall, *Hakluyt's Promise: An Elizabethan's Obsession for an English America* (New Haven, 2007), 174–178.

18. Quinn, *Roanoke Voyages*, 2: 517.

19. For shipboard experiences half a century later, see David Cressy, *Coming Over: Migration and Communication between England and New England in the*

Seventeenth Century (Cambridge, 1987), 148–149, 159–177. For meals, see Humber, *Backgrounds and Preparations*, 42.

20. Quinn, *Roanoke Voyages*, 2: 517–520.

21. Quinn, *Roanoke Voyages*, 2: 835–836.

22. Quinn, *Roanoke Voyages*, 2: 517–522, 813, 836–838. The armament of the *Lion* is an estimate derived from ordnance carried by the *Tiger* in 1585: six demi-culverin, ten sakers, two minions, two falcons, four fowlers, and four bases. She was rated at 160 tons compared to the *Lion*'s 120. Humber, *Backgrounds and Preparations*, 32–35, 104.

23. Quinn, *Roanoke Voyages*, 2: 523–524. The identity of the "gentleman" remains unknown. Was he an important investor in the voyage (or his representative), more interested in profits from piracy than the successful outcome of White's expedition?

24. White's account is the only known record of what happened on July 22, and therefore much of the preceding discussion is necessarily speculative. On Fernandes, see Olivia A. Isil, "Simon Fernandez, Master Mariner and Roanoke Assistant: A New Look at an Old Villain," in *Searching for the Roanoke Colonies: An Interdisciplinary Collection*, ed. Shields and Ewen, 74–75 (Raleigh, NC, 2003).

25. Quinn, *Roanoke Voyages*, 2: 524–525.

5. The Broken Promise

1. David Beers Quinn, ed., *The Roanoke Voyages, 1584–1590*, 2 vols. (London, 1955), 2: 525–526. Howe was one of the assistants.

2. Quinn, *Roanoke Voyages*, 2: 525–529. The dearth of corn was a result of drought and affected all the peoples of the region and those of Chesapeake Bay. David Stahle et al., "The Lost Colony and Jamestown Droughts," *Science* 280 (1998): 564–567; and Dennis B. Blanton, "If It's Not One Thing It's Another: The Added Challenges of Weather and Climate for the Roanoke Colony," in *Searching for the Roanoke Colonies: An Interdisciplinary Collection*, ed. E. Thomson Shields and Charles R. Ewen, 169–176 (Raleigh, NC, 2003). Manteo's mother may have been the *werowansqua* (chief) of the Croatoan people.

3. Quinn, *Roanoke Voyages*, 1: 377; 2: 529–530, 614.

4. Quinn, *Roanoke Voyages*, 1: 279; 2: 529–532; David Beers Quinn, *Set Fair for Roanoke: Voyages and Colonies, 1584–1606* (Chapel Hill, NC, 1985), 269; and Michael Leroy Oberg, *The Head in Edward Nugent's Hand: Roanoke's Forgotten Indians* (Philadelphia, 2007), 120–122. Towaye disappears from the narrative.

White makes no reference to him other than noting his name alongside that of Manteo in the list of colonists.

5. Richard Hakluyt, *The Principall Navigations, Voyages Traffiques and Discoveries of the English Nation*, 3 vols. (London, 1598–1600), 3: 285; and Quinn, *Roanoke Voyages*, 2: 533–535. The "testimonie" is the only direct evidence of the planters' opinions. Because it is one of the most remarkable documents of early English America, it is presented here in its entirety. See also Quinn, *Set Fair for Roanoke*, 291.

6. This version of events is considered the most plausible scenario both in regard to existing evidence and subsequent developments (for which see below and the next chapter). For the Spanish expedition, see Irene A. Wright, ed., *Further English Voyages to Spanish America, 1583–1594* (London, 1951), 232–233.

7. Quinn, *Roanoke Voyages*, 2: 535–536, 613–614.

8. Quinn, *Roanoke Voyages*, 2: 535–538.

9. Quinn, *Roanoke Voyages*, 2: 538.

10. Harry Kelsey, *Sir Francis Drake: The Queen's Pirate* (New Haven, 1998), 287–299; Quinn, *Roanoke Voyages*, 2: 554; Raleigh Trevelyan, *Sir Walter Raleigh* (New York, 2002), 129–130; and Robert Lacey, *Sir Walter Ralegh* (New York, 1973), 126–128.

11. Quinn, *Roanoke Voyages*, 2: 538, 547–548.

12. Quinn, *Roanoke Voyages*, 2: 547–552, 563.

13. Quinn, *Roanoke Voyages*, 2: 560–564, 793–794. There are frustratingly few details about Grenville's fleet. See Quinn, *Set Fair for Roanoke*, 301. Nothing is known of Grenville's instructions or how many colonists he may have carried.

14. White says nothing in his account about the fifteen settlers carried on the *Brave* and *Roe*.

15. Quinn, *Roanoke Voyages*, 2: 566–569, 794–795. It is unclear what happened to the *Roe* after she separated from the *Brave* and why she also abandoned the voyage.

16. Quinn, *Roanoke Voyages*, 2: 778–780, 804–812, 825; and Paul E. Hoffman, *A New Andulucia and a Way to the Orient: The American Southeast During the Sixteenth Century* (Baton Rouge, 1990), 281, 303–305. Gonzáles had been to the Bahia de Madre de Dios (Chesapeake) several times before. In 1570 he transported nine Jesuits and a Hispanicized Indian, Paquiquineo (named by the Spanish Don Luis de Velasco), who established a mission on the York River. He returned the following year and the year after, when it was discovered that all the Jesuits had been killed except for a boy novice, who was returned to the

Spaniards and told them about the slaughter of the priests by Paquiquineo. Clifford M. Lewis and Albert J. Loomie, *The Spanish Jesuit Mission in Virginia, 1570–1572* (Chapel Hill, NC, 1953), 179–188.

17. William Camden, *The History of the Most Renowned and Victorious Princess Elizabeth Late Queen of England*, ed. Wallace T. MacCaffrey (Chicago, 1970), 308, 318; Geoffrey Parker, *The Grand Strategy of Philip II* (New Haven, 1998), 202–268; Neil Hanson, *The Confident Hope of a Miracle: The True Story of the Spanish Armada* (New York, 2003),108–109, 113, 125, 168–170, 295–297; and Penryn Williams, *The Later Tudors, England 1547–1603* (Oxford, 1995), 320–321.

18. Trevelyan, *Raleigh*, 131–135; Lacey, *Ralegh*, 131; Samuel Purchas, *Hakluytus Posthumus or Purchas His Pilgrims . . .* , 20 vols. (Glasgow, 1906), 19: 466–506; Hanson, *Confident Hope*, 238–322, 376, 385–386; Garrett Mattingly, *The Armada* (New York, 1959), 268–373; Kelsey, *Drake*, 305–339; and Camden, *History*, 319–328.

19. Trevelyan, *Raleigh*, 135–138; Lacey, *Ralegh*, 104–107, 135–137; Nicholas Canny, "Raleigh's Ireland," in *Raleigh and Quinn: The Explorer and His Boswell*, ed. H. G. Jones, 94–97 (Chapel Hill, NC, 1987).

20. Quinn, *Roanoke Voyages*, 2: 553–559, 569–576. Three syndicate members— Sanderson, Smythe, and Richard Hakluyt—had been closely involved with the Roanoke venture already, and quite likely several others were known personally to White. Walter Bayly may have been a relative of Roger Bayly, one of the leaders of the colonists; Thomas Wade was born in St. Martin's Ludgate and married in St. Matthews, Friday Street, where several Roanoke colonists were from; and Thomas Hood, recently installed in London as lecturer in mathematics and navigation by Smythe, was surely known to Hariot as well as to White. Among the assistants, Simon Fernandes, William Fullwood, and James Platt, named in 1587, do not appear. Dimmocke was a new addition, and along with White and John Nichols was in England. Lebame houston is currently undertaking research on the 1589 group.

21. Trevelyan, *Raleigh*, 137–140; Quinn, *Set Fair for Roanoke*, 311–314; and Kelsey, *Drake*, 341–359.

22. Kenneth R. Andrews, *Trade, Plunder and Settlement: Maritime Enterprise and the Genesis of the British Empire, 1480–1630* (Cambridge, 1984), 236–239; Trevelyan, *Raleigh*, 140; Kelsey, *Drake*, 359; Quinn, *Roanoke Voyages*, 2: 579–582, 713–715, 799. According to the governor of Puerto Rico, Diego Menéndez Valdes, the *Hopewell* carried cannon for the use of the colonists, which if so would further support the argument that the purpose of the voyage was to fortify Virginia, not abandon it.

23. White's account of his return to Roanoke in 1590 can be found in Quinn, *Roanoke Voyages*, 2: 598–613.

24. Quinn, *Roanoke Voyages*, 2: 613–616.

25. Quinn, *Roanoke Voyages*, 2: 616–622.

26. Quinn, *Roanoke Voyages*, 2: 715.

6. "Into the Main"

1. Raleigh Trevelyan, *Sir Walter Raleigh* (New York, 2002), 172–182; Robert Lacey, *Sir Walter Ralegh* (New York, 1974), 145–151, 165–173; and Alison Plowden, *Elizabeth I* (Sparkford, 2004), 573.

2. John Hemming, *The Search for El Dorado* (London, 1978), 110–114, 120–123, 183; Charles Nicholl, *The Creature in the Map: Sir Walter Ralegh's Quest for El Dorado* (London, 1996), 26–37; Kenneth R. Andrews, *Trade, Plunder and Settlement: Maritime Enterprise and the Genesis of the British Empire, 1480–1630* (Cambridge, 1984), 288–290; and Sir Walter Ralegh, *The Discoverie of the Large, Rich and Bewtiful Empyre of Guiana* (1596), introduced by Neil L. Whitehead (Norman, OK, 1997), 122–128.

3. Trevelyan, *Raleigh*, 102–103; and Ralegh, *Discoverie*, 121–122. For the extraordinary career of Sarmiento de Gamboa and his attempt to found a colony in the Straits of Magellan, see Samuel Eliot Morison, *The European Discovery of America: The Southern Voyages, A.D. 1492–1616* (Oxford, 1993), 690–708.

4. Ralegh, *Discoverie*, 122–133; Trevelyan, *Raleigh*, 214–252; David Beers Quinn, ed., *The Roanoke Voyages, 1584–1590*, 2 vols. (London, 1955), 2: 715; Edward Edwards, *The Life of Sir Walter Ralegh*, 2 vols. (London, 1868), 2: 109; and Hemming, *Search for El Dorado*, 184–191.

5. Trevelyan, *Raleigh*, 348–349; David B. Quinn, ed., *New American World: A Documentary History of North America to 1612*, 5 vols. (New York, 1979), vol. 5, *The Extension of Settlement in Florida, Virginia, and the Spanish Southwest*, 165; David B. Quinn, *England and the Discovery of America, 1481–1620* (New York, 1974), 405–430, 442–452; and Philip L. Barbour, ed., *The Complete Works of Captain John Smith*, 3 vols. (Chapel Hill, NC, 1986), 1: 51. Two earlier expeditions to Roanoke may have been dispatched by Ralegh in 1599 and 1600, but no information about them has survived, which suggests they were very small-scale affairs. Quinn speculates that Mace may have accompanied Gilbert in 1603 and explored the Chesapeake Bay, which might explain why the London Virginia Company thought it unnecessary to send an exploratory voyage three years later in advance of the Jamestown expedition. See the remarks of the

Spanish ambassador in August 1607, in Philip L. Barbour, ed., *The Jamestown Voyages under the First Charter, 1606–1609*, 2 vols. (Cambridge, 1969), 1: 77. On the background to the establishment of Jamestown, see Karen Ordahl Kupperman, *The Jamestown Project* (Cambridge, MA, 2007), 12–72, 109–217.

6. Quinn, *Roanoke Voyages*, 2: 826–838; Georgia Archives, Mary L. Ross Papers, folder 44, item 16. An Anglo-French group of merchants dispatched the *Castor and Pollux* in 1605 to trade with Indians along the Florida coast and visit Croatoan Island to make contact with the English settlers left there by Ralegh. The ship was captured by the Spanish before reaching the Outer Banks. Quinn, *New American World*, 5, 108–126.

7. Ralegh would spend nearly thirteen years in the Tower before being released in the spring of 1616 to undertake another expedition to Guiana in search of the gold mines of Manoa. The disastrous outcome of the voyage and James I's eagerness to sacrifice him to the crown's pro-Spanish ambitions sealed Ralegh's fate. He was executed at Westminster on October 29, 1618. Trevelyan, *Raleigh*, 350–553.

8. The creation of the Virginia Company is summarized in James Horn, *A Land As God Made It: Jamestown and the Birth of America* (New York, 2005), 33–37. See also Charles M. Andrews, *The Colonial Period of American History* (New Haven, 1964), 1: 73–75, 84; and Barbour, *Jamestown Voyages*, 1: 13–21, 24–34.

9. Barbour, *Jamestown Voyages*, 1: 13–21, 24–34.

10. Barbour, *Jamestown Voyages*, 1: 49–54; Peter C. Mancall, *Hakluyt's Promise: An Elizabethan's Obsession for an English America* (New Haven, 2007), 227–228; and E. G. R. Taylor, ed., *The Original Writings and Correspondence of the Two Richard Hakluyts*, 2 vols. (London, 1935), 2: 456–457, 494. Thomas Hariot may have been included in discussions about settling Virginia, but there is no direct evidence of his involvement until 1609.

11. Barbour, *Jamestown Voyages*, 1: 51, 133–137; Mancall, *Hakluyt's Promise*, 227–228; Taylor, *Original Writings and Correspondence*, 2: 456–457, 494; Helen C. Rountree, *The Powhatan Indians of Virginia: Their Traditional Culture* (Lincoln, NE, 1989); and Frederic W. Gleach, *Powhatan's World and Colonial Virginia: A Conflict of Cultures* (Lincoln, NE, 1997), 22–60.

12. Barbour, *Jamestown Voyages*, 1: 79–93, 98–102.

13. Barbour, *Jamestown Voyages*, 1: 111–119.

14. Horn, *A Land As God Made It*, 42–44, 56–60.

15. Horn, *A Land As God Made It*, 61–67. For Smith's account of his capture and "discourse," see Barbour, *Complete Works*, 1: 43–47; 2: 146–147. Opechancanough was in his early sixties at the time of the encounter. He is treated at length

in Helen C. Rountree, *Pocahontas, Powhatan, and Opechancanough: Three Indian Lives Changed by Jamestown* (Charlottesville, VA, 2005). Clothed does not necessarily mean the men still wore European clothes, but was rather a way by which Indians signified European peoples: they wore or had worn European clothes.

16. Barbour, *Complete Works*, 1: 53, 55. Wahunsonacock was the chief's personal name, but the English called him "Powhatan." Rountree discusses his titles, family, and origin in *Pocahontas, Powhatan, and Opechancanough*, 25–33. For European activity in the Gulf of St. Lawrence, see Quinn, *England and the Discovery of America*, 313–336.

17. Barbour, *Complete Works*, 1: 49. Smith was just a boy when John White led the last expedition, but he had read accounts of the Roanoke colonies in Richard Hakluyt's *The Principal Navigations, Voyages, Traffiques and Discoveries of the English Nation*.

18. Horn, *A Land As God Made It*, 100–102.

19. Barbour, *Complete Works*, 1: 63, 79, 219. Also included on the Roanoke section of the map were a number of place names: "nansamund," "chisiapiack," "imhamoack," "Roanock," "Chawanoac," "Uttamuscawone," "panawiock," "ocanahowan," "morattico," "machomonchocock," "aumocawpunt," "rawcotock," and "Pakerakanick." Barbour, *Jamestown Voyages*, 1: 236–240; and Lee Miller, *Roanoke: Solving the Mystery of the Lost Colony* (New York, 2000), 245–247, 258, 322. Miller speculates that Panawiock refers to "a place of strangers" who spoke a different language from the Algonquians, namely the Mangoaks. Panauuwioc, an Iroquoian town, which De Bry places on the Pamlico River, had the same meaning. The possible location of Ocanahonan on the Roanoke River is discussed below. I am grateful to Philip Evans for generously sharing his ideas about possible locations of the lost colonists. See also Clarence Walworth Alvord and Lee Bidgood, *The First Explorations of the Trans-Allegheny Region by the Virginians, 1650–1674* (Cleveland, OH, 1912), 127.

20. Rountree, *Pocahontas, Powhatan, and Opechancanough*, 118; Barbour, *Complete Works*, 1: 234, 238, 244, 265–266; William Strachey, *The Historie of Travell into Virginia Britania* (1612), ed. Louis B. Wright and Virginia Freud (London, 1953), 33–34. The title of Strachey's work can be roughly interpreted to mean the "History of the English in Virginia." The piedmont refers to the gently sloping plateau beyond the fall line that runs up to the Appalachians.

21. Alden T. Vaughan, "Powhatans Abroad: Virginia Indians in England," in *Envisioning an English Empire: Jamestown and the Making of the North Atlantic World*, ed. Robert Appelbaum and John Wood Sweet, 51–54 (Philadelphia, 2005); and Strachey, *Virginia Britania*, xix–xxi.

22. Strachey, *Virginia Britania*, 34, 89, 91. Conceivably, the information may have been first acquired by the company from Machumps or some other source, and Strachey later included it in his history. For Strachey's comments on the southern and western limits of the Powhatans' influence, see *Virginia Britania*, 36, 56, 106. He is emphatic that the lost colonists were killed *outside* Wahunsonacock's dominions. The Powhatan chief, he writes, had ordered the slaughter "of so many of our Nation without offence given, and such as were seated far from him, and in the Territory of those Weroances which did in no sort depend on him, or acknowledge him," that is, the Chowanocs and Tuscaroras.

23. Samuel M. Bemiss, *The Three Charters of the Virginia Company of London 1606–1621* (Williamsburg, VA, 1957), 42, 47–48; and Wesley Frank Craven, *Dissolution of the Virginia Company: The Failure of a Colonial Experiment* (New York, 1932), 29–33.

24. David B. Quinn, *Explorers and Colonies: America, 1500–1625* (London, 1990), 255; Quinn, *Roanoke Voyages*, 1: 388; and Bemiss, *Three Charters*, 59–61.

25. Barbour, *Complete Works*, 1: 265–266; 2: 215; Horn, *A Land As God Made It*, 171–173. For the wreck of the *Sea Venture*, see Lori Glover and Daniel Blake Smith, *The Shipwreck That Saved Jamestown: The Sea Venture Castaways and the Fate of America* (New York, 2008), 86–170.

26. Quinn, *Roanoke Voyages*, 2: 858; William P. Cumming, *The Southeast in Early Maps*, 3rd ed. (Chapel Hill, NC, 1998), "Americae pars, Nunc Virginia dicta" (1590), Plate 14. Salmon Creek may have been the boundary between Weapemeoc and Chowanoc lands. Ralph Lane specifically identifies Metackwem ("Mattaquen") as a Weapemeoc town under the jurisdiction of Okisko. See Quinn, *Roanoke Voyages*, 1: 258. Okisko was closely allied with the Chowanocs. Thomas C. Parramore, "The 'Lost Colony' Found: A Documentary Perspective," *North Carolina Historical Review* 78 (2001): 67–83. Farther up the west bank of the Chowan River toward "Ohanoak," near modern-day Colerain, or to the south at Edenton Bay, are other possibilities. A site on the mainland near Roanoke Island, such as on the Alligator River, or on the banks of the Pamlico River, cannot be ruled out, but is unlikely in view of the hostility of the Secotans and unknown disposition of the Pamlicos.

27. The theory offered here differs significantly from the conventional interpretation that the settlers probably journeyed north to Chesapeake Bay, their original destination (see, for example Quinn, *Set Fair for Roanoke*, 290). This is highly unlikely. First, if the settlers had decided to move to the bay they probably would have agreed to meet White at one of the known rendezvous points, either Skicoak or Chesepiooc (marked on his map), before he departed.

On his return, he would have gone to the bay, not back to Roanoke Island. Second, at the time White left Roanoke Island he knew the settlers intended to head west into the mainland. The settlers had told White they intended to go fifty miles "further up into the main," which indicated that they intended to head west into the interior rather than along the coast to the Chesapeake Bay. Third, to travel north in the pinnace and their boats the settlers would have to navigate Currituck Sound and sail along the Atlantic coast to the mouth of the bay. The journey would have been extremely hazardous, and the settlers would have had to repeat it several times to move everyone off Roanoke Island. Currituck Sound had been described earlier by Ralph Lane as very shallow and dangerous owing to "flats and shoals" in the channel. By contrast, sailing up Albemarle Sound would have been much easier, was a direct route inland, and would allow the settlers to keep in contact with the small group on the island. Finally, the route to the Chowan River had already been navigated and described by Lane in 1586.

28. Strachey, *Virginia Britania*, 34; Alvord and Bidgood, *First Explorations*, 122–123, 125, 128; and Alan Vance Briceland, *Westward from Virginia: The Exploration of the Virginia-Carolina Frontier, 1650–1710* (Charlottesville, VA, 1987), 28–91. Briceland argues that Bland was sent to the region by Governor William Berkeley to look for an English man and woman who were thought to be survivors of the lost colony living with the Tuscaroras. Bland is explicit that "Hocomawananck," which I interpret as a garbled version of Ocanahonan, was near the falls of the Roanoke River. Lee Miller mistakes Hocomawananck for Occaneechee Island. *Roanoke*, 259.

29. Parramore, "The 'Lost Colony' Found," 79; and Strachey, *Virginia Britania*, 106–107.

30. Barbour, *Complete Works*, 1: 257; Edmund S. Morgan, *American Slavery, American Freedom: The Ordeal of Colonial Virginia* (New York, 1975), 108–123; and Horn, *A Land As God Made It*, 157–223, 232–234, 246–247, 280. John Pory, a former secretary to the colony, explored the Chowan River in February 1622. Like Sicklemore, he discovered a fertile country of pines and abundant silk grass but made no reference to the lost colonists. William S. Powell, *John Pory, 1572–1636: The Life and Letters of a Man of Many Parts* (Chapel Hill, NC, 1977), 101. Hopes of discovering mines in the mountains or a passage to the South Sea would reemerge from time to time, in 1626, in the 1640s, in the early 1650s, and in the 1670s.

31. Bemiss, *Three Charters*, 60. Newport reported in May–June 1607 sighting at "Port Cottage" (Poor Cottage) on the James River "a Savage Boy about

the age of ten years, which had a head of hair of perfect yellow and a reasonable white skin, which is a Miracle amongst all Savages." Barbour, *Jamestown Voyages*, 1: 140. Bland found "many of the people" above the falls of the Roanoke River "to have beards" (suggestive of mixed European-Indian ancestry). Alvord and Bidgood, *First Explorations*,126–127. The towns of "machomonchocock," "aumocawpunt," "rawcotock" between the Roanoke and Tar Rivers are as yet unidentified, although it is possible "machomonchocock" was near the copper mines on the Tar River, marked on Edward Moseley's map of 1733. See Cumming, *Southeast in Early Maps*, Plate 51, map 218. The tragic history of the Indian peoples of Ossomocomuck during the seventeenth and eighteenth centuries is briefly summarized in Michael Leroy Oberg, *The Head in Edward Nugent's Hand: Roanoke's Forgotten Indians* (Philadelphia, 2008), 146–152, 157–160. See also Douglas L. Rights, *The American Indian in North Carolina* (Winston-Salem, NC, 1957).

Epilogue: Ralegh's Ship

1. John Lawson, *A New Voyage to Carolina*, ed. Hugh Talmage Lefler, (Chapel Hill, NC, 1967), xi–xxxi, 7–69. In 1654 Francis Yeardley of Virginia reported that a small expedition had visited Roanoke Island the year before and seen "the ruins of Sir Walter Ralegh's fort." Alexander S. Salley Jr., ed., *Narratives of Early Carolina, 1650–1708* (New York, 1911), 23–29; William P. Cumming, "Naming Carolina," *North Carolina Historical Review* 22 (1945): 34–42.

Illustration Credits

1.1. Sir Humphrey Gilbert's map from *A Discourse of a Discoverie for a New Passage to Cataia* (1576). Courtesy of the Library of Congress.

1.2. Abraham Ortelius, *Typus Orbis Terrarum*, 1570. Courtesy of the Colonial Williamsburg Foundation.

1.3. Sir Walter Ralegh, c. 1590. Courtesy of the Colonial Williamsburg Foundation.

1.4. Durham House. Detail from John Norden, *Speculum Britanniae* (1593). Courtesy of the Henry E. Huntington Library.

1.5. Jacques Le Moyne, Map of Florida, c. 1565. Engraving by Theodor de Bry, 1591. Courtesy of the Colonial Williamsburg Foundation.

2.1. John White, *The Arrival of the English*, 1585–1586. Engraving by Theodor de Bry, 1590. Courtesy of the John D. Rockefeller Jr. Library, Colonial Williamsburg Foundation.

2.2. Indian Peoples of Ossomocomuck and Surrounding Regions. Drawn by Rebecca L. Wrenn.

2.3. John White, *Indians Fishing*, 1585. Copyright. The Trustees of the British Museum. All rights reserved.

2.4. John White, *One of the Wives of Wingina*, 1585. Copyright. The Trustees of the British Museum. All rights reserved.

2.5. Sir Richard Grenville, 1571. National Portrait Gallery, London.

2.6. John White, *A map of that part of America, now called Virginia*, 1585–1586. Engraving by Theodor de Bry, 1590. Courtesy of the John D. Rockefeller Jr. Library, Colonial Williamsburg Foundation.

2.7. John White, *Pomeiooc*, 1585. Copyright. The Trustees of the British Museum. All rights reserved.

2.8. John White, *Secotan*, 1585. Copyright. The Trustees of the British Museum. All rights reserved.

2.9. John White, *Indians Dancing*, 1585. Copyright. The Trustees of the British Museum. All rights reserved.

2.10. John White, *Mosquetal* and *Cape Rojo*, 1585. Copyright. The Trustees of the British Museum. All rights reserved.

3.1. John White, *Land Crab, Pineapple, Flamingo, Flying Fish*, 1585. Copyright. The Trustees of the British Museum. All rights reserved.

3.2. Explorations of 1585–1586. Drawn by Rebecca L. Wrenn.

3.3. John White, *A map of that part of America, now called Virginia*, 1585–1586, Detail. Engraving by Theodor de Bry, 1590. Courtesy of the John D. Rockefeller Jr. Library, Colonial Williamsburg Foundation.

3.4. John White, *Wingina*, 1585. Copyright. The Trustees of the British Museum. All rights reserved.

3.5. Indians Panning for Gold in a Mountain Stream. Engraving by Theodor de Bry, 1590. Courtesy of the John D. Rockefeller Jr. Library, Colonial Williamsburg Foundation.

3.6. John White, Roanoke, 1586. Copyright. The Trustees of the British Museum. All rights reserved.

3.7. John White, Map of the East Coast of America, 1586. Copyright. The Trustees of the British Museum. All rights reserved.

4.1. Detail from the Copperplate Map of London, ca. 1559. Courtesy of the Guildhall Library, City of London.

4.2. Claes Visscher, detail from a panoramic view of London, showing London Bridge, 1616. Courtesy of the Guildhall Library, City of London.

4.3. Coat of arms of the City of Ralegh and those of John White. Copy post-1660. Courtesy of the Provost, Fellows and Scholars of the Queen's College, Oxford.

4.4. Places of Origin of Some Settlers from London, 1587. Drawing by Rebecca L. Wrenn.

5.1. The Spanish Armada off the South Coast of England, 1590. Courtesy of the National Maritime Museum.

6.1. John Smith, Map of Virginia, engraved by William Hole, 1612. Courtesy of the John D. Rockefeller Jr. Library, Colonial Williamsburg Foundation.

6.2. John Smith's sketch map of 1608 (Zuñiga Map). Courtesy of the Archivo General de Simancas Ministerio de Cultura, Spain.

6.3. Detail from John Smith's sketch map of 1608 (Zuñiga Map). Drawn by Rebecca L. Wrenn.

6.4. John White, detail from *A map of that part of America, now called Virginia*, 1585–1586. Engraving by Theodor de Bry, 1590. Courtesy of the John D. Rockefeller Jr. Library, Colonial Williamsburg Foundation.

6.5. Locations of Lost Colonists, 1608. Drawn by Rebecca L. Wrenn.

Acknowledgments

This has been a wonderful book to write. Throughout, I have enjoyed the support of the First Colony Foundation, a not-for-profit group of historians, archaeologists, and enthusiasts dedicated to research related to Sir Walter Ralegh's colonies on Roanoke Island, 1585–1587. The foundation awarded me a grant in 2009 to undertake work in London on the English origins of the lost colonists, for which I am most grateful. I have benefited enormously from conversations with Phil Evans, Alastair Macdonald, lebame houston, William S. Powell, and archaeologists Nick Luccketti, Eric Klingelhofer, Carter Hudgins (senior and junior), Clay Swindell, and Ivor Noel Hume. Phil Evans has been especially generous in sharing his knowledge of Roanoke Island and the surrounding region and ideas about the lost colony.

I am grateful also for the advice and wisdom of Don Lamm, who encouraged me to pursue the project. Early versions of the argument were presented at graduate seminars at New York University, Northwestern University, and the University of Maryland, College Park. I would like to record my thanks to the participants for their thoughtful comments.

I would like to thank the staffs of the Alderman Library at the University of Virginia, the Swem Library at the College of William and Mary, the British Library, the Outer Banks History Center, the

National Park Service at Fort Raleigh, the Institute of Historical Research, the Guildhall Library, the London Metropolitan Archives, and the City of Westminster Archives Centre for their assistance. The National Park Service at Fort Raleigh was extremely accommodating in allowing me to examine Milagros Flores's recent research materials, copied from original sources in Spanish archives.

At the Colonial Williamsburg Foundation, I am most grateful to Colin Campbell for his encouragement and interest. Marianne Martin at the John D. Rockefeller Jr. Library assisted with tracking down illustrations and organizing permissions. Susan Shames's expert understanding of genealogical materials was invaluable and saved me from many errors in trying to unravel the origins of the lost colonists. Rebecca L. Wrenn drew the maps, and Kirsten Kellogg kindly gave up spare time to help with some of the Spanish translations. I would also like to thank Joan and George Morrow for many delightful conversations.

Lara Heimert, Editorial Director at Basic Books, has been a superb editor, and I owe her a great debt of thanks. I am grateful also to Brandon Proia, Renee Caputo, Sharon DeJohn, and other staff at Basic who have brought the book to completion.

My family has been a constant source of support throughout the research and writing. I could not possibly have completed the work without their forbearance and patience during the years I have spent pondering the fate of the lost colonists. I thank them with all my heart. The book is dedicated to my wife, Sally, and my children, Ben and Liz, with much love.

Index

Church of England and, 159–160
Croatoans and, 55
England and, 55, 60–61, 81, 107
English/Indians relations, 155,
    157–158
English relations, 81, 82, 93, 100,
    101
as information source, 60, 61
as Lord of Roanoke and
    Dasemunkepeuc, 159
lost colonists and, 224, 227–228
Roanoke Colony (1587), 151
Roanoke expedition (1585), 66, 71,
    75
*Map of that part of America, A, now
    called Virginia* (White), 69(fig.),
    90(fig.), 212, 225(fig.)
Marqués, Pedro Menéndez
English colonists, 165–166, 172,
    173
St. Augustine, 104
Marston, John, 216
Mary, Queen of Scots
background, 135–136, 199
Elizabeth assassination attempts
    and, 57, 59, 136
execution/consequences, 135–138
Mary Spark (ship), 195
Mattamuskeet, Lake, 72
Medina Sidonia, 174, 175, 176, 179,
    180–181
Menatonon, Chowanoc chief
capture/release of, 94–95, 97
description, 46
Lane/English and, 93, 94–95, 97,
    98, 101, 106, 109–110, 211
Roanoke Colony (1587) and, 164
Weapemeocs and, 101
Mendoza, Don Bernardino, 57,
    58–59, 64–65, 137
Menéndez, Pedro de Avilés, 13, 37,
    112

Metackwem, 225(fig.), 226, 228
Mexico and Spain, 11
Monkey (ship), 167
Moonlight (ship), 184, 185, 228
Morales, Pedro, 111
Moratucs, 94, 99
Moseley, Edward, 236
Mosquetal camp, Puerto Rico, 68,
    76(fig.), 77, 85(fig.), 86, 145
Mosquetal (White), 76(fig.)
Münster, Sebastian, 10

Namontack, 216
Netherlands
England and, 59
Protestant rebels, 56–57, 59
as Spanish possession, 56–57
Neuse peoples, 47
Newfoundland/fishing banks, 16,
    28–29, 34, 59, 75
Newport, Christopher
Jamestown Colony, 202, 203–204,
    210, 215, 218, 219, 230
returns to England, 205, 215, 216,
    219
White's return to Roanoke (1590),
    184
Nichols, John, 126
Norris, John, 183
Northwest Passage, 7–8, 8(fig.), 10,
    10(fig.), 11, 34
Nugent, Edward, 100
Nugumuit Inuits, 33

Ocanahonan location, 207, 209,
    214–215, 217, 218, 221, 228,
    229, 229(fig.), 230, 231, 234
Occaneechees, 236
Okisko, Weapemeoc chief, 46–47,
    101, 160, 164
One of the Wives of Wingina (White),
    53(fig.)